PRETEND WE'RE DEAD

PRETEND WE'RE DEAD

CAPITALIST MONSTERS IN

AMERICAN POP CULTURE

Annalee Newitz

Duke University Press

Durham and London 2006

© 2006 Duke University Press

Licensed under the Creative Commons Attribution-
NonCommercial-NoDerivs License, available at
http://creativecommons.org/licenses/by-nc-nd/2.0/
or by mail from Creative Commons, 559 Nathan
Abbott Way, Stanford, Calif., 94305, U.S.A.
"NonCommercial" as defined in this license specifically
excludes any sale of this work or any portion thereof for
money, even if the sale does not result in a profit by the
seller or if the sale is by a 501(c)(3) nonprofit or NGO.

Printed in the United States of America
on acid-free paper ⊗
Designed by Amy Ruth Buchanan
Typeset in Scala by Tseng Information Systems, Inc.
Downcome display typeface by Eduardo Recife,
http://www.misprintedtype.com
Library of Congress Cataloging-in-Publication
Data appear on the last printed page of this book.

CONTENTS

ACKNOWLEDG- MENTS

Parts of this book appeared in various forms in a few places. A chunk of chapter 1 appeared in *Cineaction* as "Serial Killers, True Crime, and Economic Performance Anxiety"; a chunk of chapter 2 was published in *Bright Lights Film Journal* as "A Low-Class, Sexy Monster"; and a chunk of chapter 5 was published in the *San Francisco Bay Guardian* as "The Corporations Have You: The Matrix Trilogy Freaks Out Over Info-Capitalism."

This book project took far too long, so I have a lot of thanking to do.

Thanks to my old colleagues and mentors in the academy: My dissertation committee, Richard Hutson, Susan Schweik, and Carol Clover, offered helpful comments and encouragement when this book was still in ridiculously bad shape. Several others helped me learn what I needed to (whether they knew it or not): Michael Berube, Laura Kipnis, Gerald Vizenor, Kathy Moran, Fred Pfeil, Henry Jenkins, and the brazen Constance Penley. Others in the academy, who shall remain nameless, also guided my intellectual development immeasurably. You know who you are.

Thanks to Ken Wissoker at Duke University Press for being a patient, kind, and thoughtful editor.

Thanks to the *San Francisco Bay Guardian* crew (past and present), especially Tim Redmond, Lynn Rapoport, Cheryl Eddy, Susan Gerhard, John Marr, and zillions of picky readers: you have truly encouraged me to print the news and raise hell. Thanks to the *Bad Subjects* gang for being totally rad: Joel Schalit, Charlie Bertsch, Megan Shaw Prelinger, Jonathan Sterne, Doug Henwood—you rock! Keep on refusing to answer the hail. And thanks to my fellow freedom-loving geeks at the Electronic Frontier Foundation, who encouraged me to choose a Creative Commons license for this book and always provide me with endless discussions of cheesy movies in between bouts of agitating against large entertainment companies, ruthless rights holders, and the government.

Thanks to my many families: the wonderful, goofy Burnses; the super-genius Kuppermans; my long-suffering housemates Ed and Ikuko Korthof; and my father, who took me to my first monster movie.

Last but not least by any means, my profoundest love and adoration to Charlie Anders, Jesse Burns, and Chris Palmer, who have helped me through much worse things and are the best friends I have.

INTRODUCTION

Capitalist Monsters

They've got us in the palm of their big hand

When we pretend that we're dead

They can't hear a word we said

When we pretend that we're dead

—L7, from *Bricks Are Heavy* (1992)

At the turn of the century, critics hailed two movies as exciting reinventions of the horror genre: *The Sixth Sense* and *Blair Witch Project*. Both are about dead people who refuse to stay that way. The signature line from *Sixth Sense*, Haley Joel Osment's whispered, creepy "I see dead people," was an instant pop cultural meme. T-shirts with this phrase and morphed versions of it ("I see stupid people") were everywhere at the dawn of the new millennium, as were parodies and rip-offs of M. Night Shyamalan's terse, quiet movie about a little boy plagued by needy ghosts.

Osment's character Cole sees spirits who cannot rest until they get some kind of closure on their lives. He's begun to go insane when Malcolm, a child psychologist, helps him understand that the dead are not there to hurt or frighten him—they just need to be heard by one of the only human beings who can. Every dead person has a story that Cole must interpret. Only by talking with these terrifying creatures, who often appear to him soaked in blood or with their brains dripping out, can he bring peace to himself and his preternatural counterparts.

Of course, some ghosts could give a crap about closure. Certainly this is the case with the bloodthirsty spirits who haunt the remote Maryland woods in *Blair Witch*. When a bunch of art students decide to slum it around the countryside to get footage for a sarcasm-laced film they're making about the legend of these spirits, they discover what documentary film-makers have known for almost a century: the natives don't appreciate their condescending attitude. Murdered in mysterious, supernatural fashion, the students in *Blair Witch* are reduced to little knots of hair and teeth because they've refused to heed stories the locals tell about the Blair Witch's power to kill from beyond the grave.

Nothing is more dangerous than a monster whose story is ignored.

Like all ghosts, the dead people in *Sixth Sense* and *Blair Witch* come to the human world bearing messages. They remind us of past injustices, of anguish too great to survive, of jobs left undone, and of truths we try to forget. Gloopy zombies and entrail-covered serial killers are allegorical figures of the modern age, acting out with their broken bodies and minds the conflicts that rip our social fabric apart. Audiences taking in a monster story aren't horrified by the creature's otherness, but by its uncanny resemblance to ourselves.

One type of story that has haunted America since the late nineteenth century focuses on humans turned into monsters by capitalism. Mutated by backbreaking labor, driven insane by corporate conformity, or gorged on too many products of a money-hungry media industry, capitalism's monsters cannot tell the difference between commodities and people. They confuse living beings with inanimate objects. And because they spend so much time working, they often feel dead themselves.

The capitalist monster is not always horrifying. Sometimes it is, to borrow a phrase from radical geneticist Richard Goldschmidt, a "hopeful monster."[1] Instead of telling a story about the destructiveness of a society whose members live at the mercy of the marketplace, this creature offers an allegory about surmounting class barriers or workplace drudgery to build a better world.

Regardless of whether its story is terrifying or sweet, capitalist monsters embody the contradictions of a culture where making a living often feels like dying.

✳ Economic Disturbances

Stories about monstrosity are generally studied from psychoanalytic and feminist perspectives, but I argue that an analysis of economic life must be synthesized with both in order to understand how we define "monsters" in U.S. popular culture. Capitalist monsters are found in literature and art film as well as commercial fiction and movies. Certainly we can find dramatic differences between its literary and B-movie incarnations. But, even as they cross the line between one form of media and another, the stories' fundamental message remains the same: capitalism creates monsters who want to kill you.

It's crucial to acknowledge that the people creating the books and movies I analyze in *Pretend We're Dead* may not have self-consciously intended to draw connections between what is monstrous and what people do for money. The "capitalist" part of capitalist monsters is usually a subtext and may not even be the most important part of a narrative. It lurks in the background, shaping events and infecting the plot line.

And it must be contained, figured, talked around, repressed. Stories where economic concerns rise to the surface and become overt are generally marginal affairs, embraced only by audiences of the highly educated or hardcore fans.

As an example, consider the strange case of Brian Yuzna's brilliant 1989 monster movie *Society*. Set in Beverly Hills, this low-budget gore fest follows the paranoid adventures of teenager William Whitney, who discovers that his adoptive parents and sister are polymorphous, incestuous, human-eating aliens who have raised him for food. As the story unfolds, Yuzna draws an overt connection between the ruling class and evil beasts who eat the poor for fun. While *Society* is intentionally ironic and playful at times, the message is unmistakable: the rich are repulsive alien monsters. Further, these elite aliens are literally incestuous, so we are unable to avoid the implication that wealth is being hoarded by a few inbred elites who have no intention of sharing it with anyone who isn't part of their "family." *Society* culminates in a grotesque, skin-dripping orgy at the mayor's house where all the rich white folks of Beverly Hills melt into one, throbbing body which sucks the flesh off a human "meal."

While *Society* boasts all the standard fare of a horror film, complete with gloppy makeup effects and gratuitous nubile teenagers, it was never released theatrically in the United States. Theatergoers in England got a chance to see it on the wide screen, and gave it rave reviews, but in the United States it went straight to video. Yuzna speculates that this discrepancy has everything to do with how Americans view class. Interviewed about *Society*, he said:

> I realized that the British don't have a hard time realizing that there are classes. Americans, it's like messing with their mythology; you're threat-

ening their whole world. The American world view is predicated on this idea that those who have more really deserve it. . . . One of the points of *Society* is that not only do a very small number of people control the world, but . . . whatever class you are born in is the class you will grow up in.[2]

Clearly, Yuzna's open depiction of class warfare made his film too disturbing, too economically horrifying, for a mainstream American audience. Even *The Psychotronic Video Guide*, known for its promotion of weird, underground films, describes *Society* as "very anti-establishment."[3] Thus, while we might say *Society* is a success artistically and certainly within its own terms as a capitalist monster movie, it hardly qualifies as "popular." It rests on the extreme edge of the pop culture spectrum, a film too overt for its own good. Like one of the nineteenth-century literary novels I will talk about in chapter 2, Frank Norris's *McTeague*, *Society* reaches only a small audience which is already willing to accept the basic idea that wealth generates monstrosity.

A more "standard" entry in the capitalist monster genre might be *Silence of the Lambs* (1991), a popular and Academy award–winning horror film about serial killers, released just two years after *Society*. Certainly one would not want to argue that *Silence* is an unself-conscious production; Jonathan Demme, its director/*auteur*, is well known for his thoughtful, critical films about U.S. culture. Yet *Silence* is hardly the blanket condemnation of class warfare that *Society* is.

We are reminded repeatedly in *Silence*, through flashbacks and scenes between hero Agent Starling and seductive psycho Hannibal Lecter, that Starling's traumas are related to her class background (Lecter calls her a "rube"), yet her preoccupation with her poor, rural background is sutured neatly into a splashier narrative about gender and the art of violence. Judith Halberstam notes that *Silence* "dramatizes precisely . . . [how] monstrosity in postmodern horror films finds its place in what Baudrillard has called the obscenity of 'immediate visibility' and what Linda Williams has dubbed 'the frenzy of the visible.' "[4] It participates in a hypervisual and distracting gore aesthetic of oozing wounds and skinned flesh. The spectacles of murdered and mutilated bodies are so heavily foregrounded that the questions about social class and economic mobility which fuel the narrative are safely contained as subtext.

✳ Dead Labor

A number of theorists and literary critics such as Halberstam have dealt with monster stories as something more than sheer entertaining spectacle. Perhaps most famously, Carol Clover's groundbreaking study, *Men, Women and Chainsaws: Gender in the Modern Horror Film*, paved the way for an analysis of monsters as rooted in anxieties around masculinity, urbanization, and sexual desire. Other critics, such as David J. Skal and William Paul, have investigated the political and social meanings of horror in film. Some studies of the horror genre, such as James Twitchell's *Dreadful Pleasures*, Drake Douglas's *Horrors!*, and even David Kerekes's and David Slater's *Killing for Culture: An Illustrated History of the Death Film from Mondo to Snuff*, offer a way of blending aesthetic appreciation with cultural criticism.[5] I think the "appreciation" approach is still by far the most common in work on monsters, which indicates the degree to which many people remain uncertain as to whether one can call something "aesthetic" if it is also disgusting or outright goofy the way many monster movies are.

I take it for granted that pop culture stories are worth analyzing in my work. What matters to me is not aesthetics, but why monster stories are one of the dominant allegorical narratives used to explore economic life in the United States. As Clover explains, something about the flagrant violence of generic horror lends itself well to allegorical reading. Addressing the problem of gender in slasher films, she writes:

> The qualities that locate the slasher film outside the usual aesthetic system . . . are the very qualities that make it such a transparent source for (sub)cultural attitudes toward sex and gender in particular . . . the slasher film, not despite but exactly because of its crudity and compulsive repetitiveness, gives us a clearer picture of current sexual attitudes, at least among the segment of the population that forms its erstwhile audience.[6]

Like slashers, narratives in the capitalist monster genre are often too violent to fit within "the usual aesthetic system." And yet, as I will argue, such violence offers an intensely raw expression of what it means to live through financial boom and bust, class warfare, postcolonial economic turmoil, and even everyday work routines. Like gender, capitalism is a social construction which gets passed off as natural only by means of psychological repression and various forms of public coercion. Understandably, then, it is in extreme images of violence and misery that we find uncensored fears of capitalism.

Perhaps above all else, capitalist monsters represent the subjective experience of alienation. As Karl Marx and other philosophers have explained, there is a particular kind of social alienation attached to labor in free market capitalism. Marx describes alienation as the sensation of being brutalized and deadened by having to sell oneself for money. Alienation is what it feels like to be someone else's commodity, to be subject to a boss who "owns" you for a certain amount of time. Capitalist forms of work, Marx writes:

> Mutilate the laborer into a fragment of a man, degrade him to the level of an appendage of a machine, destroy every remnant of charm in his work and turn it into a hated toil . . . they transform his life-time into working-time . . . Accumulation of wealth at one pole is, therefore, at the same time accumulation of misery, agony of toil, slavery, ignorance, brutality, mental degradation, at the opposite pole.[7]

Elsewhere, Marx has stated simply that "capital is dead labor." Of course, the accumulation of wealth does not literally mean the death of laborers, although often it does; more importantly, capitalist work implies a symbolic death. It is the death of individual freedom, of pleasurable, rewarding activity, and of a rich social life. In short, it is the transformation of "life-time into working-time." Capitalism, as its monsters tell us more or less explicitly, makes us pretend that we're dead in order to live. This pretense of death, this willing sacrifice of our own lives simply for money, is the dark side of our economic system.

✳ Great Monsters in American History

In this book, I deal with five types of monsters: serial killers, mad doctors, the undead, robots, and people involved in the media industry. I use each chapter to trace the evolution of stories about these monsters from their late-nineteenth- and early-twentieth-century incarnations up through early twenty-first century ones. As we tell and retell these monster stories over time, their meanings gradually shift to reflect changing social conditions and economic anxieties. Moreover, these monsters tend to jump from one form of media to another. They can be found in b movies, pulp fiction, and classic American novels. My choice of texts from all these media reflects this diversity of venues.

Every monster story I discuss in this book is North American, and all except for a tiny subset were created in the United States.[8] I chose to narrow my focus in this way so that I could focus explicitly on the kinds of fantasies produced by a nation devoted to capitalism as both an economic and a moral system. Many of the financial concerns shared by people in the United States are quite different from those experienced by people in Japan, Brazil, Italy, and other countries whose pop culture is full of stories about ghosts and otherworldly beasts. Analyzing stories about monsters produced in the United States gives us a window into what Fredric Jameson would call the "political unconscious"[9] of a powerful but troubled nation.

I've also chosen to examine monster stories beginning with ones published in the 1880s and continuing through to the present day. I start with the 1880s because it was an important turning point in U.S. economic history. Aside from being a time of tremendous financial crisis, it was also the era immediately following the Civil War Reconstruction. The United States no longer depended on slave labor to fuel a large portion of its economy, and labor unions were beginning to make their presence felt. Moreover, civil rights for people of color and several waves of immigrants meant that new workers were pouring into the free market and changing its character forever. At the same time, technological innovations allowed the United States to develop industries devoted to the manufacture and maintenance of communications devices, among them the machines that later became radios, cameras, film projectors, and televisions. Analysts later termed the economic relations spawned by these devices "the culture industry." The culture industry changed the way we tell stories in such a profound way that its hegemony could be compared to the rise of print culture after Gutenberg built the first press.

The monsters in this book reflect the character of the American economy in the years since the 1880s. They rampage through narratives preoccupied with postslavery economics, the culture industry, and new definitions of labor.

I locate the literary roots of capitalist monster stories in late nineteenth century naturalism rather than in gothic romanticism of the same era. Halberstam and many other theorists such as Marie-Hélène Huet[10] have made a strong case for tracing monstrosity in literature back to the gothic and romantic traditions. But I argue that the naturalist novel, featuring what Donald Pizer has called "melodramatic sensationalism and moral confusion," provides perhaps the first glimpse of certain thematic and spectacular obsessions that come to dominate the capitalist monster genre.[11] Stephen Crane's attention to gore in his naturalist classic *The Red Badge of Courage* certainly influenced later disturbing images in film and fiction related to economic horror, and the overt connections between class, brutality, and murder in Frank Norris's *McTeague* might be said to make his novel a slightly more staid and realistic version of Yuzna's *Society*. A concern with yoking the surreal extremes of human behavior with socioeconomic status make naturalist aesthetics an obvious precursor of capitalist monster tales.[12]

The twentieth-century modernist and postmodernist fixations on what Theodor Adorno and Max Horkheimer call "the culture industry" are also deeply important to capitalist monster narratives, especially after the 1950s.[13] As the market in images, culture, and information came to replace industrial mass production, the issues foregrounded in these stories shifted. Simultaneously, the mid-century movement toward decolonization in the United States and abroad changed the stakes for global capital and for race relations. Put simply, forms of ownership and production that were immediately relevant in the early twentieth century became what Raymond Williams calls "residual formations" within dominant culture.[14]

The media industry may be an "emergent formation" that is still in the process of achieving market hegemony, but it nevertheless underwrites the ways we have experienced and expressed alienation over the past fifty years. Frank Norris represented a monster created by capitalism in the 1880s by putting a gigantic mining drill into the hands of his demented protagonist McTeague; in the 1980s, David Cronenberg offered us a similar kind of monster in *Videodrome* (1983) by surrealistically inserting a mind-controlling videocassette into the body of his media mogul antihero. Both stories disturb us by showing what it means to become the "appendage of a machine," but the forms of capitalist production associated with these machines are very different.

✸ The Nightmare of Social Construction

Capitalist monsters may be the bearers of stories, but they are also protagonists in them, individuals propelled by (and often attempting to propel) social circumstances they cannot control. For this reason, a cluster of issues which came to be called "identity politics" in the late twentieth century are central to how economic horror maps its social terrain. Gender, race, sexuality, and national identity are crucial to how we are asked to imagine (or not imagine) our economic identities in these stories. I don't mean to imply that any of these categories come to stand in for class. Rather, they provide a context for economic crisis; they complicate the idea of class by providing alternate models of oppression and liberation; and most importantly, they operate alongside capitalism as overwhelming social forces which help to create monsters as often as they create "normal" individuals. A capitalist monster story is, like a naturalist one, quite profoundly interested in social structures. But it is also focused on how specific individuals—often marginalized ones—cope with them.

What the monsters I deal with in this book share in common are position(s) which place them at the mercy of social, rather than "natural," forces. Theirs is a monstrosity that grows out of what Judith Butler has called "subjection,"[15] the process by which an individual is granted psychological interiority—subjectivity—only by assimilating (often unspoken) social norms and taboos. That subjection results in monsters points up the degree to which economic horror narratives are trying to articulate a connection between "civilization" and human disturbance. By contrast, many other horror genres locate "terror" in the realm of nature: humans in such tales are menaced by wild animals, creepy nonhuman beings, aliens, natural disasters, etc. Capitalist monsters are, to put it succinctly, freaks of culture, not freaks of nature.

It is therefore no surprise that the monsters I examine here are all *made* monstrous, rather than *born* monstrous. Serial killers are created by "bad environments"; mad doctors build or concoct monsters in their labs; the undead are reanimated as monsters; robots are always built by someone else; and of course people in the media industry are only made monstrous by virtue of the narratives they produce and consume. Indeed, the constructedness of these monsters is often at the crux of their stories. It underscores their connection to human-made institutions like the economy, demonstrating the degree to which ideology is "made material" in individuals as well as their social apparatus.[16]

One might say that in the stories I look at in this book, monsters are always constructed. This forces us to question the human agency behind their creation, socialization, and education.

Westworld (1973), Michael Crichton's proto–*Jurassic Park* film about a cyborg revolt at a theme park, foregrounds the horrifying implications of what it means to construct identities for the sole purpose of maintaining a service labor force. Protagonists Peter and John visit the "Delos" park, which promises "vacations of the future." Peopled by cyborgs who are "there to serve you," and paid for by the exorbitant 1,000-dollar-a-day guest fees, the park is divided into Medieval World, Roman World, and Westworld, each populated by robot "natives." Peter and John stay in Westworld, a simulation of the Old West complete with gunfights, prostitutes, and wild saloons. As it turns out, all the most exciting forms of entertainment in Westworld require using the robots: John has a gleeful adventure shooting a sheriff robot, both men get in a barroom brawl with more robots, and later they enjoy a night of sex with robot whores. Yet Peter is made uneasy by the robots' obvious resemblance to slaves and kept women. Late at night, we see workers hauling away all the robots who have been "killed" by their human masters. Clearly, the robots' constructed social position at the park is more than a little disturbing. Seeing their dead bodies left behind like so much litter underscores just how problematic the human/robot relationships in *Westworld* actually are.

Created by and for the entertainment economy, the robots of *Westworld* are effectively slaves of the culture industry. Yet due to their programming, the robots' options for revolt are fairly limited: they manage to kill several humans but can't escape the park's boundaries. This, finally, is the dark side of social construction, the moment when subjection becomes teratogenesis. In *Westworld*, as in other narratives, we see how the market (inflected by a history of racial slavery and sexism) helps to create antisocial monsters who are destructive of human life precisely *because* of how and why they were constructed. *Westworld*'s cyborgs were *made* dangerous to fill a market niche for specialty vacations and to fulfill a human desire for interactive entertainment. Allegorically speaking, individuals in this fabricated race of cyborgs are so thoroughly alienated during the subjection process that they can only imagine an end to suffering in violence and murder. But ultimately, humans are the biggest problem in this movie. They are so thoroughly alienated themselves that they get amusement out of producing servants they can kill without guilt. The monster's construction is simply a more literal version of his human counterpart's.

Capitalist monsters are the fantasy outcome of social constructivism in a class-stratified world. Their tales demonstrate why identity constructed under capitalism is a nightmare.

✳ Pretend We're Dead

I have divided my analysis of economic horror into three clusters: mental monstrosity, bodily monstrosity, and narrative monstrosity. What's at stake here are three basic ways that economic forces "mark" us. The economy structures not just the way we think, but also (as many people have noted) the shape and health of our bodies. It also affects how we tell stories about transformations in both our psychological and physical states under capitalism.

In chapters which focus on serial killers and mad doctors, I explore mental monstrosity in tales about people who go insane because they lead lives which they perceive as forced on them by profit-driven institutions. I argue that the serial killer is a figure whose brutality condemns methods of capitalist production by taking them to their extreme, ultimately mass producing dead bodies. This grisly mass production is what drives the "publicity machine" in Norman Mailer's *The Executioner's Song*. As Mailer details how serial killer Gary Gilmore turned himself into a commodity image for the culture industry with his public pleas for execution, it becomes clear that the professional media are an integral part of Gilmore's homicidal mania. I consider *The Executioner's Song* in the historical context of naturalist fiction, especially Stephen Crane's *The Red Badge of Courage*, and in light of movies about serial killers made during and after the 1970s. Tracing their aesthetic origin to Mathew Brady's Civil War photographs of dead bodies, I ascribe the relevance of films like *Henry: Portrait of a Serial Killer* and *Private Parts* to a continuing cultural association between image consumption and the act of serial killing.

I turn next to the madness of doctors in narratives that are about the importance of professional middle-class work. Doctors in the Jekyll/Hyde tradition (in which I include Frank Norris's crazed dentist from *McTeague*) are driven mad partly because they feel they must be at work all the time, performing intellectual labor which involves selling off one's ideas to professional institutions. To express their nonprofessional sides, they make monsters of themselves.

Bodily monstrosity comes to the fore in my chapters on the undead and robots, beings who are, in many cases, physically disfigured by the very economic practices which grant them immortality and superhuman powers. The undead, in my analysis of short stories by H. P. Lovecraft and a variety of zombie movies, represent the horrifying return of beings whose identities were forged in a colonial-era, slave-based economy. Comparing fantastical horror stories with D. W. Griffith's racist epic *Birth of a Nation*, I explore why both whites and people of color live in fear that their colonial ancestors will rise again to bring the world back to an earlier, more overtly brutal phase in capitalist history.

Robots are also marked as physically "other," but not in a racial sense. They are a "lower class," usually cast as the new manual laborers in a global capitalist future. Having assimilated technology into its body, or vice versa, the robot is a monster who is programmed and manufactured to serve a specific purpose: usually, its job is to perform intensive labor and to fight for a human society which does not view cyborgs as human equals. Beginning my analysis with Charles Chaplin's *Modern Times* and Isaac Asimov's classic *I, Robot* and continuing with contemporary movies like *RoboCop* and cyberpunk novels by William Gibson, Rudy Rucker, and Marge Piercy, I connect representations of the robot's mechanical body to its degraded social status. I conclude my chapters on the undead and cyborgs with an analysis of how both monsters are portrayed as engaging in revolutionary acts aimed at overthrowing the people who created them.

I conclude with a chapter on narrative monstrosity, which deals with the hideous and sometimes pathetic creatures who participate in the culture industry as producers and consumers. From hack writers and bloodthirsty actresses trapped in Hollywood hell to prisoners of television and video games, these are media monsters whose lives are ruled by commodity images and corporate propaganda. Trapped inside a storytelling machine which exists solely to make money, characters in these tales struggle to tell the difference between narrative truth and the slick, commercial lies that do well at the box office. Often, their conflicts turn them into rampaging monsters—or, worse, pieces of media themselves come to life and eat the audiences who watch them.

Pretend We're Dead is ultimately an extended meditation on how works about monsters represent economic crisis. The extreme horror we see in these stories—involving graphic depictions of death, mutilation, and mental anguish—is one way popular and literary fictions allegorize extremes of economic boom and bust in the United States during the past century. What becomes clear when we analyze monster stories is that the capitalist culture industry hasn't simply generated happy fantasies of self-made men with good, clean work ethics. It is just as likely to spawn gore-soaked narratives of social destruction. The history of capitalism can be told as a monster story from beginning to end.

1. SERIAL KILLERS

Murder Can Be Work

Affixed to the lid of the box was an old daguerreotype, very similar in style and com-
position to the Civil War work of the eminent photographer Mathew Brady. Based on
the picture's aged and battered condition, I judged it to be about the same vintage
as Brady's work. The image displayed was that of a dead white man: scalped, eviscer-
ated, and emasculated, with arrows protruding from his arms and legs. His eyes were
missing. — Caleb Carr, *The Alienist*

In his critically acclaimed bestseller *The Alienist*, Caleb Carr tells the story of
a late-nineteenth-century serial killer named Japheth Dury who becomes a
murderer because his cruel, frigid mother humiliates him constantly during childhood.[1] Dury is the owner of the box and picture described above,
which a team of investigators find in his tenement flat along with a bottle
of human eyeballs floating in formaldehyde. Inside Dury's box, under the
photograph, the investigators find his mother's dried heart. Dury's parents,
we discover, are the first of many people he has murdered in imitation of
the photograph on the lid of his box—itself one of many photographs taken
by his missionary father depicting white people killed by the Sioux in South
Dakota. Having endured his mother's mistreatment, his father's photography, and life as a social outcast because of a disfiguring facial tic, Dury
turns to murdering unruly young children (particularly cross-dressing boy
prostitutes) who remind him of himself as a child.

Dr. Laszlo Kreizler, the alienist (i.e., psychiatrist) of the book's title, constantly reminds his team of investigators that murderers are created by
their social context. The nature of their crimes can be ascribed to traumatic
events in their early—or not so early—lives. Dury, for example, cuts out
his victims' eyes in part because of the photographs he saw as a boy and in
part because he has suffered under the scrutiny of his mother and other

people who taunt him about his facial tic. And yet there is more to this "context" than childhood trauma, for Carr's novel traces not just Dury's personal history, but the history of an entire nation, in the process of revealing its killer. Set in the New York City of 1896, and including in its cast of characters Police Commissioner Theodore Roosevelt and Professor William James, Carr suggests that intellectual and material history are just as responsible for "inventing" Dury as his mother's abuse is. *The Alienist* is ultimately about how late-nineteenth-century philosophy, science, and economics help set the stage for a team of investigators who will be capable of finding a serial killer. This is not exactly a novel about serial killers, but rather about a social apparatus which detects them. Quite frequently, this apparatus is contingent upon historical developments such as the inventions of "alienists" and fingerprinting techniques. But just as importantly, the network of sociohistorical forces Carr associates with the origin of serial killers and their trackers is bound up with the pursuit of "real" history and human beings' relationship to it.

Carr's own novel follows the trajectory of this desire to possess knowledge of history—writing about serial killers, a fashionable topic in recent decades, he takes readers back nearly one hundred years to the first serial killer investigation ever conducted. Something about the random, apparently unmotivated violence of serial killing seems to send us to the history books, the research room, and psychoanalytic case histories. What is it about this particular form of violence that brings up history and historical "truth"?

Serial killings are characterized by their relative randomness and a lack of any personal connection between the killer and his or her victim. But the literature and popular culture surrounding serial killing, like *The Alienist,* are dense with explanations which clarify both the killers' motivations and how society helped to create them. In a general sense, then, the serial killer narrative relies upon historical analysis of various kinds to establish what Fredric Jameson has called a "cognitive map" of what would otherwise appear to be meaningless brutality.[2] The cognitive map provides a layout of the totality of social and historical relations which go into the creation of a given situation. Thus, the cognitive map provided by serial killer narratives tries to chart the way that human history and social relations can create random, senseless violence between people who do not know each other. To put it simply, these narratives try to answer one question often asked by people confronting (and participating in) a culture of violence: *how did we come to this?*

Narratives about serial killers have tried to answer or at least to present the question for audiences to puzzle out themselves. In their urgent need to figure out why people kill each other, stories about the past century's most glamorous type of sociopath share stylistic and thematic concerns with nineteenth-century antiwar novels like Stephen Crane's naturalist master-piece *The Red Badge of Courage* as well as current turn-of-the-century narratives about terrorism. While most contemporary horror narratives have their roots in eighteenth- and nineteenth-century gothic tales, serial killer stories are preoccupied with realism. To understand why books and movies about these murderers take the shape they do, it's crucial to understand their origins in literary naturalism, whether that's the old-school sensational realism of Crane or that of contemporary writer (and war chronicler) Norman Mailer. Following in these authors' narrative footsteps, turn-of-the-century portraits of serial killers in pop culture treat their subjects as real-life monsters, and as a result many of these stories are based in fact or have a pseudo-documentary feel to them. Perhaps the most extreme examples can be found in fake documentaries like *Blair Witch Project* and in true crime biographies of notorious killers like Jeffrey Dahmer. But the realist's urge to get at some kind of social truth haunts every story in the pantheon of serial killer tales.

At the same time, no storyteller—and especially no Hollywood movie-maker nor a writer with a major publishing house—wants to be the bearer of bad news. And thus the "truths" that our serial killers reveal to us in these stories often become comforting if creepy tautologies. Death is truth, they tell us, and truth is death. Other stories, however, offer a more complicated and tantalizing snapshot of social reality: there are many ways to be dead, and being executed by a serial killer might be less terrifying than many of them.

✳ Naturalist Origins

Like today's gleefully blood-spattered serial killer stories, naturalist tales of murder in the late nineteenth century have often been viewed with critical disdain because of their preoccupation with topics unacceptable for drawing room chatter and small talk. American literary critic Donald Pizer sums up objections to naturalism in an essay defending it:

> Because much naturalism is sordid and sensational in subject matter, it is often dismissed out of hand by moralists and religionists. . . . Many

readers have also objected to the fullness of social documentation in most naturalistic fiction. From the early attack on naturalism as "mere photography" to the recent call for a fiction of "fabulation," the aesthetic validity of the naturalistic novel has often been questioned.[3]

The classic naturalistic style walks a strange line between "mere" photographic reproduction of social reality and an extreme interest in the "sordid and sensational," or those events which deviate (perhaps a great deal) from ordinary experience. Later, Pizer continues, "A naturalistic novel is . . . an extension of realism only in the sense that both modes often deal with the local and the contemporary. The naturalist, however, discovers in this material the extraordinary and excessive in human nature."[4] Therefore, we would expect a naturalistic story about murder to offer realistic—even "photographic"—portraits of exceptionally violent outbursts; but we would also expect those outbursts to "deal with the local and contemporary" or to gesture toward "the fullness of social documentation." We would be anticipating a narrative which would use violence as a metaphor for ordinary human relations, while at the same time pointing out the ordinariness of extreme violence.

This is precisely what critics have argued *The Red Badge of Courage* provides. While *Red Badge* is not explicitly about serial killing, it is certainly preoccupied with mass killings—and its (anti-) hero Henry Fleming kills a number of people he does not know in a manner which is quite intentionally depicted by Crane as both senseless and basically meaningless. Death in *Red Badge* is not simply a matter of quick, "necessary" killing to survive. It is often romantically intimate, and dead bodies themselves become textualized—that is, readable or interpretable—functioning as aspects of the plot itself. *Red Badge* provides an aesthetic template for later stories about serial killers, and also underscores the similarities between serial murder and warfare. Crane's corpses are windows on social truth: we learn about the context of Fleming and his comrades' lives by "reading" the dead or mutilated bodies they create.

In a famous scene, Fleming happens upon a dead soldier, his first encounter with actual death in the war. Up until this point, he has had access to death only through stories which make him imagine "red, live bones sticking out through slits in the faded uniforms" (11). While he's prepared for mutilation and indeed yearns to earn "the red badge" of a wound for himself, Fleming is "horror-stricken" when he sees a dead man who was seated with his back against a columnlike tree. The corpse was dressed in a uniform that once had been blue, but was now faded . . . The eyes staring at the youth, had changed to the dull hue to be seen on the side of a dead fish. The mouth was open. Its red had changed to an appalling yellow. Over the gray skin of the face ran little ants. One was trundling some sort of a bundle along the upper lip (41–42).

This is not the text he expected to find. The dead man does not have a "torn" body, nor do his bones stick out of him at fantastic angles. Indeed, he is strangely ordinary, except for the fact that he has "faded" all over. Terrifyingly, he is just a "thing" which ants step all over as they go about their business. The dead soldier's body is itself a battlefield—discolored and faded from exposure to war, he is covered by busy creatures very near his eyes who don't care if they have to march on something delicate and vulnerable to get where they need to go. From this highly codified dead body, then, we move forward in the narrative toward a generalized explanation of the social context which produces it.

The Civil War in *Red Badge* is—as Crane writes in a frequently quoted passage—"an immense and terrible machine" which "produce[s] corpses" (43). It is thus associated with industrial production and a repetitive, inhuman process. Soldiers in the war consider themselves industrial workers whose product is corpses. Fleming is "grimy and dripping like a laborer in a foundry" (33).

The war is also filled with numerous internecine conflicts which produce as much violence as the ostensible "real fight" against the Confederacy: Fleming, for example, earns his "red badge of courage" from a fellow Union soldier who is so eager to flee a battle that he hits Fleming on the head with the butt of his gun. Fleming, having already anticipated humiliation and scapegoating from his comrades after running in terror from the attack, lies about the wound and pretends he earned it in battle. Meanwhile, his superior officers lie in order to keep their soldiers fighting. The Civil War here is less a series of military engagements involving two opposing armies than it is a workplace where the laborers fight each other, lie, and unfairly use one another at every turn.

The dead soldier's body may be a war zone, but the war zone itself is something else—a place packed with factories, workers, and petty (or large-scale) conflicts between men on various levels of the social hierarchy. It is, in short, something like urban environments of the late nineteenth century, an era famous for its deathtrap industrial factories, class-based conflicts such as the Chicago Haymarket Riots, and generally miserable conditions which many politicians tried to ignore or misrepresent to the public. Crane's Civil War can function as an allegorical stand-in for another geographical space, but it more meaningfully stands in for another temporal space—Crane's contemporary America.

As a journalist, Crane wrote scathing social satires and exposés about urban life and American militarism abroad in the Philippines, Spain, and Cuba. Amy Kaplan has suggested that *Red Badge* is an effort to reinterpret American history as an explanation, and justification, for its current domestic and foreign conflicts. She writes, "Crane's novel participates in a widespread cultural movement to reinterpret [the Civil War] as the birth of a united nation assuming global power and to revalue the legitimacy of military activity in general."[5] To comprehend present-day American violence and global engagements, Crane goes back to what might be called an episode from America's "original" violence—a war which fragmented the nation, then solidified its boundaries by force.[6]

And yet what amazed Crane's contemporaries most about *Red Badge* was its historical accuracy. Only twenty-four years old when he wrote *Red Badge*, Crane had never been in a war of any type. In a defense of *Red Badge* written in 1896, social reformer and Civil War veteran Thomas Wentworth Higginson congratulates Crane on being the only novelist besides Tolstoy who "brought out the daily life of war so well" and is particularly impressed with Crane's refusal to paint a falsely heroic or noble portrait of war, like the "well known engraving of the death of Nelson, where the hero is sinking on the deck in perfect toilette."[7] Higginson contrasts this absurdly perfect picture of battlefield behavior with what Higginson calls Crane's "bit of war photography." While literary critics such as Milne Holton[8] have discussed the possibility that Crane's style is influenced by his training in journalism, and many others have noted that he modeled his descriptions after contemporary military engagements, none seem to have considered the possibility that his "photographic" style might, in fact, have been influenced by photography. Considering that the Civil War is the first American war which was extensively photographed, it seems possible that *Red Badge*'s "accuracy," particularly in visual terms, might have been inspired by camera images of the Civil War.

Pizer's invocation of the complaint that naturalistic writing is "mere photography" makes it clear that many critics consider the literary analogue of photographic representation to be almost redundant ("*mere* photography"). Yet a photographic style, as Higginson implies, comes across as more historically accurate than an impressionistic one—it seems to represent events as they actually happened rather than how we imagine them in retrospect or memory. Of course, as both makers and theorists of film have noted, a photographic image can be as manipulative as a painting.[9] If Crane's history is photographic, it may not be "realism" which is at stake, but rather a realist aesthetic of the sort preferred by naturalists.

And this aesthetic owes a great deal to pioneering photojournalist Mathew Brady's photographs of the Civil War. These are arguably the most famous and often-reproduced photographs taken during the mid-nineteenth century. Like Crane, who went on journalistic missions to report on American military engagements overseas, Brady set up his photographic equipment, assistants, and labs in the field so that he could send to newspapers the most accurate and up-to-the-minute visual images of the war.[10] By 1862, Brady had thirty-five separate "bases" from which he could take and develop photographs of the war—he had, in other words, a small-scale photographic factory which produced images of combat. Due to the limitations in photographic technology, Brady and his crew shot only one (very hazy) photograph of action in the field. For the most part, he focused on portraits and still scenes, photographing soldiers, officers, and dead bodies left in the aftermath of battle. Brady's images of dead bodies are quite similar to Crane's descriptions of them—the men in them appear only to be resting save for their discolored faces. They also resemble crime scenes in that their authors (the killers) are gone: We cannot "read" these dead bodies in the context of political struggle without the aid of captions supplied by Brady, such as "Confederate Dead, Antietam, 1862." In this particular photograph, the "Confederate Dead" are literally part of a battlefield: sprawled out along a wooden fence, their bodies seem at points to blend into their environment—legs disappear into patches of grass, and limbs that lean against the fence are (in black and white) nearly the same color and shape as the wooden fence poles. Another photograph ("Behind the Stone Wall on Marye's Heights, Fredericksburg, Virginia, 1862") shows Confederate soldiers, bloody, limp, and dead, piled in a trench behind a stone wall. Their guns lean into and above the trench. It is easier to tell the guns apart from each other than it is to identify individual dead bodies. Prominent in the foreground, one dead soldier is clearly clenching his fist. His is the only body that seems to have been human once. The others look like "things," as Crane would put it.

The effect of these images is hardly an unproblematic realism. They may be records of how dead bodies look when shot with bullets, but they are not accurate recreations of historical events. *Red Badge* and Brady's photographs make it seem that dead bodies are as close as you can get to "real" war, but in fact isolated shots of corpses (even in battle postures, with their guns) still require captions to orient their viewers.

Like Brady's photographs, *Red Badge* deploys a very specific type of realism—one where people must be given or supply a social context to understand what is really going on in each spectacular image. Key here are the implications of the term "spectacular." As Michael Rogin argues, spectacle functions as ideology. It can serve to erase or radically alter historical events. "Spectacle is the cultural form for amnesiac representation," he writes, underscoring how political spectacles of various types can encourage audiences to forget the histories (often of brutality and oppression) which created contemporary politics in the first place.[11] Crane plays with this idea, using photographic-style spectacle to call our attention to the way objective reportage is a sort of a fantasy which satisfies our desire to find truth but allows us to forget it at the same time.

I explained earlier that Brady's photographs of the Civil War were mass produced, both in the field and in newspapers which later reprinted his work. As a result, the Civil War was the first American war which mass produced corpses and realistic images of them. It was a war that Crane, thirty years after the fact, could look at in photographs as if he were reviewing evidence at a murder scene. He could investigate violence just as the detectives in Carr's *The Alienist* do: by examining the images of bodies left behind. Such images—and, more importantly, their subsequent interpretation—are heavily dependent upon the kinds of industrial and mass production techniques Crane refers to in description after description of the Civil War.

Crane writes that Fleming's "mind took a mechanical but firm impression, so that afterward everything was pictured and explained to him, save why he himself was there" (87). Although Fleming can see battles "over there, and over there, and over there," as if in an assembly line, he cannot understand why he himself is there watching or fighting. But as the novel closes, all becomes clear: "Later he began to study his deeds, his failures, and achievements . . . At last they marched before him clearly. From this present view point he was enabled to look upon them in spectator fashion and to criticise them with some correctness" (107). The mission of naturalistic writing is to produce accurate depictions of "real life" so that people become spectators of their own social situations and learn to analyze them. Of course, as Crane hints, this will also produce misinterpretations or even sheer miscomprehensions like Fleming's on a huge scale. This problem is the main source of naturalism's anxieties. Despite mountains of real evidence, sometimes truth cannot be found or it is as ambiguous as a William Faulkner novel. But the fantasy of getting at the truth is what drives us to consume story after story about murder after murder: perhaps this time we will discover the real story behind our social experiences.

✷ How Murder Became Hip

Walter Benjamin's early-1930s essay *The Work of Art in the Age of Mechanical Reproduction* is a meditation on what happens to audiences who are unable to contextualize—historically and spatially—the images they consume. Because film and photography are always reproductions, rather than "originals," he worries that they lead to a "tremendous shattering of tradition," or historical context. He traces this decontextualization to the kinds of social relations produced by industrial capitalism, in which the masses produce and consume goods, including art, which are standardized or mass produced. Certainly this makes art more widely available, and Benjamin remarks hopefully that in certain circumstances "photographs [can] become standard evidence for historical occurrences, and acquire a hidden political significance." At the same time, movies and photographs have the potential to be deeply alienating, like commodities, "because [in film] an unconsciously penetrated space is substituted for a space consciously explored by man."[12] What is unconscious, of course, is the apparatus which produces the film—audiences are alienated when images or scenes come to them without their knowledge of how they were created or, as Benjamin puts it, "penetrated." Like Karl Marx's commodity fetish, the photographic image seems to come to us as if by magic, and not out of social relationships and various means of production.

The serial killer can be understood as Benjamin's nightmare of what mechanically reproduced works of art will do to audiences: alienated from what they see, they want to get "closer" to it, but have no idea what it takes to do so. They are left with nothing but "unconscious penetration" as a means of interacting with the social world. "Unconscious penetration" is a vague epithet, and this is precisely the point. With no idea how they might "consciously explore" human relations, people who consume those relations in photographs or film might just decide to possess other people in the most violent possible manner. You might say that the twentieth-century serial killer narrative speculates about what could happen to a person who has been socialized by watching movies or television. More generally, however, it expresses a fear about what will happen to human relations in a culture which is saturated by mass produced, alienated images that can be consumed by anyone, anywhere—repeatedly and meaninglessly.

Benjamin's fears and hopes for mass mediated image culture are magnified and played out in Norman Mailer's "true life novel" *The Executioner's Song*, which attempts to explain why Gary Gilmore went on a killing spree as a result of his socialization in 1970s America. Mailer's overarching argument connects the social forces responsible for creating Gilmore's violent personality to the same forces that make him famous and help to circulate his image and story in the mass media. As critics have noted, there are really two heroes of *Executioner*: the murderer Gary Gilmore and his publicist/promoter, a media producer named Lawrence Schiller. Schiller went on to direct an award-winning television miniseries based on Mailer's novel about Gilmore. Most of *Executioner* is about how Schiller buys the rights to Gilmore's story and what he does with them. Though he would agree with Benjamin that the mass media is linked inextricably to alienation, Mailer's conclusion is more extreme than Benjamin's. He ultimately implies that mechanically reproduced art leads to psychotic, homicidal social relationships. But unlike Benjamin, Mailer thinks that's cool.

In a 1957 essay called "The White Negro," Mailer writes: "The psychopath murders—if he has the courage—out of the necessity to purge his violence, for if he cannot empty his hatred then he cannot love, his being is frozen with implacable self-hatred for his cowardice."[13] His essay extols the strength and vision of "hipsters" in postwar America, individuals who are mostly young, male, and violent. The hipster registers his protest of the social order by taking violent action; Mailer celebrates the kind of animalistic or "instinctual" form of power that murderous hipsters represent. And while it is commonplace for critics like Judith Scheffler to compare *Executioner*'s Gilmore to Mailer's hipster figure,[14] what gets left unexamined in this admittedly useful comparison is why the hipster must turn to murder as a means of rebellion in the first place. Mailer claims it is to "purge his violence" and that it is a sign of "courage." Therefore we need to ask in what context it is that the murderous act comes to occupy so privileged a position as that thing which can both purify and exalt the courage of rebellious men.

As a journalist and novelist, Mailer returns often to the idea that death is somehow the most meaningful and creative force in American culture. Mailer's hipster hero Stephen Rojack in *An American Dream* (1964) is liberated when he kills his wife, for example, and Mailer rewards him with a fabulous postmurder sexual experience (not with his dead wife) and eventual escape from the law. Gilmore, it turns out, also finds death liberating—especially his own. Gilmore's notoriety grew out of his insistence that he receive the death penalty. Sure, his random killings of two men on consecutive nights were worth a few local headlines, but they weren't particularly outlandish or grisly—it was really Gilmore's death wish that brought him fame. Mailer is obsessed with Gilmore's desire to die rather than remain in prison for the rest of his life, and he spends a great deal of time discussing the kinds of "cosmic" and "karmic" forces that will make Gilmore's death meaningful as an act of justice and responsibility. Death, especially a death over which he has a degree of control, is the most "real" or authentic form of action available to Gilmore. As it is Mailer's intention to describe true life America in *Executioner*, he seizes upon Gilmore as a figure who embodies this spirit of truth as both a murderer and an executed man.

Mailer takes up many of Crane's concerns from *Red Badge*—certainly, both Mailer and Crane seem to think of death as the ultimate reality in their narratives, and they are also interested in generating a kind of critical spectator position which opposes and compliments the perspectives of their protagonists. In *Executioner*, this position is highly developed, as the book's structure gives the reader an omniscient point of view. Mailer includes detailed personal anecdotes from the lives of nearly everyone who participated in the Gilmore case, from the love life of rookie reporter Tamera Smith (who first wrote about Gilmore and his girlfriend Nicole's love letters in *The Deseret News*) to seemingly more important facts about how Gilmore spent half of his life in prison. Because Mailer organized the massive amount of information in *Executioner*, one would expect that the omniscient spectator position here would be, in fact, Mailer's own. But in an unusual move for the notoriously egocentric author, Mailer is completely absent from *Executioner*: the book ends right before Schiller hired Mailer to write it.

Readers are in some sense alienated from the novel's "means of production" because Mailer excuses himself from the narrative. We are left with an unknown, unexplained storyteller who can nevertheless see into the thoughts, histories, and actions of all the people who are part of Gilmore's life and death. Yet Gilmore himself remains opaque. He refuses to explain what inspired him to kill and then allow himself to be killed. Early on, Mailer describes Gilmore's interview with Nielson, a detective: "Nielson then asked him if he would have gone on killing, if he hadn't been caught.

Gilmore nodded. He thought he probably would have. He sat there for a minute and looked amazed. Not amazed, but certainly surprised, and said, 'God I don't know what the hell I'm doing. I've never confessed to a cop before.' "[15] Here we find confirmation that Gilmore considers himself a serial killer in the making—he would have killed more random strangers had he not been caught. But no explanation.

But Mailer (and Schiller) want more than Gilmore's confession. Somehow, if they could just get him to explain why he wanted to kill and be killed, the real truth about everything might be revealed. In search of this truth, Schiller and his assistants frantically try to find out about Gilmore's homosexual experiences in prison and his relationship with his mother.[16] Gilmore refuses to answer their questions about both, claiming that he had no homosexual sex in prison and that his mother was a "good" mother (although he seems to dislike her). They are overjoyed when they discover a letter from Gilmore to Nicole in which he describes being raped in reform school, and how he later became the lover of another young man whom he protected from being raped. And yet, even when Schiller interviews Gilmore for the last time on the night before his execution, he continues to evade questions which might reveal his inner life.

Trying to get Gilmore to describe details from his past which might have led up to his homicidal impulses, Schiller

> took his last crack at the question they could not get Gilmore to respond to. "I believe you had rough breaks," said Schiller. "You got into trouble, and had a temper . . . but you weren't a killer. Something happened. Something turned you into a man who could kill Jensen and Bushnell, some feeling, or emotion, or event."
>
> "I was always capable of murder," said Gilmore. . . . It wasn't exactly the answer Schiller was hoping to hear. He wanted an episode. (906)

Mailer is forced to guess what made Gilmore a murderer by reading the man's social context. Coming up with no answers, he finally attempts to learn something from Gilmore's dead body.

After the execution, we see Gilmore autopsied. This scene is perhaps most revelatory of Mailer's need to know what is going on inside Gilmore. We see it through the eyes of Jerry Scott, the official witness:

> They started removing different parts of Gilmore's body . . . Jerry Scott had seen a lot of bodies . . . but just sitting there, watching them cut away, got to him. . . . Now the fellow who was at the head of Jerry's table

made an incision from behind Gary's left ear all the way across the top of his head . . . after which he grabbed the scalp on both sides of the cut, and pulled it right open, just peeled the whole face down below his chin until it was inside out like the back of a rubber mask. (982–83)

This is the reality of death, but Mailer's language also implies a literalized version of looking inside Gilmore's head, under his skin, to see what is "truly" there. This is what Mailer and Schiller's team have been trying to do all along, and failing. Alive, Gilmore does not give them the confessions that they want—he cannot or will not explain what it felt like to kill, or be violent, or what it meant to grow up in prison and with his troubled family. Trying to know Gilmore intimately finally leads to a complete knowledge of his physical death, and little else.

"Truth" may be absent, but Schiller and Mailer are ultimately able to manufacture an arresting vision of Gary Gilmore for the mass media. It is within the context of this image production, I want to argue, that the "hip" of Gilmore's murderousness matters. By the time Mailer wrote *Executioner* in the late seventies, the slang terms "hipster" and "hip" meant something slightly different from the 1950s "rebel." To be hip in the seventies was to be on the cutting edge of popular culture, to be in the know about what things were cool and what things were not. Perhaps most importantly, being hip meant being able to negotiate and manipulate the flow of images, styles, entertainment, and goods available in consumer culture. *Executioner* features both kinds of hipsters: the murderous, fifties-style "white negro" rebel Gary Gilmore and the swingin' seventies pop media promoter/producer Lawrence Schiller. What unites these hipsters is an ability to control death, whether that's through action or representation. Gilmore kills people and then insists upon going through with his execution; Schiller is known as "the journalist who deal[s] in death."[17] Both men have control over Gilmore's death story, although the murderous rebel is doomed to die and place his image in Schiller's custody. Gilmore and Schiller's brands of hipness are—at least in Mailer's novel—dependent upon each other.

As a notoriously violent American celebrity,[18] Mailer clearly fancies himself a version of Gilmore. And yet what he seems to share most with Gilmore is less a violent streak than a desire for self-promotion. One of Mailer's early books is in fact called *Advertisements for Myself*. Robert Merrill describes Mailer as a man who wished to invent a series of self-images which would eradicate who he had been in the past, or give him the ability to control what other people would see when they consumed him as an author-celebrity. He notes that Mailer never discusses his early life as a "nice Jewish boy from Brooklyn," and that after publishing the hit novel *The Naked and the Dead*, "Mailer did begin to refashion his life. . . . By the middle of the 1960s Mailer had pretty well established himself as the most notorious literary figure in America," a fact which Mailer himself referred to as the "Mailer legend."[19] Like Gilmore, Mailer wanted to generate an image of himself which other people could consume — only he didn't want to hire a publicist like Schiller to do it. He did the job himself.

Converting yourself into a spectacle, as Gilmore demonstrates, is often connected with violence. Mailer describes negative portrayals of himself on the radio and in books as "murder in the mass media."[20] Despite the pitfalls, these men pursue publicized identities because marketing yourself as spectacle is also a way of taking power in a culture which is, after World War II, increasingly dominated by image production and consumption. Whereas murder in *Red Badge* is associated with factories and industrialism, murder in *Executioner* is connected to the postindustrial media economy.

For Mailer, celebrity is one of the only methods by which a person in postwar America is able to control his or her life. Becoming famous for murdering is a quick and easy way for people to seize control of the means of production and engage in a truly rebellious, or revolutionary, act. Finally, Mailer seems to offer the three figures of Gilmore, Schiller, and himself as allegories for identity in a culture where death and truth are indistinguishable from a promotional campaign.

✸ Pop True Crime and Economic Performance Anxiety

> Torture. Dismemberment. Rape. Cannibalism. Incest. Murder. His crimes make Ted Bundy and Charles Manson sound like choirboys! . . . Complete with never before published photos including artwork by Lucas himself!
> —From the blurb on serial killer Henry Lee Lucas's biography, *Henry Lee Lucas*, by Joel Norris

For Americans living after Gary Gilmore's celebrity in the late seventies, serial killers like Henry Lee Lucas and Ted Bundy are media icons. This is so widely known, and so generally condemned, that film auteur Oliver Stone made an entire movie, *Natural Born Killers*, based on the critique of serial killer celebrity. Like *The Executioner's Song*, *Natural Born*

Killers focuses—often ironically—on the promotion and popularization of charismatic young Americans who murder people and commit other violent crimes. For Mailer and Stone, the murderers themselves are less problematic than the media industry which makes them famous; Stone ends his film with Mickey (one of the killers) telling a tabloid TV reporter that he's the morally bereft "Frankenstein" who made Mickey possible in the first place. Mickey and his wife Mallory then shoot the reporter, filming it all on a portable TV camera.

In movies like *Natural Born Killers*, Americans can look critically at their pleasure in murder as much as they celebrate murder itself. One might make a similar observation about the ongoing American obsession with high school shootings like the one at Columbine. Although these stories consistently make front page news, op-ed pieces blasting Americans for sinking to a new low in their love of exploitation and sensationalism are just as popular. There's often something like social criticism going on when Americans consume stories about murder. This social criticism even seems to have a specific historical context: serial killers and stories about them are associated with the period beginning roughly near the end of the 1950s.[21] What might the culture and society of post-fifties America have to do with the eruption of a new kind of homicidal pathology? And what exactly is it about serial killer narratives which makes them so seductive, particularly when that seductiveness is so easily and quickly criticized? What I want to suggest is that the serial killer—as both allegory and "reality"—acts out the enraged confusion with which Americans have come to regard their late twentieth century economic and social productivity.

Hitchcock's film *Psycho* (1960) is often cited as the original serial killer movie, which spawned an entire genre of serial killer or "slasher" stories popular throughout the seventies, eighties, and early nineties.[22] However, the film *Psycho* is itself based upon an "original" narrative, the life story of Ed Gein,[23] who in 1957 was discovered to have killed and ritualistically mutilated two elderly women who reminded him of his dead mother. Gein, like *Psycho*'s Norman Bates, was a seemingly ordinary and shy man who lived an isolated life in a rural American town. While Hitchcock's shocking ending to *Psycho* introduced Americans to transvestitism, Gein had already done Hitchcock one better in the shock department: rather than dressing up in his mother's clothing, he used to dress up in her (cured and preserved) skin.

Decades later, American audiences finally got treated to a dose of Gein's true crimes in a film about serial killers called *Silence of the Lambs* which won Best Picture, Best Actor (Anthony Hopkins), Best Actress (Jodie Foster), and Best Director (Jonathan Demme) at the 1991 Academy Awards. In homage to both *Psycho* and Gein's life story, Demme directed a film about a serial killer who wears the female skins of his victims. And it was at this moment—when the cinematic serial killer's crimes were at their most shocking and "true"—that he achieved the status of allegorical figure in what powerful cultural institutions like the Motion Picture Academy name "art."

Because fictional representations of serial killers are often based on the biographies of actual killers, one might say the serial killer narrative spans both fictional and nonfictional genres. Biographical portraits of famous serial killers are available to consumers of the popular genre known as "true crime." Interestingly enough, true crime sections in bookstores are frequently located within or next to sociology sections.[24] True crime seems to consider itself the nonfictional generic counterpart—and the theory of—fictional narratives about crime and criminality. Criminological and true crime accounts of serial killers agree on serial killer demographics and on their personality types. Joel Norris, a "psychobiologist" and author of many true crime accounts of serial murder, writes in his trade paperback *Serial Killers* that most serial killers are white men under forty.[25] His point is reiterated in a scholarly textbook on the topic, Eric W. Hickey's *Serial Murderers and Their Victims*. Hickey notes that "in this study, males were responsible for 88% of all serial murder cases[;] . . . male offenders tended to be in their late 20s[;] . . . 85% of male offenders were white."[26] A great deal of overlap exists between pop true crime and what might be called authentic criminology. Indeed, Hickey introduces his book by acknowledging the contributions true crime authors like Ann Rule (a former police officer, now a best-selling true crime author) have made in his field.

True crime authors and criminologists postulate that serial killers' psychopathology allows them to function normally in most situations; many are able to hide their periodic moments of homicidal psychosis. Most are drifters who commit similar crimes in a number of regions over a period of time. The most noteworthy and characteristic aspect of serial killing is the relative randomness of its victims. Serial killers are rarely acquainted with the people they kill, and for this reason serial killings are sometimes called "stranger murders."[27] Serial killers are also known as "recreational killers" or "lust killers,"[28] indicating the degree to which their acts are associated with the pursuit of leisure and sexual desire.

Often in true crime books we find a kind of self-reflexive cultural analysis of American masculine identity gone awry. As Lynne Segal has observed, masculinity is constituted by a reaction against what is perceived to be "feminine" or "other" in all human beings. That is, for a man to identify himself as masculine, there must exist a series of identities which he refuses to claim as his own. He projects these identities onto subordinated others, which in an American context are most often women, children, and ethnic or sexual minority groups. The other is then generally associated with vulnerability, passivity, domesticity, and emotionality, while the man is "free" of them. "No one can be [masculine] without constantly doing violence to many of the most basic human attributes," Segal writes.[29] To maintain his identity, he must do a kind of psychic violence to himself; he excises and disavows a portion of his feelings and social experiences.

One can see where a purely feminist analysis of serial killing might go, and perhaps rightly: the serial killer, in this analysis, kills off the "feminine vulnerability" in himself when he kills women, and thus proves himself a man. While this reading is a good start, both true crime literature and its subjects are more complex than that—men sometimes kill other men, and women kill too. While clearly there is a deep connection between cultural constructions of masculinity and serial murder—as true crime authors almost unanimously acknowledge—it may not be enough to understand this simply in terms of the violence of gendered hierarchies.

As Mark Seltzer points out in his discussion of serialized violence, masculinity is also associated with dominant modes of economic production and reproduction.[30] Seltzer draws a connection between repetitive male violence and "machine culture," which he links to industrialized mass production and information-processing bureaucracies. In other words, he offers us a way of understanding masculine violence in terms of the kind of work men do in a bureaucratic capitalist culture. This work is repetitious, blurs the boundaries between what is natural and artificial, and takes place in a consumer-oriented economy. Seltzer suggests that serialized violence is a kind of social corollary to working conditions under consumer capitalism. Indeed, the American "ideal" of masculinity is based as much upon what it means to be economically productive as it is upon a repudiation of femininity. The man who makes a great deal of money is seen as more potent, more masculine, than the man who (for example) makes a pittance teaching cultural studies for a living.

Keeping this in mind, I want to take a look at what Ted Bundy referred to in a series of interviews as his "professional job"—kidnapping, raping, and murdering women.[31] Bundy's effort to achieve normal masculinity was profoundly dependent upon his sense of himself as a successful worker. Ann Rule—his former colleague and true crime biographer—reports that during the time he was murdering women in Colorado, Utah, and Seattle, Bundy was pursuing—rather successfully—a career in law and politics. He volunteered with the Republican Party, served on various local committees for the prevention of violent crimes, and matriculated as a law student at the University of Utah. With a bachelor's degree in psychology, he also did a good deal of social work such as volunteering with Rule at a suicide-prevention hotline in Seattle. His background, as Rule puts it, was "stultify-ingly middle-class,"[32] and Bundy was ambitiously pursuing both economic and social upward mobility.

In her biography of Bundy, *The Stranger Beside Me*, Rule is explicit about the relationship between Bundy's crimes and his desire to be upper class. His victims resembled each other quite closely—all were conventionally beautiful and "feminine"; all had long hair parted in the middle; and all of them tended to be middle- to upper-middle-class. His final killing spree in Tallahassee, Florida, took place in a "top" sorority house, a virtual factory for the production of middle-class women. Moreover, Rule and other commentators on Bundy's crimes have noted that Bundy began killing women shortly after being rejected by Stephanie Brooks, a wealthy woman he dated for a year in college who wore her long dark hair parted in the middle. Rule believes that Bundy felt Brooks "outclassed him,"[33] and his subsequent murders of women who resembled her would seem to indicate that his victims were chosen not just for their gendered characteristics but for their apparent class backgrounds as well. One might say that Bundy, rather than marrying up, killed up instead.

Ultimately, Bundy's crimes got him the best job of his career as a fledg-ling lawyer: his own case. When on trial in Colorado and Florida, Bundy acted as his own defense attorney and spent vast amounts of time and energy in law libraries working on his own defense. His state-appointed lawyers served as "counsel" for the most part, and Bundy became famous for discrediting his attorneys, asking that the state reassign him different ones, and generally making a nuisance of himself in court and out with his requests for special treatment and delays. At one point during his Florida trial, he was witness, defendant, and defense attorney all at once.

Bundy wasn't the only one making a career out of his murders. Rule her-self, a single mother of four trying to make ends meet on a police officer's salary and the money she got writing articles for true crime magazines, got her first big break when she realized that she was actually acquainted with Ted Bundy from their work at the suicide prevention hotline. Because she knew him, Rule was able to scoop the story and get exclusive interviews with the recently apprehended killer. One of the most fascinating aspects of *The Stranger Beside Me* is Rule's personal story of her growing fame and success as she writes the book. Her concerns about money, writing, and raising her family are interwoven with Bundy's life story, which often echoes—perversely—her own. Both Bundy and Rule desired professional success, and both used true crime to get it.

✴ Homo Economicus

Economic identity, especially after World War II, is associated with the ability to produce effectively, but more notably with the ability to consume. Juliet Schor describes what economists of this period dub "homo economicus," or economic man: "The most important personality trait of homo economicus is that he can never be satiated. He will always prefer more to less. Although he can become tired of any particular good, there is never a point at which having more goods overall will make him worse off. And because more will always make him better off, his desires are infinite."[34] His dominant trait appears to be a desire to consume infinitely—and, as a result, he must work infinitely as well. Indeed, the premise of Schor's book *The Overworked American* is that homo economicus must essentially become a workaholic in order to support his consumer habits. Serial killers, in true crime and in Hollywood, often seem trapped in what Schor calls the "treadmill" effect of consumer capitalism, where the American Dream is dominated by a frantic desire to work hard enough to maintain it. For these serial killers, the murderous act is a result of their inability to stop working and consuming. They kill after reaching a point when they confuse living people with the inanimate objects they produce and consume as workers.

Tim Cahill names his biography of serial killer John Wayne Gacy *Buried Dreams* in ironic reference to the American Dream of prosperity and political success for which Gacy longed. Gacy had nearly achieved that success when he was caught; he had even had his picture taken with First Lady Roselyn Carter after he organized a large civic parade. Cahill repeatedly calls Gacy a workaholic—and Gacy's criminal acts did indeed become notorious because they appeared to proceed so directly from the contracting work he did in his everyday life. When Gacy was finally arrested, he gave a series of voluntary statements about his crimes. He admitted to killing over thirty boys and claimed many were buried in the crawl space under his home. Later, he drew a concise map of where each of the graves was located in the crawl space. They had been laid out with the precision of a contractor, in such a way as to conserve space and utilize every foot available. Gacy also had a tendency to kill his young employees; they were often told to dig trenches in his crawl space for "laying pipes," which led to reports about the way Gacy had his victims dig their own graves. This was true in some cases, apparently. Gacy, one might say, did not always make a distinction between people and commodities. He used his skills as a contractor to produce buildings and to dispose of dead bodies in a systematic way. The dead bodies created by his criminal acts were literally built into the structure of the house he produced while working as a contractor.

Jeffrey Dahmer, another notorious serial killer, seemed unable to distinguish between murdering men and the labor he performed as a chocolate factory worker. Dahmer's modus operandi was to kill men in his apartment, dismember them, and dissolve their body parts in a fifty gallon drum of acid he kept for that purpose. He occasionally ate parts of his victims' bodies. At work, Dahmer stirred liquid chocolate in large drums. Essentially, Dahmer was treating his victims just as he treated the commodity he produced at the chocolate factory: sometimes he stirred them into large drums of liquid, and sometimes he ate them.[35] Dahmer, as his biographer Don Davis explains, was an utter failure as a worker. Although his family was very middle-class, Dahmer was downwardly mobile: he went from the army to low-paying factory jobs in Milwaukee. Davis draws a telling parallel between the economic depression in Dahmer's birthplace of Akron, Ohio, and Dahmer's own emotional depression. He writes, "In the same way that Akron cannot keep its young [workers], Jeffrey Dahmer had a hard time keeping friends."[36] Just as we find a correspondence between Gacy's overwork and murder, we also find one between Dahmer's underemployment and murder. Ultimately, what matters here is that true crime biographers frequently link serial murder to economic conditions no matter what those conditions might be.

Dahmer has stated that part of what motivated his homicidal behavior was a fear of "abandonment." This fear is an emotional structure associated with interpersonal relationships, but it is also a primary economic relationship between workers and commodities. In a capitalist culture, the commodity is an object which appears to abandon the workers who make it. Marx has called this process "alienation": workers find themselves deprived

The cover of a true crime book about Henry Lee Lucas reads like a grisly resume.

of what they produce because they do not own the means of production nor do they own the products of their labor.[37] Therefore, it would appear that the mass production of commodities is a kind of mass abandonment, for nothing that workers create while on the job belongs properly to them — they cannot keep what they make. One might say that serial killers attempt to mend the wounds of alienation by turning into consumers of death. With each dead body, they are able to bring the dead labor they've wasted back into their bodies or into their zone of influence.

We can see the logic of alienation and its violent repair at work in the biography of Henry Lee Lucas. Lucas, a drifter famous for killing hundreds of people in the South, reported to biographer Joel Norris that his child-hood abuse gave him the sense that he never owned or loved anything. He says: "I was worth nothing. Everything I had was destroyed. My mother, if I had a pony she'd kill it. . . . She wouldn't allow me to love nothin.' . . . She wanted me to do what she said and that's it. That is, make sure the wood is in, the water's in, make sure the fires are kept up. . . . Work! That's it!"[38] Here Lucas connects his sense of alienation to performing endless work for his mother in their rural home. Because his mother worked at home as a prostitute, one might say that Lucas never learned to distinguish between emotional alienation and economic alienation. His mother was a commodity (she sold her body for money) and also an abusive, neglectful parent. He later murdered her. For Lucas, people and commodities were intertwined sources of pain and alienation. Killing his mother was just a way of literalizing her status as a commodity, an inanimate thing.

Marx uses the metaphor of "dead labor" to represent how value is produced and measured in a capitalist culture. This metaphor is useful here as well, for it serves to define the performance of economic and psychological identity we find in the serial killer's repeated acts of murder. Marx writes that "Capital is dead labor. . . . The time during which the laborer works, is the time during which the capitalist consumes the labor-power he has purchased of him. If the laborer consumes his disposable time for himself, he robs the capitalist."[39] When a person is working, he is experiencing what might be called "dead time" because at work, the worker belongs to his employer, the capitalist.[40] The worker feels dead while working, for nothing he does at work enriches his life in any way. His work time, you might say, is dead for him. Moreover, what he produces at work is also dead to him because he does not own it. And yet because he earns a salary, he is rewarded economically for being dead; his worth as a human being is measured for him in terms of how long he is willing to play dead for money. Marx continues his analysis by pointing out that the worker in capitalism is just another commodity which can be purchased and used. He is merely an object among objects, rather than a subject with agency and self-determination. You might say that the message capitalism sends to workers is this: the longer you stay dead, the more you'll get paid. And, as a corollary: the more death you make, the more you'll be paid as well.

One of the basic and painful contradictions a worker must face is that his source of social power is also the source of his degradation as a subject. His work may give him power, but the price he pays is the "death" of his subjectivity, or various parts of his subjectivity over time. When this contradiction becomes too much for him to bear, he may develop a psychopathology which compels him to literalize Marx's metaphoric notion of "dead labor" by killing people who represent it. Murder is, for these men, a way of projecting onto others the destructive feelings inspired by the workplace. This logic is particularly clear in Gacy's case, as he converted his employees (dead labor) into dead people. Dahmer and Lucas, on the other hand, killed and consumed people as if they were commodities. Indeed, Lucas felt he could only possess and love people if they were dead—he reports to Norris that most of the sex he had was with the bodies of women he killed. Lucas's confession is testimony to how far outside the bounds of social acceptability he had to go in order to reclaim the objects capitalism had snatched away from him.

✸. First You Work and Then You Die

In novels such as Patricia Cornwell's *Postmortem* and *All That Remains* we find serial killers who use their work skills to advance their careers as murderers. The heroine of Cornwell's novels, Dr. Kay Scarpetta, is chief medical examiner in Richmond, Virginia. Scarpetta's own job brings her into close contact with the serial killers of both novels, whom she tracks down based on postmortem evidence she gathers from the bodies of their victims during autopsies. In *Postmortem*, Scarpetta ultimately tracks the killer down when she discovers he is a dispatcher for the local 911 emergency service. The killer, Roy McCorkle, has been choosing female victims to rape and murder when they call into the 911 service and their home addresses appear on his computer screen. "All of the calls were made from their homes," Cornwell writes, "Each address immediately flashed on the 911 computer screen. If the residences were in the women's names, the operator knew they probably lived alone."[41] McCorkle's murders, committed when he is off duty, are in some sense the direct antithesis of his job as a person who is supposed to summon help for endangered people. And yet he cannot commit his crimes without the aid of his job, where he gains information about his possible victims. Cornwell describes 911 operators as people for whom "the entire city was a video game." Certainly McCorkle behaves as if his victims—the people he helps at work—are targets in a video game when he chooses to murder them.

Scarpetta locates the killer in the sequel to *Postmortem*, *All That Remains*, by discovering where he works as well as what kind of work he wishes he could do in his spare time. Steven Spurrier is the wealthy proprietor of a bookstore whose first murders are a young lesbian couple who have been buying newspapers from him for several months. Later we discover that part of the fantasy he acts out when stalking and killing couples goes along with what might be called a work fantasy. Spurrier is obsessed with the military, the CIA, and other branches of the secret service: he owns videos, weaponry, and other paraphernalia associated with jobs in these organizations. He also kills his victims with weapons used primarily by the FBI, which initially leads Scarpetta to suspect that the murderer might be an agent. The killer in *All That Remains* commits his crimes as part of a fantasy in which he is not a lonely bookstore owner, but an action hero working for the government on a secret mission. Describing Spurrier's video collection, one investigator notes that "they're all *Lethal Weapon*-type shit, flicks about Vietnam, vigilantes."[42] Spurrier escapes from his life on the job by assuming the identity of a spy or assassin in his fantasies. Believing he was cheated out of a career in the military because he had to care for his sick mother, Spurrier pretends to be the "ultimate soldier." Here we find that fantasy work—used as an escape from real work—is directly related to the serial killer's violent crimes.

Work is also a source of anguish and violence in Bret Easton Ellis's *American Psycho*, the story of a yuppie serial killer named Patrick Bateman set during the 1980s. Like Cornwell's killers, Bateman commits murders which are related to his actual and fantasy experiences of work. For Bateman, the wealthy son of an upper-class East Coast family, work is all about conspicuous consumption. He has a sketchily defined job at an investment firm, but most of the novel is concerned with his voracious appetites for expensive commodities and killing. Several of Batemen's murders explicitly involve the use of pricey widgets. During a typical murder scene, Patrick says:

> Her breasts have been chopped off and they look blue and deflated, the nipples a disconcerting shade of brown. Surrounded by dried blood, they lie, rather delicately, on a china plate I bought at Pottery Barn on top of the Wurlizer jukebox in the corner . . . a bag from Zabar's loaded with sourdough onion bagels and spices sits on the kitchen table while I grind [her] bone and fat and flesh into patties . . . I just remind myself that this thing, this girl, this meat, is nothing, is shit, and along with a Xanax (which I am now taking half-hourly) this thought momentarily calms me.[43]

Images of mutilated bodies are, throughout the novel, interspersed with references to brand name items, gourmet food, and expensive prescription drugs. Unlike the vast majority of serial killer narratives, *American Psycho* is told entirely from the perspective of the serial killer, who remains free at the end of the novel. I would suggest that one reason Bateman is able to escape detection in this narrative is precisely because he makes no attempt to free himself from his work as a consumer. While Cornwell's serial killers perform their murders as reactions against their work lives, Ellis represents Bateman's murders as consumerism taken to its logical extreme. His homicidal activities do not appear to contradict his work life, whereas both McCorkle and Spurrier kill in ways which undermine or cancel out what they do in the workplace. When Bateman kills, he's just going the extra mile, continuing his work during off-hours. In the film version of *American Psycho*, it's strongly suggested that Bateman hasn't been caught because he's imagining all the killings (a possibility that the book keeps much more ambiguous). Whether fantasy or reality, Bateman's murders are a direct reflection of his yuppiedom.

We might conclude that serial killer narratives are generally about the failure to escape economic identity. But as the epithet "recreational killer" suggests, serial killing is also supposed to take place outside the realm of work, like leisure or family time. Henri Lefebvre has theorized that as bourgeois society developed, "family life became separate from productive activity. And so did leisure."[44] If we consider serial killing as a pathological form of recreation, it is logical that we would find serial killing represented as a pathological extension of family relations too. Narratives that connect serial murder with the stresses of fatherhood, motherhood, and even childhood are quite common. When seemingly ordinary family members become serial killers, we find that their pathological transformation is often caused by their discovery that home life is as difficult and demanding as work.[45] Lefebvre's contention that capitalism sets up families and leisure in opposition to labor helps explain why a man who wishes to escape from work might hope to find a safe haven in his family. What seems to convert fathers into murderers is the realization that work does not end when they come home to their wives and children.

The Stepfather (1987), a "sleeper" horror film followed by two sequels, demonstrates the congruence between fatherhood and work, as well as one man's unsuccessful effort to escape both. The movie opens with our antihero Jerry altering his appearance and identity after having brutally murdered his family. Jerry is, we discover, not just a serial killer, but a serial father. His modus operandi is to move from family to family, marrying women with children, all of whom he kills once they "disappoint" him. Jerry facilitates his movement from one family to the next by quitting his job and getting a new one somewhere else; hence, he murders the family he's leaving behind only after he is sure he will be employed afterward. His ability to repeatedly murder his family is contingent upon finding work in a place far enough away from the scene of his crime that he will not easily be noticed.

Having gotten a job as a real estate agent, Jerry quickly ingratiates himself with a new family. Once this occurs, we see Jerry and his new family almost entirely from the point of view of his teenage stepdaughter, Stephanie. She immediately senses that Jerry is dangerous, and Jerry is equally suspicious of her. Stephanie's problems at school force him to confront the fact that his family is not perfect, although he continues to pretend as if it is. When Stephanie is expelled for starting a fight with another student in art class, Jerry insists that "girls don't get expelled." Later, he nearly beats up Stephanie's boyfriend when he kisses her goodnight, insisting that the young man is "trying to rape her." His alternately dismissive and aggressive responses to Stephanie finally alarm her mother, who yells at him for not making an effort to talk to her first about how to raise Stephanie. It is at this point that his new family becomes too much work. In response to his wife's request that they have a talk about family issues, he says menacingly, "I'm taking care of it." His wife asks, "By yourself?" and Jerry nods. This scene in particular is key to finding out what exactly Jerry's murders might mean in the context of American economic identity, which is deeply connected to a "do it yourself" ethos.

At a company barbecue, Jerry says to his fellow real estate agents, "I truly believe that what I sell is the American Dream." Part of the American Dream, of course, is individualism. At work, Jerry is able to be the ultimate autonomous individual—even as he is plotting to kill his present family, the free market always provides him with an opportunity to rebuild himself, get a new identity, and find a new place to raise a family. The free market is explicitly what allows Jerry to individuate himself from his family before he murders them. His comment to his wife, that he can fix their family "by himself," tips us off to his main problem with family life. Family life is work which relies upon social interdependence, rather than individualism. As much as he desires family life—he returns to it again and again—his training as an individual in the free market makes it impossible for him to perform his work in the home.

But why does the father's refusal of family life get represented with such brutal violence in serial killer narratives? Charles Derber, referring to the Menendez brothers, famous for having murdered their millionaire parents, concludes that their "pathology was that they allowed themselves to be socialized so completely." For Derber, the Menendez brothers are a version of Jerry. Their act of violence was a logical extension of the behavior they observed growing up in a family which valued making money above all else.[46] The problem with the Menendez family—and Jerry's fictional fathering—might be that ideals of the marketplace have fully invaded the home.

Rules which are intended to regulate economic exchange serve to regulate socialization in the family. For example, the individual who must aggressively compete with other individuals "works" within the economic sphere, but within the domestic sphere a ruthless pursuit of autonomy and promotion disrupts family life. Violence erupts in the serial killer narrative when family life resists complete assimilation into economic life; a character like Jerry goes homicidal when he must compromise his status as an autonomous individual. In attempting to organize the family by economic principles, he is left with seemingly no choice but to destroy it entirely and move on to the next one.

✳ Taking Pictures

Describing how the name "serial killer" was invented to categorize people who murder repeatedly for seemingly no reason, FBI veteran and ex-Army CID colonel Robert Ressler writes:

> I think what was . . . in my mind were the serial adventures we used to see on Saturday at the movies (the one I liked best was the *Phantom*). Each week, you'd be lured back to see another episode, because at the end of each one there was a cliff-hanger. In dramatic terms, this wasn't a satisfactory ending, because it increased, not lessened the tension. The same dissatisfaction occurs in the minds of serial killers. The very act of killing leaves the murderer hanging, because it isn't as perfect as his fantasy.[47]

This diagnosis is familiar to any consumer of the serial killer narrative, in which we are often told (most famously by serial killer psychiatrist Hannibal Lecter in *Silence of the Lambs*) that the killer is acting out, or creating, some kind of fantasy in his murders. What is interesting here is the way Ressler, who studies serial killers, is himself participating in the same type of serialized, unsatisfying fantasy. When he came up with the name "serial killer," it was *he* who was thinking about adventure serials like *The Phantom*. Along these same lines, we might postulate that part of the pleasure an audience gets out of consuming serial killer narratives is in the way serialized homicidal crimes seem so well-adapted to the mass cultural form.

As Guy Debord points out in *Society of the Spectacle*, late capitalism sells us images as often as it sells us goods. Jean Baudrillard's *Simulations* elaborates on Debord's insight by looking at the way everyday reality is permeated by "simulacra," objects and events which exist only as reproductions and have no proper original version. Simulacra flourish in a culture where mass production and the mass media have altered the way people interpret reality. A culture of simulation encourages people to understand all objects (including other people) as simultaneously fictional and real. Furthermore, simulacra always seem to come in a series of reproductions precisely because fiction in late capitalism is associated with mass production. If indeed homo economicus confuses himself with commodities, Baudrillard's discussion of commodity culture serves to explain why contemporary murder could involve a series of acts designed to make their author—and their object—into simulations. In fact, Joel Black's fascinating analysis of celebrity murderers in *The Aesthetics of Murder* suggests that the fantasy many killers are after is one of media fame. Like Gary Gilmore, they kill precisely in order to see themselves mass produced as simulations in the newspapers and television reports.[48]

Several films and novels about serial killers suggest a connection between image production and murderous acts. In the movie *The Eyes of Laura Mars*, for example, a fashion photographer, Laura Mars, has a telepathic link to the mind of a serial killer. She views murders through his eyes and then duplicates several of the murder scenes in her highly successful photographs of models who appear to be wounding or killing each other. Famous for her provocative photography, she is indebted to a serial killer for her inspiration. In Dennis Cooper's novel *Frisk* we see a similar narrative where an artist simulates murder. Dennis, the novel's point-of-view character, tells the story of his obsessive fantasies about having sexual relations with beautiful, dead men. Throughout most of the novel, the reader is unsure whether Dennis is actually killing men, or if he is merely writing a novel about it. Finally, we discover that his descriptions of murdering young men in Holland are actually a series of letters he's been writing and sending to his old lovers, two brothers named Julien and Kevin.

The violence of serial killers, as I argued earlier, is associated in particular with the aesthetic production of photographs or film. In *Frisk*, we discover that Dennis traces his fascination with eroticized dead bodies back to a series of "snuff" photographs he saw as a teenager in the back room of a magazine shop. *Frisk* begins and ends with short sections titled only with the symbol for infinity. Each is a description of the snuff photographs; in the opening section, we are unsure of whether the boy in the photographs is actually dead, and in the closing section we know that what appears to be a wound in his anus is "actually a glop of paint, ink, makeup, tape, cotton, tissue, and papier-mâché sculpted to suggest the inside of a human body. . . . You can see the fingerprints of the person or persons who made it."[49] Dennis's quest, it turns out, has been to recreate those photographs he saw as a teenager. Once Julien and Kevin answer his letters, the three of them photograph a willing young man, and the result is the description we get in the last section of the book (quoted above). The process of this kind of production, however, is still dependent upon Dennis having seen images of a (possibly) dead boy—just as Laura's photographs are dependent upon her having seen actual murders take place.

Not surprisingly, these fantasy images of murder have their true crime counterpart. Robert Ressler's book *Whoever Fights Monsters* is like other true crime narratives in that it features a series of photographs in the middle of the book, much like a centerfold. These photographs are of Ressler himself, the serial killers he interviewed, many of their victims, the crime scenes, and the law enforcement officers on various cases. Other books—such as Norris's *Henry Lee Lucas*—include photographs of the victims' dead bodies. Such photographs add to the scientific, or ethnographic, feel of true crime, but they are also clearly for entertainment. They seem to ask: Can we read "evil" in this criminal's face? Can we imagine what it must have felt like to be murdered when we look at the dead, chopped up, naked bodies of his victims? Asking these questions, we are invited to engage in a simulation of our own, inseparable from the "truth" of true crime.

Private Parts is a cult film where a photographer's work is inextricable from his murderous acts, which involve killing beautiful young women who find him attractive. We discover that George, the photographer, is actually a woman whose mother essentially forced her to become a man because she thinks all women are whores. George lives in her mother's hotel, where she photographs beautiful women whom she later kills with a hypodermic. Her particular ritual—which is acted out in detail during several scenes—is to attach a photograph of her victim's face to a transparent, blow-up sex doll filled with water. When she gets excited enough, she uses a hypodermic to inject the doll with her own blood in an obvious reference to the act of ejaculation. In order for George to have a sexual relationship with anyone, it would seem, they must be converted into a photograph and blood must be shed. Furthermore, George's obsession with photography and murder is linked to her own desire to pass as a man. Although the photographic image is often understood to reproduce "reality," George must constantly confront the contradiction between realistic images and reality itself. While she *appears* to be a man, she in fact is not. Her murders are a way to maintain her sense of herself as a man and to keep her masculine appearance intact. It is only when a woman is dead or in a photograph that she cannot discover the difference between George-the-male image and George-the-female body.

George—like many serial killers—is torn apart by a desire to appear masculine and, more importantly, productive. Serial killers are represented as people who long desperately to appear ordinary on the outside: they are intriguing because they *succeed* at seeming normal while engaging repeatedly in highly deviant, antisocial acts. We can understand the serial killer's identity in terms of a desire to be consumed as if he were a photographic image which does not have any "real" or "truth" behind it.[50] The serial killer wishes to be looked upon as if he has nothing to hide, as if his normal image conceals nothing, so that he may do his "work" as efficiently as possible. However, people who *consume* the serial killer image in narrative enjoy it precisely for the opposite reason: they "know" the image isn't real, and are thus given the chance to feel as if they've outsmarted their own simulated culture. Viewers of photographic images generally do not expect a photograph to hide or alter any aspect of reality—they expect reality to be *revealed* in it. But viewers of the serial killer image can "know better," and that's the hook.

Nowhere is this tendency more obvious than in *Martin* and *Henry: Portrait of a Serial Killer*, two movies in which serial killers try to convert themselves into photographic or filmic images which an audience gets to "see through." Both films hinge on the audience's ability to get at the "truth" of the killer's image and understand him for the criminal that he is. In George Romero's *Martin*, the teenage protagonist Martin believes that he's a vampire, having been told so by his crazed, religious grandfather. Martin convinces himself that he's a vampire by murdering people and drinking their blood. But he also needs publicity to complete his image, so he calls a radio talk show and describes his "vampiric" deeds. Throughout *Martin*, the audience is generally led to believe that he is not a vampire: he requires a syringe full of drugs to subdue his victims, and kills them human-style, with a razor. We are also given plenty of clues, such as Martin's strange home environment and his sexual uncertainties, that Martin has many reasons to be mentally unbalanced. While there remains some doubt about Martin's "true" nature, it seems fairly clear that this is a movie portraying a person who *seems like* a vampire—so much so that his grandfather finally kills him by driving a stake through his heart. Part of the pleasure in watching this film is in knowing the "truth" about Martin's crimes. He's no vampire, but a serial killer.

Henry: Portrait of a Serial Killer, loosely based on the life of Henry Lee Lucas and his partner Otis Toole, is about a prolific killer who feigns an image of normalcy and consumes movies of his own murderous acts. One of the most graphic and disturbing points in the film comes when Henry and Otis shoot home movies of themselves torturing and killing a family. Subsequently, they watch it and drink beer, joking around with the "slo-mo" and "reverse" buttons. Earlier in the film, after Henry and Otis murder two prostitutes, we discover that Henry views all human relations as a matter of life and death; for him, killing is an ordinary response to human interaction. "[Killing] is always the same and always different," he says, "It's either you or them—one way or the other." The pseudo-documentary style of the film calls attention to Henry's "normal" act—the grainy photography and cinema verité acting invite audiences to see it as artfully constructed. In some ways, *Henry* is actually a boring narrative—although its content is often gruesome and terrifying, we are always returned to scenes of characters eating dinner or playing cards in an almost exaggeratedly normal manner.

What appears to be ordinary in this film turns out to be both realistic and fake at once. Henry's "normal" facade conceals his violence and brutality. But the docudrama artificiality of *Henry*'s realism works to enhance our sense that Henry and Otis's ordinariness is sheer performance, and utterly extraordinary. While an audience can see through Henry's "ordinary guy" act, doubts about what is ordinary remain. Just as *Martin* encourages an audience to ask if in fact Martin's vampiric image might not be reality, *Henry* offers us the possibility that serial killing might indeed be more normal (or, at least, common) than we think. Even when audiences are offered a way to deconstruct images in these movies, there remains a kind of escape hatch for simulation. One can believe and not believe in these serial killers at the same time, as it were. And in the end, this escape hatch provides a way for audiences to ignore the critical aspects of these narratives as they apply to economic relations under postwar capitalism.

✳ The Forensic Fetish

In the late twentieth century, serial killer narratives take a turn for the clinical. Probably influenced by the runaway success of *Silence of the Lambs*, which gets into the gory details of the relationships between forensic pathologists and serial killers, a spate of late-1990s and early-2000s movies deal with people who are professionally trained to read murders and figure out who perpetrated them. Rather than focusing on the killer and his economic pathologies, these movies deal with the professionals who are trained to catch serial murders. These movies are, in essence, about the economy which grew up in response to serial killing.

The moody, baroque *Se7en* epitomizes the forensics subgenre with its arcane literary references and fanatically allegorical killer. David Mills is a new cop learning the ropes from his wise partner William Somerset in an unnamed industrial wasteland of a city. They're hot on the trail of a new killer in town, whose carefully planned murder scenes are like Victorian-era *tableaux vivants*, each victim carefully made up and positioned in his or her deathbed to represent one of the seven deadly sins. As David and William examine each scene, we learn that the killer is an intellectual artist. He spends a great deal of time on each victim, in one case representing "gluttony" by forcing a man to gorge himself to death on fattening foods while he's strapped into a chair over a period of weeks.

While David wants to leap into action and get the murderer, William knows that the only way to find their killer is to head straight to the library, where they can fortify themselves with the scholarly knowledge needed to solve the mystery. After all, they're dealing with a killer who pads out his murder *tableaux* with references to *Paradise Lost* and Dante's *Inferno*. In fact, the library serves as a laboratory in *Se7en*: the detectives discover the murder's identity by tracking who has checked out particular books. Starling hangs out in the lab reading the bodies of Buffalo Bill's victims in *Silence of the Lambs*, but the men in *Se7en* have to read the books their killer reads.

The point is, it takes training and education to trap a serial killer. Not just anybody can do this kind of work.

This represents a sea change in movies about catching killers. In her appealing and brilliant *Men, Women and Chainsaws: Gender in the Modern Horror Film*, Carol Clover identifies "the final girl" as one of the most important generic elements of serial killer movies in the late 1970s and early '80s. A female foil to their masculine killer, the final girl is a tough-minded, tomboyish, and usually nonsexual person who manages to elude certain death by outwitting the killer, often aiding the police in tracking him down. Sometimes, she kills him single-handedly after he's slaughtered all her friends.

Traditionally, the final girl has only a tenuous connection to the economy: she is a teenager or high school student, not a worker. But after *Silence of the Lambs* and *Se7en*, she gets a job as a forensics expert. She plays nearly the same role within these narratives—compare Starling's final showdown with Buffalo Bill to that of countless final girls in movies from *Halloween* to retro-slasher *Scream*—but she gets paid to do it. The serial killer's hideous relationship with labor and his anguished attempts to integrate lost lives into himself through murder and self-simulation finally give women something to do other than merely escape death.

Copycat, another movie clearly inspired by *Silence of the Lambs*, helped make 1995 the year of forensic heroism.[51] In a story that's far too meta for its own good, Helen Hudson is a nationally known expert on serial killers whose best-selling books have made her a recent target of a particularly vicious murderer. After police manage to rescue Helen while the killer is trying to hang her in a bathroom stall, she sinks into depression and agoraphobia. Refusing to leave her high-rise apartment, she spends all her time online, talking to other neurotic shut-ins in chat rooms. She's pulled out of self-imposed exile when a new serial killer comes on the scene. His MO is to kill women in ways that re-create famous serial killer crime scenes from history—especially the history that Helen has described in her books.

The killer is the ultimate copycat criminal, a kind of postmodern artist whose work is all done in reference to other people's crimes. (Interestingly, a few years later in 1998, Gus Van Sant released a shot-by-shot remake of *Psycho*, implicitly acknowledging that the art of serial killing is all about stylish imitation.) Only an academic criminologist like Helen, who has devoted her life to serial killer history, can possibly help the FBI track down the killer. Plus, her own life is at stake: the killer wants his crowning achievement to be a re-creation of Helen's own brush with death. Helen teams up with federal agent M. J. Monahan to track down the killer, leading to a climactic scene featuring two professional serial-killer-hunting women facing off against a man who studies the same things they do. The final girl has truly become the final forensic analyst, and her anxieties are as much economic as anything else.

The Bone Collector and *The Cell* take place inside the minds of people who hunt killers. Both register the anxieties of being a professional woman in a male-dominated field, and both draw parallels between serial killing and being a working woman. In *The Bone Collector*, Amelia Donaghy is a shaky, rookie forensic analyst who is being mentored by the brilliant but recently paralyzed Lincoln Rhyme. Hot on the tail of a *Se7en*-style allegorical killer obsessed with New York history, Lincoln does a *Rear Window* with Amelia, guiding her through crime scenes and freaky dark places via cell phone. She's the eyes, ears, and body; he's the brains. To catch the killer, they have to figure out why he's decorating his murder scenes with old bones. More importantly, Amelia has to learn to use a male brain to become a forensics expert. Lincoln's wisdom animates her body until she is able to retrain herself to think the way he does.

In *The Cell*, our psychologist hero Catherine penetrates the mind of a killer and ultimately sucks him into her own mind in order to solve the mystery of where he's hidden his last victim. Just as Amelia uses technology to bring Lincoln's voice into her ear, guiding her through each step in the investigation, Catherine uses a science fictional machine called a "neuromed" to literally plug herself into the brain of the catatonic killer. Trained to understand the symbology of the unconscious mind, she wanders through the killer's childhood memories of abuse and his adult messianic fantasies about artistically mutilating women. Her hope is to gain his trust and convince him to tell her where he's left his final victim trapped inside a tank that is gradually filling with water. But there's more at stake than saving a woman's life. Catherine's job is on the line.

At the Campbell Center where she works on the experimental neuromed, her main focus is on a psychologically disturbed little boy whose father is providing all the funding for her work in the hope that she can cure his son. As the movie opens, she's been given six months to prove that her methods will work. If she gets no results, her funding will be yanked. Luckily, her violent psychological encounters with the killer teach her something valuable about how to use the neuromed. When she goes inside the killer's mind, she has no control and can't seem to win any battles with him. But when she brings him inside her own mind, she squeezes the information she needs out of him and is able to make him come to terms with his mental anguish. Her encounter with him inside her own mind ends with a strange baptism scene, where Catherine dips the killer in water and forgives him before he dies.

As the film closes, we see that this encounter has taught Catherine that her mind is stronger than a killer's—and now she can work more effectively. She invites her young patient into her mind, surrounding him with beautiful images, and begins to draw him out of his shell. Serial killing may be a dead-end career for men, but for women it's a great resume-builder.

At the turn of the twenty-first century, several events conspired to change representations of serial murder in public life and the mass media. The apprehension of Ted Kaczynski, also known as the Unabomber, created a new breed of human monster: the serial killer terrorist. Like John Doe in *Se7en*, Kaczynski was a prolific writer and his motives could not be understood without the aid of political philosophers. Kaczynski could hardly be called a lust killer; there was nothing fun about his dense manifesto, "Industrial Society and Its Future." Then, after terrorists destroyed the World Trade Center in 2001, the serial killer figure began to recede in the public imagination. He was replaced by the terrorist.

Thus, the so-called sniper killers in the Washington, D.C., area during 2002 were treated like terrorists rather than recreational murderers. During John Muhammad and John Lee Malvo's killing spree, law enforcement called on the Department of Homeland Security to help with the investigation, and newspaper articles speculated about whether the random shootings were a new kind of terrorist tactic. When the snipers were caught, much was made of the fact that the elder sniper, John Muhammad, was Muslim. Both men were charged in Virginia under a new antiterrorism statute. And yet to anyone familiar with serial killer history, the killers' MO was much closer to that of a Jeffrey Dahmer than a member of the Taliban. The snipers killed random victims, for reasons that seemed primarily emotional. Perhaps their emotions were a response to what Kaczynski calls "industrial society," but neither man articulated their motivations in those terms. They certainly put a lot of work into their killing apparatus, creating a hidden sniper lookout in the trunk of Muhammad's car and using fairly sophisticated weapons. But despite all the labor and expertise the snipers poured into murder, they had no political motivations nor did they have any wish to undermine state power.

Stories about the snipers and Kaczynski, as well as the ongoing American obsession with images of the twin towers exploding, demonstrate the degree to which terrorists have replaced serial killers in the social imaginary as the sorts of pathological individuals who are most in need of forensic analysis and containment. Although Hollywood types are attempting to exercise good taste by not manufacturing very many stories about terrorists in the wake of 9/11, there is no paucity of tales about the Unabomber.

Apprehended from his tiny Montana shack in 1996, Kaczynski has been the subject of countless books (academic and popular), TV shows (including extensive trial coverage on Court TV), and the subject of a cheesy TV movie called *Unabomber: The True Story*.[52] The so-called *Unabomber Manifesto* has been printed by various small presses and posted all over the Internet. As his manifesto makes clear, Kaczynski killed people in a protest against industrialization and its effect on the media. In a telling passage, he writes, "Freedom of the press is of very little use to the average citizen as an individual. The mass media are largely under the control of large organizations that are integrated into [the industrial-technological] system. . . . In order to get our message before the public with some chance of making a lasting impression, we've had to kill people."[53] Many of his murders were also aimed at undermining the kind of intellectual labor he'd been forced to engage in as a mathematics PH.D. student and professor. He sent his bombs to academics and scientists, and in his writing he blames universities for the rampant technologization of everyday life.

While Kaczynski killed for consciously political reasons, I would argue that this doesn't push him over into the category of terrorist. As I explained earlier, one could easily make the case that Ted Bundy and John Wayne Gacy killed for unarticulated but nevertheless salient politico-economic reasons. Is the difference between a serial killer and a terrorist only a matter of being someone who is capable of self-consciously writing a manifesto rather than unconsciously responding to political forces?

Two narratives about terrorism, the movie *Fight Club* and footage of the Al Qaeda attacks on New York and Washington, D.C., demonstrate the cultural logic at work when we confuse serial killing with acts of terrorism. In *Fight Club*, directed by *Se7en* scribe and director John Fincher, a nameless corporate drone narrator meets an exciting, visionary man named Tyler Durden. Tyler leads the narrator into an underground world of male violence called Fight Club, a place where men meet to beat one another senseless as a way of coping with the maddening effects of consumer culture. Gradually, under the leadership of Tyler and the narrator, Fight Club morphs into a string of terrorist cells across the country. Tyler becomes an underground cult celebrity, and at the end blows up some buildings in a major metropolitan center. A hyper-ironic critique of capitalist culture, *Fight Club* glamorizes Tyler and the narrator's anticonsumer crusade. In a twist ending, we discover that the narrator is schizophrenic and has a split personality. Tyler is a figment of his commodity-addled imagination. Like the Unabomber, Tyler/narrator is clearly mentally ill and has a fairly thoughtful critique of his culture.

What makes *Fight Club* a movie about a terrorist rather than a serial

The unnamed hero of *Fight Club* lectures his fellow terrorists in Project Mayhem.

killer is its emphasis on community. Although the narrator has invented his muse Tyler Durden, he hasn't invented Fight Club nor its many incarnations across the country. The people working with him to undermine corporate capitalism are quite real, as is the lurid downtown explosion as the film ends. Tyler/narrator may be nuts, but he has an army. In *Se7en*, by contrast, John Doe acts alone. He has a very explicit message that he wants to convey by posing his victims in the postures of the seven deadly sins: contemporary culture is carnal, degraded, driven by greed. But John Doe hasn't attracted anyone to his cause. He is a murderer rather than a terrorist because he isn't part of a movement.

And yet in the year before 9/11, the U.S. State Department defined terrorism as "Premeditated, politically motivated violence perpetrated against noncombatant targets by subnational groups or clandestine agents, usually intended to influence an audience."[54] There is no mention of terrorism having to do with communities of like-minded individuals, despite the fact that the State Department's annual report on terrorism defines every terrorist organization in terms of its "strength" (meaning number of members).[55] What these two definitions of terrorism reveal is that there is a fundamental confusion at the core of how the U.S. government imagines terrorism. All terrorists engage in political violence, but it's unclear whether terrorists are "groups" or individual "agents." This slippage between groups and individuals mirrors the cultural confusion that has merged the figures of terrorist and serial killer in the mass media.

Footage of the Al Qaeda terrorists driving jets into the Twin Towers and

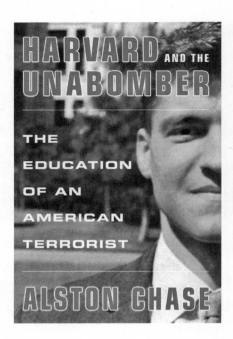

THE
EDUCATION
OF AN
AMERICAN
TERRORIST

HARVARD AND THE UNABOMBER

ALSTON CHASE

The cover of a Ted Kaczynski biography emphasizes that he's a terrorist rather than a serial killer.

the Pentagon illustrate one possible outcome of this problem. News media repeatedly played movies of the towers collapsing, bodies falling from their upper floors, like a hideous preview of a scene from *Matrix Reloaded*. Frantic with fear and sadness, audiences for these images could only see death; they weren't sure how to interpret what had caused it.[56] Into this void of meaning stepped President George W. Bush, whom you might in this narrative situation call the nation's forensic analyst. He called the terrorists "evil" and refused to acknowledge any kind of political context for their acts (which should have been by definition political, since they were terrorists). Al Qaeda's acts of terrorism were, if you took the president's word for it, indistinguishable from acts of serial murder. Most media audiences understood the 9/11 attacks as recreational violence, the work of sociopathic freaks rather than a political organization with coherent if disturbing goals. A year after the attacks, Bush said that a Muslim engaging in terrorism is "just a murderer."[57] The litany of horrifying 9/11 attack images allowed Bush to persuade the vast majority of Americans that the terrorists could not be stopped unless the country went from its attack on Afghanistan to "Operation Iraqi Freedom." Polls conducted during the invasion of Iraq showed that over half the people in the United States believed that Saddam Hussein had been directly involved in 9/11.[58] I don't mean to point out simply that one form of confusion leads to another; rather, I want to underscore how the inability to distinguish terrorism from serial killing is fundamentally related to the urge to drain all violent homicidal acts of their political meaning. If Al Qaeda attacks are treated like serial murder, then it "makes sense" to march into whatever country we choose to destroy others like them because terrorists are evil individuals who could be anywhere. They are not groups of people with a political and social context, but merely autonomous deviants who could come from anywhere and fly planes into any old place they think might be fun to blow up.[59]

Framing Ted Kaczynski's crimes as terrorist acts performs the same ideological function that Bush's antiterrorist rhetoric does. Narratives about the Unabomber as a terrorist conflate the acts of a lone individual killer—albeit a well-read and politically minded one—with those of terrorist organizations who represent a social force. A recent scholarly work, *Harvard and the Unabomber: The Education of an American Terrorist*, is a perfect case-in-point: even on the book's jacket copy, Kaczynski is referred to as both a serial killer and a terrorist. But like John Doe in *Se7en*, Kaczynski acted alone.

When the unconscious social motivations of serial killers are confused with the conscious, collective actions of terrorists, it becomes hard to tell psychosis apart from politics. While it may be useful to know that politics can be insane, and vice versa, deliberately confusing the two ideas does little to help audiences orient themselves in anything remotely like reality. It undermines Americans' ability to interpret the sources and contexts for the violence they see erupting around them every day.

Consuming serial killer tales is all about alienation—but not the good kind that Bertold Brecht once praised when he imagined a "theater of alienation" that would awaken audiences to the social forces constructing their lives. Instead, stories about serial killers come to us as commodities, safely framed as entertainment. Even as audiences learn about the profound violence to which alienated labor can lead, they are alienated from their own discovery. All that's left for us to do is consume these stories—again and again and again.

2. MAD DOCTORS

Professional Middle-Class Jobs Make You Lose Your Mind

Under tremendous pressure from his funders to create the ultimate fusion energy source, renowned physicist Dr. Otto Octavius has been experimenting around the clock with a hideously dangerous fireball. Just as a little side project, he's invented huge, artificially intelligent robotic arms that are capable of interfacing with his nervous system. When he dons the arms, Octavius can use them as prostheses to manipulate his energy source without exposing himself to radiation.

At last, the big day arrives: Octavius will be demonstrating his powerful, self-renewing energy source for corporate sponsors, research colleagues, and a young college student named Peter Parker who has expressed interest in the doctor's work. But something goes terribly wrong. The experimental fireball explodes, and in the chaos that ensues Octavius's robotic arms fuse permanently with his nervous system, taking over his brain and turning him into an energy-obsessed maniac with four fantastically strong, serpentine arms growing out of his back. Converted into the evil Dr. Octopus, dubbed Doc Ock in the press, he rampages through the city stealing chemicals and machines to use in his secret lab, where he plans to build another energy source like the first. Controlled by the artificial intelligence in his robot arms, the once-kindly doctor has become violently focused on succeeding with his research at any cost. Instead of using the robot arms to do his job, the arms are using him to do theirs. And the only person who can stop him is Spider-Man, the alter-ego of Peter Parker, who has also become a superpowered being named after a multilegged creature in a weird brush with radiation.

Doc Ock needs one more preposterously named chemical to complete his fireball brew. So he strikes a bargain with Harry Osborne, Spider-Man's enemy from way back, who has a big jar of the stuff. If Doc Ock brings Spider-Man to Osborne, the chemical will be his. As *Spider-Man 2* (2004) careens into its action-packed conclusion, Spider-Man has escaped from Osborne's clutches and is swinging from building to building in a race against time. He must rescue the imperiled Mary Jane from Doc Ock and stop the mad doctor from carrying out his insane plan to reignite the potentially earth-destroying power source. As Mary Jane screams and the fireball grows to predictably disastrous proportions, Spider-Man wrestles with Doc Ock.

Their physical fight is nothing compared to the mental struggle Doc Ock undergoes at the last minute, when Spider-Man helps Dr. Octavius recapture his own mind from the tentacular bonds of his arms. Octavius realizes that saving lives is more important than completing his crazy experiments and heroically plunges to his death in the ocean so he can douse the ever-expanding fireball. Doc Ock is the archetypal mad doctor of fantasy cinema, a professional whose drive to succeed ultimately induces him to merge with his own experiments. His mind is literally consumed by work, and he can only reclaim it in a spectacular act of self-destruction.

Narratives charting the descent of a doctor into madness register profound cultural anxieties about the medical and scientific professions, which are driven almost entirely by the minds of their practitioners. Because these professionals also occupy some of the highest class positions in the U.S. economy, with access to tremendous resources and power, we are left with the uneasy sense that our social fabric is one mental breakdown away from being consumed by a whacked doctor's corporate-funded fireball.

Definitions of professional work nearly always contrast it with manual or physical labor. Former U.S. Secretary of Labor Robert Reich calls professional labor a form of "symbolic-analytic services," noting that "symbolic analysts solve, identify, and broker problems by manipulating symbols. They simplify reality into abstract images that can be rearranged, juggled, experimented with, communicated to other specialists, and then, eventually, transformed back into reality."[1] Professionals thus work in a liminal space between "reality" and "abstract images." But certain professions, such as the applied sciences and clinical medicine, are entirely dedicated to making abstract claims "real."

What I want to explore here are the ways fictional narratives grapple with anxieties about what can go wrong when doctors make abstract claims into material conditions. Bound up with the figure of the mad doctor are a whole host of social terrors: doctors who go mad can hurt or kill their patients; they can transform human bodies and other living beings; they can impose "immoral ideas" about reality onto the physical world; and they can sever the connection between human bodies and minds. Each of these fears is intimately connected to discomfort with the process by which professionals translate ideas and abstractions into material reality. They are also, I will argue, connected to the often-brutal process by which academic and other institutions turn people into doctors and then use them for their minds.

As early as 1922, philosopher Georg Lukács laid the foundations for a critique of professional labor in his essay "Reification and the Consciousness of the Proletariat." What is most disturbing about mental labor, he writes, is the way it alienates workers from their own minds. Because what they sell to an employer is their ability to think and have ideas, professional workers are put into a position where they literally do not own portions of their own minds for those parts of the day when they are on the job. Lukács describes this process as "the structure of reification sink[ing] more deeply . . . into the consciousness of man." He continues:

> Here it is precisely subjectivity itself, knowledge, temperament, and powers of expression that are reduced to an abstract mechanism functioning autonomously and divorced from the personality of their "owner." . . . His qualities and abilities are no longer an organic part of his personality, they are things which he can "own" or "dispose of" like the various objects of the external world.[2]

Lukács offers us one possible reason for cultural anxieties about doctors going mad: the more these professionals labor, the more they lose control of their minds. Their very thoughts no longer belong to them, and their ideas are reified, turned into commodity things which belong to "the medical profession" or "science." Looked at from this perspective, it is no wonder that the terrifying underbelly of professionalism often gets represented in the popular imaginary as mental disintegration.

In Frank Norris's late-nineteenth-century naturalist novel *McTeague*, a foundational narrative for the mad doctor genre, we discover that the process of maintaining a professional identity is so brutal that it ultimately turns the novel's eponymous dentist into a homicidal maniac. Movies and novels in the tradition of *Dr. Jekyll and Mr. Hyde* take up this theme in stories of mad doctors who achieve professional status only by turning themselves into tragic scientific experiments. Finally, post–World War II "brain" movies like *Donovan's Brain* and *Pi* dramatize what happens when professional minds become commodity fetishes. Ultimately, I argue that narratives about the mad doctor can be read as one way pop culture grapples with the contradictions implicit in the idea of intellectual property. How can we sell our intellects and yet remain ourselves? Mad doctors are each a kind of Jekyll and Hyde figure: bearing and treating sickness, experimenter and experimented-upon, they embody both the horror of mental productivity and the horror of discovering you've become a product.

✳ "Ain't I a doctor?"

After working as a dentist in San Francisco for over a decade, McTeague receives a letter from City Hall which informs him "that he had never received a diploma from a dental college, and that in consequence he was forbidden to practise his profession any longer."[3] When his wife Trina tries to explain what this means, McTeague asks, "Ain't I a dentist? Ain't I a doctor?" Trina retorts, "But, Mac, you ain't a dentist any longer; you ain't a doctor. You haven't the right to work. You never went to a dental college" (148).

The defrocked dentist of Norris's novel makes several half-hearted attempts to continue working as a doctor, but when he is served with a second notice prohibiting him from practicing dentistry, he finally quits. Driven into manual labor jobs, deprived of the prosperity he has enjoyed for many years, and increasingly more "brutish," McTeague becomes an unemployed alcoholic who beats, abandons, and ultimately murders his wife.

The only "college certified" dentist we meet in *McTeague* is referred to merely as "the other dentist," and, more elaborately, "that poser, that rider of bicycles, that courser of greyhounds" (85). This "other dentist" has middle-class consumer tastes—he rides bicycles, which were a new invention at the time *McTeague* was written, and he courses (i.e., bets on) greyhounds, an activity which requires surplus money and leisure time. McTeague, as Norris puts it, is a "poor crude dentist of Polk Street, stupid, ignorant, vulgar, with his sham education and plebeian tastes, whose only relaxations were to eat, to drink steam beer [which is very cheap], and to play upon his concertina" (17). He is, in other words, neither modern, educated, nor a man of "taste."

And yet the only important difference between the "other dentist" and McTeague is a college degree—a symbol designed to classify some minds as more capable of abstract thought than others.

McTeague's education has given him skills, but no abstract symbols. He learns dentistry from a "quack" who comes through his little mining town and agrees to take on the impoverished boy as an apprentice. As if he were working in the trades, McTeague trains to be a dentist by watching the "quack" fix teeth. He doesn't study medicine or biological science. He merely observes physical actions and learns to imitate them successfully. In the end, McTeague loses out because he learned dentistry as manual labor—although he's good enough at his job to pull patients' teeth with his bare hands, he can't claim the approval of a professional institution like the "other dentist" can. McTeague's body is an excellent commodity, but his mind isn't. This lack of mental muscle destroys his prospects. But his education, as poor as it may have been, does allow him to compete with "the other dentist"—until a chance falling-out with his best friend Marcus inspires Marcus to report McTeague to the city for practicing without a license.

A work of economic theory published in the same year as *McTeague*, Thorstein Veblen's *The Theory of the Leisure Class*, proposes a version of economic Darwinism as one way to understand McTeague's competition with the "other dentist." Veblen comments sarcastically on the work of social Darwinists like William Graham Sumner, who argues that "the well-to-do could be equated with the biologically fittest." Indeed, Veblen contends with no little irony, the rich are fit—and they got that way by clawing their way to the top of the food chain like savages. "The tendency of the pecuniary life is, in a general way, to conserve the barbarian temperament," he writes, "but with the substitution of fraud and prudence, or administrative ability, in place of the predilection for physical damage that characterizes the early barbarian." Competition for survival in the leisure class selects for "administrative ability" (getting a college degree or knowing how to report people to City Hall) rather than "mechanical industry" (knowing how to pull teeth).[4] No matter what tools are used, the process is still hopelessly brutal.

We might call McTeague's ruthless, animalistic behavior an illustration of what Veblen describes as "the barbarian temperament" of people attempting to achieve membership in the leisure class. Thus McTeague's "brute" strength and violence are not so much symptomatic of his working-class background but rather of his intense, thwarted desire to escape it. McTeague's problem is that he doesn't properly belong to any class: he's failed to professionalize himself adequately, and yet he's too well-trained in dentistry to be a manual laborer. For most of the novel, we see McTeague being hurled back and forth between classes. Either he is on his way up, with aspirations to "six rooms and a bath," or he is shooting downward into the criminal underworld, where he murders, steals, and is finally on the lam. He is unable to remain fixed in any position, or any direction, for very long. This economic instability is a side effect of the war every aspiring professional must wage to achieve and maintain his class position. Regardless of whether the person achieves professional status or not, the process strips him of his humanity and turns him into what Norris refers to repeatedly as "the brute."

✳ Whatever Happened to Dr. Jekyll?

A somewhat similar problem—where doctors go mad in the pursuit of professional class status—crops up in a number of popular American narratives based on Robert Louis Stevenson's novel *Dr. Jekyll and Mr. Hyde*. Although Stevenson himself was Scottish and his novel takes place in England, Jenni Calder writes that "*Jekyll and Hyde* has been curiously detached from [Stevenson's] authorship." Moreover, she adds, the novel was especially well received in America, where it became a wildly popular book.[5] Hollywood finally converted *Jekyll and Hyde* into an American tale. The story has been retold in American popular culture so often that its national origins and author are often downplayed to the point of occasionally being forgotten entirely. Indeed, *Jekyll and Hyde*'s mad doctor has become perhaps the quintessential allegorical figure for the horrors of professionalization in America.

Why Dr. Jekyll instead of Dr. Frankenstein? Frankenstein's monster, as Franco Moretti points out, can be read as a metaphor for the proletariat in early industrial capitalism:

> Like the proletariat, [Frankenstein] is a *collective* and *artificial* creature. . . . The monster is disfigured not only because Frankenstein wants him to be like that, but also because this was how things actually were in the first decades of the industrial revolution. . . . Frankenstein's invention is thus a pregnant metaphor for the process of capitalist production, which forms by deforming, civilizes by barbarizing, enriches by impoverishing.[6]

Dr. Frankenstein stands in for a capitalist class that produces the proletariat as its degraded opposite. Moretti tries to fit Dr. Jekyll into this same schema but ignores the very different historical context of Stevenson's tale as well as its monster's origin. Published roughly fifty years later, after industrialism had reached its peak, *Jekyll and Hyde* is concerned with a monster whose "otherness" is never entirely established. In *Jekyll and Hyde*, doctor and monster share the same body, and to a certain extent the same madness. This, I would submit, is not a novel about the production of a proletarian class—which *Frankenstein* arguably is—but rather about the production of a professionalized class that vacillates sickeningly between the capitalist and proletarian classes.

Professionalization in America, especially for medical doctors, was in full swing during the 1880s, the same decade which saw *Jekyll and Hyde* first hit print. During the fifty years following the Civil War, the number of hospitals in America increased by roughly 6,000 percent.[7] Along with hospitals came professional medical organizations, and the peculiar configuration of the "research institution" for professional production. Such institutions, which are integral to the consolidation of professional power, are places where "the production of knowledge and the production of producers are unified into the same structure."[8] Professionals are trained not only to produce commodities like proletarians do, but they are also trained to produce workers like capitalists do. Where the capitalist produces "others" as workers, the professional produces himself as one. Hence the dissimilarities between *Frankenstein*, a novel of proletarian production, and *Jekyll and Hyde*, a novel of professional production.

Jekyll, after all, produces *himself* as a kind of proletarian other, rather than making someone else into it. Like McTeague, Jekyll's problem is that he finds himself traveling between two class positions: he is a proletarian slaving over his idea commodities, yet he is also a potentially high-status professional doctor. And like McTeague, Jekyll finds that his inner "brute" maddens and undoes him. Jekyll's fantastical transformations figure the economic transformations in capitalist production during professionalization; they also figure the identity transformations required of the emerging professional middle class. Importantly, as Magali Sarfatti Larson argues, "the medical doctor" has come to epitomize professional labor and success over the past century. For this reason, Larson concludes, "the *general* demystification of the professional model and of its ideological functions may, indeed, begin with the attack on the archetypal profession of medicine."[9]

Hollywood films of *Jekyll and Hyde*, as well as popular books and movies deeply influenced by it, might be interpreted as an "attack" on the professional model, although they are hardly efforts at "demystification." Rather, such narratives amount to a remystification of professional ideologies, even as they seem to reveal the darker side of professional work. While most critics of the *Jekyll and Hyde* tale agree that Hyde is in some sense the "dark half" of bourgeois respectability, Mark Jancovich takes his analysis a step further, arguing that it is the *relationship* between Jekyll and Hyde which should be interrogated. "[Jekyll and Hyde] are the public and private faces of a bourgeois male," he writes. "[The novel] suggests that bourgeois morality is destructive, that it creates conflicts and contradictions within both the self and society. Both Hyde and Jekyll are products of a society which forces human beings to assume contradictory social roles."[10] That is, the horror of *Jekyll and Hyde* is not Hyde, but the existence of both Jekyll and Hyde in the same person.

Jancovich's point that the Jekyll/Hyde split resembles the public/private split is certainly right on the money, but here I want to suggest that this split can also be understood as another notorious "contradiction" of capitalist life: the split between those who own the means of production and those who work for them to produce commodities. For professional workers, this split would be an internal one, dividing the personality against itself. We might read *Jekyll and Hyde* as a narrative critical of this split in the sense that it is registered as a painful, monstrous condition. As long as Jekyll insists—and, indeed, scientifically *proves*—that his identity as a professional doctor is contradictory, he is a monster. But most tales in the tradition suggest that this contradiction can be resolved. If only the doctor would just stop his infernal questioning and assimilate "Jekyll" and "Hyde" into one personality, these narratives suggest, his work would go more smoothly. But Jekyll's problem is that he refuses to lie to himself and regard his split self as seamlessly whole.

While Jekyll attempts to "professionalize," Hyde refuses to buy into Jekyll's goals and ideals—particularly in the films, which I'll discuss in a moment. In Stevenson's novel, however, Hyde is simply cast as a kind of foil to the professional that Jekyll isn't quite sure he wants to be: "I had not yet conquered my aversion to the dryness of a life of study . . . my pleasures (to say the least) were undignified . . . this incoherency of my life was daily growing more unwelcome . . . I had but to drink the cup [of transformative potion], to doff at once the body of the noted professor."[11] "The hand of Henry Jekyll . . . was professional in shape and size; it was large, firm, white and comely. But [Hyde's] hand which I now saw . . . was lean, corded, knuckly, of a dusky pallor, and thickly shaded with a swart growth of hair."[12] We hear Jekyll compare his own "professional" identity with that of Hyde, who at least in the second of these statements seems both proletarian (his hand is "corded" and "knuckly" as if he does manual labor) and racially other (his skin is "of a dusky pallor" as opposed to Jekyll's "white"). Put simply, Hyde is what keeps Jekyll from maintaining his professional identity. The problem of assimilating Jekyll and Hyde's contradictory positions into one fixed identity is cast as the problem of assimilating Hyde's point of view into Jekyll's.

This is an especially important point in light of Hyde's evolving role in the film versions of *Jekyll and Hyde*. Often, it is the character of Hyde who changes most from one version of the story to the next. As James B. Twitchell points out in his discussion of the various *Jekyll and Hyde* films, it is not simply Hyde's persona and bearing which change, but perhaps more notably his relationships to Jekyll and other characters.[13] For my purposes here, I'll be considering Hyde's makeovers in the three most famous American cinematic versions of *Jekyll and Hyde*: the 1920 "John Barrymore version," the 1931 "Frederic March version," and the 1941 "Spencer Tracy version." I'll turn to contemporary incarnations of this narrative later. Several women have been gradually added to the plot of *Jekyll and Hyde*, all of whom have significant relationships with Hyde and Jekyll. Stevenson's novel has virtually no women in it all, and for this reason it has been read quite persuasively as an allegory for homosexual pleasures and their repression.[14] As Judith Halberstam and others have argued, one of the most terrifying impulses Hyde's character might suggest would be a secret (and sadistic) desire for sex between men. Giving Jekyll a fiancée, as nearly all the film versions do, and simultaneously giving Hyde some sort of "kept woman," allows *Jekyll and Hyde* to escape getting pinned down as a narrative propelled by its repression of "perverse" forms of sexuality. Sexuality, however, always returns as a major theme: in the heterosexual versions of *Jekyll and Hyde*, Victorian puritanical values are responsible for keeping Jekyll from marrying his fiancée quickly enough to satisfy his desire for her. In all three of the versions I'm discussing here, Jekyll is portrayed as deciding to drink his transformative potion *first* as an escape from what appears to be sexual frustration, and *second* in order to prove his theory that, as the 1920 Jekyll says, "We all have two selves." As these stories would have it, heterosexual desire drives us to mad experimentation more than science does.

Yet it is not exactly sex that Jekyll gets to have when he becomes Hyde. It's some form of class cachet. In the 1920 version, Jekyll drinks his potion shortly after having been invited to "give in to temptation" and go to a music hall with his upper-class friend, Sir George Carew. At the music hall, Jekyll is infatuated by the sexually inviting Gina, a cockney who dances seductively and is available to him in all the ways his potential fiancée Millicent, Sir George's daughter, is not. Later, when Jekyll undergoes his transformation, we see Sir George's leering face superimposed over him as he turns into Hyde. Clearly, there is a connection between the kinds of pleasures a gentleman like Sir George can afford to indulge in and Jekyll's desire to change into Hyde. Hyde, unlike the morally confused Jekyll, is able to sink to the depths of depravity, going to opium dens and visiting prostitutes. Jekyll's stable middle-class world is anchored down by lab work and a future marriage, but Hyde gives him access to volatile social extremes of poverty and decadence.

The problem, however, is not that Jekyll *wants* to partake of these extremes—it's that he doesn't believe he can partake of them and remain himself. Unlike the upper-class Sir George, Jekyll isn't rich enough to go slumming in the ghettos frequently and come out unscathed. Yet he isn't integrated enough into working-class life to participate in its stereotypical culture of black market pleasures either. He has to become someone else, Hyde, in order to move about freely in the dance halls and opium dens that Sir George can visit on a whim. In this version of *Jekyll and Hyde*, it seems clear that Hyde is not so much Jekyll's proletarian side, but rather his upper-class side—the part of him which can go slumming without guilt or consequences. This particular Hyde, unlike most later Hydes, is very white, thin, and tall. He looks something like the vampire in *Nosferatu*—a creature so white and Germanic that he is nightmarish.[15] Hyde's emphatic whiteness (and Europeanness), in an American context, underscores my point: in the United States, European whiteness often symbolizes the wealth and power of upper-class status.[16] That upper-class Sir George tempts Jekyll into the pleasures of slumming and that Hyde ultimately kills Sir George in a rage drives home Hyde's association with Sir George. Before Hyde kills Sir George, Jekyll screams at him, "You with your cynicism . . . made me long for a life of evil!" Hyde is Jekyll's "life of evil," the life of a decadent, white, upper-class gentleman—a life which remains utterly incommensurate with the life of a middle-class doctor.

In the two Hollywood versions following this one, released in 1931 and 1941, Hyde is no longer a decadent upper-class man. Instead, he is clearly "dark" and savage, portrayed like a monstrous caricature of a working-class man. As Hyde's class position sinks—and as his skin darkens—his romantic attachment to the lower-class woman (Gina in the 1920s version, Ivy in the later versions) grows more elaborate and grotesque. Hyde beats and rapes Ivy, forces her to do his bidding under the threat of violence, and ultimately kills her during the films' climactic moments. Both the 1931 and 1941 versions of *Jekyll and Hyde* underscore Hyde's proletarian character by demonstrating how thoroughly he fits into working-class culture as a brutish, wanton member of it, rather than as a visitor.[17] In both films, Hyde seems to be leading a relatively complete life as a member of the working-class, renting a cheap apartment in London and maintaining his "kept woman" Ivy there. Indeed, he experiences far more domestic stability as Hyde than he does as Jekyll, who must wait an interminably long time to marry his fiancée. Jekyll, meanwhile, is given a sense of moral mission in regard to his "charity cases" at the hospital. That is, in these versions, Jekyll has a legitimate, professional connection to the working classes—they are his beloved "charity cases." While the upper class virtually disappears from the 1931 and 1941 films, both Jekyll and Hyde deepen their relationships to—and antagonisms with—the working classes.

Taken together, the three versions of *Jekyll and Hyde* I've discussed indicate that within the space of a few decades, the unassimilable threat to professional success changed dramatically. In 1920, the aristocracy represented a social group which professionals needed to assimilate; in the thirties and early forties, the working class got cast as the social group which stood in the way of, and needed to be absorbed by, middle-class professionalism. Hyde's problem is no longer his decadence, but his violence and strong resistance to Jekyll's point of view. We see him behaving in a violent manner toward Ivy, but his violence is mostly aimed at hurting Jekyll, of whom he is jealous and contemptuous. He is particularly disgusted by Jekyll's altruism toward the working class, and in the 1931 version calls Jekyll "a sniveling hypocrite" after he treats the battered Ivy as one of his "charity cases."

Hyde's consciousness about his lower-class position vis-à-vis Jekyll often gets represented as a form of psychopathology. As many critics have noted, the later *Jekyll and Hyde*s are quite self-conscious of psychoanalysis, and both account for Jekyll and Hyde's relationship with one another in largely psychological terms. Hyde feels envy, hatred, and fear for his "superior" and better-off counterpart. The 1941 version, for example, depicts Jekyll's transformation into Hyde using highly symbolic—and almost parodically Freudian—hallucinatory sequences where Jekyll at one point has his fiancée and Ivy harnessed to a chariot and whips them like horses. Jekyll and Hyde's new psychological interiority is, however, another way of depicting their class struggle. That the 1941 version wants to cast Hyde as Jekyll's unleashed "id" is an ideological sleight-of-hand which allows Hyde's association with working-class life to be converted into a kind of middle-class dementia. The extent to which Hyde is able to exploit the impoverished Ivy gets played out as a fable about how middle-class men like Jekyll secretly harbor perverted sexual desires.

Indeed, the "realities" of working-class life, such as we see them, are explained away by the film using the popular symbols of psychoanalysis. When Hyde "keeps" Ivy in a cheap flat, we are given to understand Ivy's capitulation to Hyde purely as a result of Hyde's sexual sadism rather than Ivy's economic dependence on him. Yet we know that Ivy cannot flee Hyde in part because she is too poor to pay rent herself and is unemployed. Hyde's taste for tarty women like Ivy is here, also, presumably an aspect of his sexual incontinence. However, Hyde could hardly afford to keep a woman under his control unless she were lower class, that is, "tarty." Jekyll himself can barely afford to woo his middle-class fiancée. Ultimately, fore-grounding Hyde's sexual relationship with Ivy over his economic relationship with her sets up a scenario in which both Hyde and Jekyll are read through and subsumed by professional discourses of psychiatry. Depicting Hyde as Jekyll's sexual "madness" allows the film to convert class difference into psychological deviance, and thus the film implicitly assimilates Hyde into a professional point-of-view by making him into psychiatric medicine's familiar "object of study."

Contemporary versions of *Jekyll and Hyde* elaborate on many of the same problems raised by the pre-1950s movies and continue to use Hyde as a figure for those ideas or people which professionalism fights to absorb or repulse. Beginning in the 1970s, there are a few movies which feature a female Hyde, perhaps in response to the new female workforce in the West. Hammer Studios in England released *Dr. Jekyll and Sister Hyde* in the early 1970s, and in the 1990s two female-oriented *Jekyll and Hyde* narratives appeared: the comical *Dr. Jekyll and Ms. Hyde* and *Mary Reilly*, based on a bestselling novel, which is the *Jekyll and Hyde* story told from the point of view of Jekyll's maid. Mary Reilly is a character invented solely for this version of the story—she does not appear in any of the other movies nor is she in Stevenson's novel. With *Mary Reilly*, the "unassimilated" perspective in *Jekyll and Hyde* is made both working class and female.[18] Mary is also implicitly the romantic object for both Jekyll and Hyde. In this version, then, Mary comes to be associated with the unassimilated Hyde position for more reasons than her class. As their maid and the object of Jekyll and Hyde's sadistic heterosexuality, Mary alone is aware of the hypocrisy and horror in their shared identity. One might argue that Mary is Hyde and Ivy

rolled into one. That her perspective becomes sympathetic and stable re-
inforces our notion that Jekyll and Hyde's problem is their class instability
and internal contradiction; Mary can observe them without splitting herself, as it were, because she occupies only one place in their class hierarchy.

Yet all these changes in Hyde's position, and Jekyll's relative to him, are
not reflected in the historical settings of the films themselves—all the *Jekyll
and Hyde* movies, with a few notable exceptions,[19] take place at the time
Stevenson's novel was written in the 1880s. Nearly all the films take place
in England as well. Although originally a novel about contemporary life,
Jekyll and Hyde has become a period piece for twentieth-century audiences.
The question is why that might be, considering that filmmakers and writers
have changed so many other parts of the story. I would suggest that the repeated return to the late nineteenth century is important to the status of
this story as it depicts the rise of professionalism: for the late nineteenth
century, when Stevenson wrote his novel, was indeed the historical moment at which professionalism gained momentum and began to eclipse
earlier forms of middle-class employment and modes of production associated with primitive accumulation or heavy industry.[20] There is, in other
words, something about the *Jekyll and Hyde* story which invites a "return to
origins," or perhaps more accurately, a return to its own origins in the burgeoning industry of professional writing and all kinds of other professions
as well.

Even contemporary B-movie remakes of *Jekyll and Hyde*, like *Edge of
Sanity*, starring Anthony Perkins as Jekyll, fetishize the historical setting
of the novel, bringing in period details like Jack the Ripper in order to suggest a realistic historical context. Like earlier remakes of *Jekyll and Hyde*,
however, *Edge of Sanity* brings in plenty of contemporary details—in *Edge*,
Jekyll's "potion" is actually crack cocaine, which he smokes before brutally
murdering prostitutes. It is obvious that each remake of *Jekyll and Hyde* is
really about its contemporary period, but what is less obvious is that each
subsequent film and book can be said to return to the 1880s as a means of
mapping a historically changing relationship between the middle class and
the underclass. The rise of professionalism in the late nineteenth century
marked a point at which the middle-class reconsolidated itself and created a
new boundary between the work it was capable of performing and the work
it assigned to its social inferiors (or, in a more liberal language, its "charity
cases"). *Jekyll and Hyde* stories depict the boundary between one form of
labor and another, and the maintenance of that boundary over time.

Representing the history of professional labor, no matter how falsified and fantastical that history might be, is also a way of remarking that the boundary between professionals and other workers is not natural (or supernatural), but historically constructed. *Jekyll and Hyde*, therefore, can function as a record of the social construction of professionalism—particularly when we consider that *Jekyll and Hyde* is quite literally about how one professional is so riddled by internal contradictions that he literally self-deconstructs. As much as *Jekyll and Hyde* stories try to imagine ways of assimilating "Hyde" (that is, aristocrats, workers, women, people of color, etc.) into professionalism, they also remind us that such assimilation is only intermittently successful. Usually, Jekyll and Hyde die at the end of their story because Hyde refuses to toe the line and keep quiet while Jekyll goes about his middle-class business. The *Jekyll and Hyde* tradition is as much about why certain people are kept out of the middle-class professional world as it is about the need to invite them in.

Two contemporary versions of the *Jekyll and Hyde* story set in the late twentieth century, one a movie called *The Doctor* (1991) and the other a novel by Greg Bear called *Blood Music*, demonstrate alternative directions taken by the *Jekyll and Hyde* genre which nevertheless continue its work of delineating professional boundaries. In *The Doctor*, our Jekyll figure is a surgeon named Jack MacKee who is so emotionally bereft that he remarks to his students, "A surgeon's job is to cut . . . [and] caring is about time . . . I'd rather you cut straight and cared less." He becomes "Hyde" when he discovers that he has throat cancer and must engage with the medical profession as a patient. His patient identity, like Hyde, is associated with illness and discomfort, but also with new emotional and social possibilities. Distancing himself from his wife and children, Jack forms an intense bond with a working-class woman, June, who has terminal brain cancer. Unlike Hyde's relationship with Ivy, however, Jack's relationship with June is portrayed as nonsexual, healing, and spiritual. She teaches him to appreciate life even as he confronts death, and later she inspires Jack to say, "I see my tumor giving me freedoms I never allowed myself before." Discovering the inhuman negligence and cruelty doctors dish out to patients like himself, Jack realizes that, as another doctor says, "the system stinks," and that his attitude as a surgeon has been hypocritical (just as Hyde notes that Jekyll is a hypocrite in a number of the film versions).

Jack's tumor, like Jekyll's potion, splits the doctor into two halves which are contradictory. Yet *The Doctor* ends with a reconciliation between Jack's surgeon and patient selves, whereas in a traditional *Jekyll and Hyde* story reconciliation proves possible only in death. *The Doctor* is one narrative where Hyde is successfully assimilated into Dr. Jekyll. "Every doctor becomes a patient somewhere along the line," Jack asserts, and when he has recovered he assigns his students an exercise in which they are admitted to the hospital as patients so that they will understand the patients' perspective. How does this doctor manage to remain whole? Aside from the fact that his transformation is not caused by some unknown force or weird chemical he concocted, Jack is also not split into two halves which occupy different class positions. Jack-as-patient may not have the same kind of professional powers that Jack-as-doctor does within the hospital, but he still has access to the middle-class (indeed, upper-middle-class) privilege of choosing a top doctor to treat him. He is even able to reject that doctor, a callous specialist like he once was, and switch to a more caring one when he realizes that he needs some compassion. In other words, Jack's sickness forces him to switch social roles, but he does not lose social status. As Fred Pfeil argues:

> The painful wisdom Jack MacKee has had to learn has not reduced his power; on the contrary, it has made him an even better doctor than he was before, not to mention that much more justified in ordering his resident staff around. . . . The point is not finally to give up power, but to emerge from a temporary, tonic power shortage as someone more deserving of its possession and more compassionate in its exercise.[21]

This particular Jekyll is "cured," and, as Pfeil puts it, "emerge[s] from a temporary, tonic power shortage" in part because his class affiliations remain unaffected by his transformation. Most traditional *Jekyll and Hyde* stories tend to conflate bodily transformation with a downward plunge in class or social hierarchy (becoming "dark," proletarian, or female). *The Doctor* does not.

A very different story of Hyde's assimilation unfolds in Greg Bear's *Blood Music*, a novel set in the near future. Mad genetic researcher Vergil Ulam injects himself with "smart" lymphocytes he's created that evolve in his bloodstream, transform his body, and then eventually escape and reconfigure the entire human species. Here, Hyde has been converted into a massive civilization (of lymphocytes) which ultimately assimilates the mad doctor who created it—and ingested it as a "potion"—in the first place. Initially, we are invited to view the activities of the cells—called "Noocytes" —as simultaneously horrifying and revolutionary in a political sense. Vergil's mother, hearing that her son has injected himself with his experiment, says, "Anyone who's ever sanitized a toilet or cleaned a diaper pail would cringe at the idea of germs that think. What happens when they fight back?"[22] Later, as Vergil and others are transformed by the Noocytes, we are treated to gruesome descriptions of the ways they modify bodies which certainly rival Jekyll's cinematic "transformation scenes": "Work [by the Noocytes] had proceeded on her much more rapidly. Her legs were gone; her torso had been reduced to an impressionistic spareness. She had lifted her face [which was] covered with ridges as if made from a stack of cards" (91). The Noocytes convert human bodies into the building blocks of a new civilization, converting flesh into what appear to be cities, roads, and new life forms. Unlike a *Jekyll and Hyde* movie, *Blood Music* looks to the future, rather than to the past. It is still about the historical construction of professionalism, but this novel charts the end of professional labor—indeed, the end of human labor as we know it. Within days of evolving beyond Vergil's body, the Noocytes have spread across North America. Flying over the United States, observers note that, "All familiar landmarks—entire cities— have vanished beneath, or perhaps been transformed into, a landscape of biological nightmare. . . . New York City is an unfamiliar jumble of geometric shapes. . . . It is as if we have passed over an entirely new planet" (166–71). North America is still swarming with activity and labor which requires the substance of human bodies, but not in a recognizable manner. Tellingly, we see this "new labor" close up when the simple-minded Suzy, who remains unchanged by the Noocytes, wanders through an abandoned, Noocyte-infested corporate headquarters in New York City. Climbing the stairs, she wanders in and out of empty offices and labs, finally stopping in an executive's well-appointed office to get drunk. All that remains of the executive are his expensive clothes, as his body—like everyone else's—has been broken down and utilized by the Noocytes. As Suzy looks out the window over his empty clothes, she notices that "most of the city, what she could see of it, was covered with brown and black blankets. . . . Someone had come along and wrapped surplus army blankets all the way to the tenth or twentieth floors of all the buildings in Manhattan" (157). These "blankets" are, we assume, one of the structures Noocytes have built out of dismantled human bodies. Interestingly, the empty professional's clothes are contrasted with a city wrapped in "surplus army blankets," items associated with the poor and unemployed. This brings us back to an earlier image, that of the germs who "fight back," making the Noocytes sound a little like revolutionary masses who have killed off the power elite and set up their own society. Such an analysis would convert *Blood Music* into a literal enactment of the Marxist prediction that capitalist production will generate its own demise.[23]

There is, however, another reading to be done here, although it is important to stage it against a backdrop of a professional middle-class world turned into proletarian "surplus army blankets." If the Noocytes are a version of Hyde, a Hyde who takes over, we need to consider the content of this Hyde's character. Scott Bukatman notes that the "Noosphere" where the Noocytes exist is "another dataplane, still another visualization of information circulation and control."[24] The Noocytes are in some sense a vast computer, and when human beings are absorbed by them, their memories and experiences become data which is "alive" in the Noosphere. As the Noocytes put it to one scientist, "The part of you which stands behind all issued communication may be encoded, activated, returned. It will be like a *dream*, if we understand fully what that is" (174). In human terms, then, joining with the Noocytes is to leave the body behind and enter a realm which is pure information, pure thought. Labor, such as it is, becomes a matter of moving information around. Noosphere life, put like this, sounds less like the end of professional labor and more like an intensification of it. Indeed, late-twentieth-century economists such as Alvin Toffler and Tom Peters describe the future of information economies in language not unlike Bear's description of the Noosphere. Toffler's *Future Shock* invokes a "post-service economy" of "experiential industries" which produce commodities by and for the mind. "Attention will be paid to the psychological overtones of every step or component of the product," Toffler writes.[25] To create and manage the circulation of such products, one would need to be more than a professional as we know them—one would want to be a kind of human computer, capable of performing great feats of mental, rather than physical, labor. I would argue that the Noocytes-as-Hyde subsume their "Dr. Jekyll" precisely because they prove to be better professionals than he is: they are prepared for a "post-service economy" of mental and psychological experiences unhampered by the physical limitations of the human body.

* The Brain Fetish

A brain without a body—alive!—Dr. Patrick Cory, in *Donovan's Brain* (1953)

As professional labor becomes associated with a stable middle-class position in the United States, and as "the organization man"[26] becomes a well-known stereotype and problem, mad doctors in popular culture begin a new operation which splits professional identity in the service of profit, scientific progress, and even freedom. In the postwar period of the 1950s and beyond, we find mad doctors who exist in a world where the mind has become so fetishized that brains are literally leaving their bodies behind. Doctors like the addled Patrick Cory of *Donovan's Brain* and the demented Bill Cortner of *The Brain That Wouldn't Die* learn that brains do not need their bodies in order to do work. But as brain labor becomes more common, it also suffers a demotion: like Hyde's hands in Stevenson's novel, brains in the late twentieth century are rather "knuckly." In fact, they must compete with hands, feet, and even internal organs for jobs. Brains are not so special after all. Mental labor may, in fact, be the new manual labor.

The 1987 video packaging for *Donovan's Brain* invites viewers to "Find out [what happens] in this unforgettable and frightening film that will make you wonder if your thoughts are really your own!" This particular fear— that one's thoughts are not one's own, that one indeed has literally lost one's mind—propels the "detachable brain" narrative. *Donovan's Brain* stages this fear in explicitly economic terms. It all begins when the devious capitalist Warren Donovan dies in a plane crash which somehow leaves his brain intact. Patrick Cory, who has been experimenting with keeping monkey brains alive in a tank, is called in to pronounce Donovan dead. But when he realizes it might be possible to preserve Donovan's brain, he can't help himself.

"Science could use Donovan's brain," he tells his friend Frank, justifying his theft and resuscitation of it. As it turns out, however, Donovan's brain is going to use science. Soon the brain is more than merely "alive" in Patrick's tank—it is growing, glowing, and throbbing, emitting "beta frequencies" which mean the brain is "thinking systematically." In his effort to communicate with it, Patrick tries using telepathy and starts researching Donovan's life to find out more about him. Donovan, we discover, was a ruthless millionaire who "was notoriously antagonistic toward organized charity . . . carried to an extreme the independence of the self-made man . . .

[and] scorned taxes." Even his children and business associates hate him, and are relieved that his death has freed them from his greedy clutches.

Gradually, through telepathic communication, Donovan's brain begins to take over Patrick's mind, controlling his actions and thoughts. Patrick concedes, "I make myself receptive and submit to the brain's will, that's all." All that Donovan's brain cares about is reconsolidating his financial empire: for the most part, we see him using Patrick's body to write checks, withdraw money in Donovan's name, and make sure his government "connections" continue to help him cheat on his taxes and aid him in his quest to "dominate the international financial scene." As Frank and Patrick's wife Jan watch in horror, Patrick's personality is slowly eclipsed by Donovan's, leading Jan to remark, "This Jekyll and Hyde thing—it's weird." Yet Hyde here is not an aspect of Patrick's personality, but a brain which replaces his thoughts with its own. Finally, Frank and Jan realize they've got to do something. "I don't like it," Frank says, "He says he submits [to the brain]— what happens if he can't stop submitting?" In the climactic moments of the film, we realize the brain can control anyone's mind and he intends to kill Frank and Jan, who are coming between Patrick and the brain. Luckily, they—with some help from the disappearing Patrick—are able to rig up a lightening rod connected to the brain tank, which sets Donovan's brain on fire and kills it.

Even a cursory analysis of this plot reveals much: the interests of big business threaten to control science; the brain of a capitalist takes over the brain of a professional doctor; and the ownership of your thoughts becomes of paramount importance in a world where mental capacity, rather than physical strength, equals power. But why the spectacle of a brain, why this conversion of "thought" into the organ we assume creates thought? And how does the repeated image of a brain work to structure—and contain— the fear of losing our minds? In *Donovan's Brain*, and the brain narratives which follow in its footsteps, losing control over one's mind is accompanied by the possession or desire to possess a brain. The question then becomes: what is the connection between the popularity of cinematic images of brains and social anxieties about professional labor?

To answer, we must turn to theories of fetishization.[27] In the Marxist tradition, fetishization is a process by which commodities come to stand in for social or symbolic relations; in Freudian terms, a fetish is a sexualized object that guards men against a fear of powerlessness (generally represented by castration). If we understand Donovan's brain as a commodity

Patrick Cory, controlled by the capitalist Donovan's brain, has taken to reading materials more suited to a tycoon than a doctor.

fetish, then one of the social relationships it stands in for is certainly that of Patrick-the-professional-laborer to his products, which in this case are experiments on brains. Patrick considers the brain to be his property, since he "produced" it by thinking up the idea to keep it alive in the first place. But the brain escapes from his control and takes on a life of its own. Indeed, it takes over Patrick's mind. "Capitalists," Andrew Sayer and Richard Walker remark, "continually try to appropriate the powers of social labor, including the knowledge in every worker's head."[28] Here we find fantastical confirmation of their point: the brain of capitalist Donovan appropriates Patrick's experiment and "the knowledge in [his] head." In this way, the brain functions as a commodity fetish, something produced by Patrick's mental labors which he doesn't in fact own. It is, appropriately enough, owned by a capitalist instead.

The brain, however, is more than just an allegorical figure for "commodity" in a story about how capitalists "appropriate the powers of social labor." I want to argue that it also functions as a visual and even a sexual fetish, an image which exists to cover up, to disavow, some kind of deep anxiety. Brain images, in this formulation, function in some ways like images of women's bodies in traditional cinema. Using Freud's ideas about the fetishization of female bodies, Laura Mulvey famously postulated that women's bodies in film are the object of a fetishizing "look" from both camera and audience. They are presented to the (male) viewer as fetish images in order to cover up men's fear of becoming disempowered (like women).[29] As Mulvey has it, fetishized female bodies or fetishized female body parts (legs, breasts, lips) are used in movies to substitute for a frank look at the woman who threatens male power with her difference from it.[30] The cinematic fetish is quite literally a way of averting our eyes from what scares us: instead of looking at a frightening, powerful woman, for instance, we check out her sexy breasts instead.

A fear of castration in the brain movie grows out of our scientists' fears that they may be losing their mental potency to a greater force, usually a more powerful man who employs them. The idea that one's mind is not one's own is a source of incredible anxiety, particularly when mental labor is the principle source of middle-class income. The brain-as-fetish covers over the professional's fear that he may not actually own the thoughts in his head—that he may, like Patrick Cory, be losing his mind to a capitalist. Instead of playing on anxieties about losing one's penis, then, the brain movie plays on anxieties about losing one's mind. These are movies where the phallus, the seat of knowledge and power, can truly get cut off—in gory, excruciating detail. Fetishizing images of brains may be one way audiences are being invited to disavow the horror of losing one's cognitive prowess and personal thoughts.

"Look at my brain!" Donovan's voice commands Jan when she attempts to save Patrick from his control. The camera moves in on the repulsive organ in its tank of "solution" as it pulsates and grows larger. Then, lightening strikes, and the brain is burned. Rather than looking at Patrick's disempowered body and his lost mind, our gaze has been directed to the brain itself, which is easily contained and dispatched. Gazing at fetishized brains in movies, especially where people are able to possess those brains, allows for the pretense that professionals who do mental labor are not "submitting" or losing the power to possess their own ideas, as Patrick Cory does.

Tellingly, fetishized brains are coupled with gender issues in several narratives about men who possess women's brains. Most spectacularly, *The Brain That Wouldn't Die* is the story of how Dr. Bill Cortner rescues his girlfriend Jan's head from a car wreck which leaves her body sliced to pieces while he—in the driver' seat—somehow comes out intact. Bill has been conducting experiments with "grafts," mostly unsuccessfully, using a few (male) human subjects. Using a special "solution," he keeps Jan's head alive, hoping to "graft" it onto the body of another woman. "I've got to find her

The Brain That Wouldn't Die's lumpy "man thing," controlled by Jan's angry brain, jumps out of the closet to kill their tormentor so quickly that he brings the closet door with him.

a body," Bill announces, heading off to a series of burlesque dance bars and trying to pick up a prostitute to kill and use in his experiment. Jan's head, meanwhile, is in agony, calling itself a "freak" and begging to die. Like Donovan's brain, however, Jan's brain develops telepathic powers, and she begins to communicate with one of Bill's failed experiments, a creature who groans behind a door and is not revealed until the movie's final scenes. Secretly, they plot revenge upon Bill for subjecting them to experimentation. "Together we are both more than things," Jan tells the thing behind the door, "we are a power. I shall create power and you shall enforce it." Later, on his quest to find a body for Jan, Bill seduces Doris, a "body model" who has the "best body in the world." At the moment when he has Doris drugged and prepped for the head transplant, Jan shrieks, "You must be stopped!" and a giant, lumpy man-thing bursts from the closet and tears out Bill's throat.

Here we have what would appear on the surface to be a fairly standard, antifeminist story of a woman "losing her head," thinking she has power, and wreaking havoc. Jan's head and brain would seem to fit the definition of Mulvey's fetish, diverting our fear from the female body and directing our attention to a female head instead. Yet, unlike the female fetish Mulvey describes, Jan's brain is hardly "reassuring." Indeed, her head poses more of a threat without its body than it ever did when it was attached. What remains unseen in this movie, however, and what Jan's brain *does* divert our attention from, is the monstrous male body locked away behind a door, whom we assume is being telepathically controlled by Jan.[31] Using her brain's tremendous new powers, Jan orders the deformed man-thing to kill Bill; thus, the image of her head is in fact a diversion from the degree to which her mental capacities overwhelm the men around her. Like Donovan's brain, her brain is also capable of "taking over," and to a certain extent taking away, people's thoughts. In the final violent confrontation, she takes over the mind of the deformed man-thing so she can use his body to keep Bill from producing another "mad" experiment, another demented product of his mind. The thing is therefore left with no mind, and the doctor is killed before he can possess the product of his mental labor. Jan's brain poses a double threat: that of a powerful woman *and* that of powerful thoughts.

Two other tales of women's brains, the movie *The Man with Two Brains* and Robin Cook's popular novel *Brain*, are also about how female brains undermine professional work. Importantly, they reveal another fear which the brain fetish disavows: what Barbara Ehrenriech has referred to as a professional middle-class "fear of falling" into a lower class position.[32] Considered this way, *The Man with Two Brains* and *Brain* recall late versions of the Jekyll and Hyde story which cast Hyde as a woman. With these texts we are reminded again that women are often associated with downward mobility.

The Man with Two Brains is a satiric love story which pokes fun at movies like *Donovan's Brain* and *The Brain That Wouldn't Die*—in case we hadn't got that idea already, there is an early scene in the film when mad brain surgeon Michael Hfuhruhurr watches *Donovan's Brain* on television, exclaiming happily, "That's my favorite movie!" Betrayed by his philandering, gold-digging wife Dolores, Michael falls in love with Anne, a telepathic brain which is being kept alive in a jar by his equally mad colleague, Dr. Alfred Necessiter. Michael's "two brains," that of his wife Dolores (whom he performed brain surgery on early in the movie) and his love Anne, are explicitly associated with money. Dolores is scheming to steal Michael's $15 million inheritance, and she's prostituting herself on the side to make even more money. Dolores's brain and body are going to cost Michael a fortune. Anne's brain, on the other hand, ends up costing Michael only six quarters.[33]

After Dolores is murdered by Merv Griffin in a random plot twist, Michael and Dr. Necessiter use a "thought transfer" machine to place

Anne's thoughts into Dolores's body. This transfer machine, Necessiter reveals to us, was put together out of old video game parts, and it costs Michael six quarters to get it up and running for the transfer. The arrival of Anne's brain removes the threat of Dolores's desire for huge amounts of money. As the film closes, Michael only has one (cheap) brain, and he doesn't even have to worry about Dolores's expensive body anymore. Anne is a compulsive eater, and her brain makes Dolores's beautiful body so chubby that it is unrecognizable. Michael has no need to fear losing his money once he has a relationship with the brain he loves. The financial threat represented by Dolores's brain and body are removed completely when Anne's brain enters the picture. Here, the neutralized threat is not losing one's mind, but losing one's money.

✷. Proletarian Minds

Robin Cook's *Brain* extends the logic of *Two Brains* by arousing the same fear—losing money to a brain—but combines it with anxieties about the market value of professional mental labor. Two mad doctors, Dr. Michaels and Dr. Mannerheim, have been experimenting on the brains of (female) university students visiting the ob-gyn clinic at their hospital. Using various chemicals, they induce seizures and extreme dissociation in the patients; later, they take them to a lab and reconstruct their bodies in order to study their brains more easily. When sane Dr. Martin discovers Dr. Michaels's laboratory, he finds one of their human subjects:

> Submerged in what Martin later learned was cerebrospinal fluid, were the living remains of Katherine Collins. . . . But her brain had been completely exposed. There was no skull. Most of the face was gone except for the eyes, which had been dissected free and covered with contact lenses. . . . Her arms had also been carefully dissected to extract the ends of the sensory nerves. These nerve endings looped back like strands of a spider web to connect with electrodes buried within the brain.[34]

Dr. Michaels explains that this setup creates a "feedback system" in the human brain, making it more like a computer which can essentially comment upon the input it receives. "We've used the human brain to study itself," Michaels says to Martin, who is utterly appalled. But the mental labor performed by Katherine Collins's brain (and, we assume, the brains of the other women too) is actually intended to make human mental labor replaceable by computers. The experiments Michaels and Mannerheim conduct are part of secret government research on artificial intelligence. *Brain* ends with an enigmatic "*New York Times* article" published shortly after the sane Dr. Martin vows to go public with information about this project and its unlawful use of human subjects. Having been threatened with death if he leaks the story, Martin is hiding out in Sweden and has told the press only that he has a story which "suggests that the field of medicine is not immune to having its own Watergate" (301).

Brains in *Brain* are different from those in the narratives I've discussed up to this point in two important ways: they are totally at the mercy of medicine, and they are likened to computers, which are passive tools rather than powerful agents like Donovan, Jan, or even Dolores. Mental labor in this story is not only exploitable, it can be replaced with machines. Andrew Ross has noted that certain contemporary discourses about high technology resemble those about union labor. Broken down computers or Xerox machines are talked about as if they are hostile laborers on strike, fighting against a managerial class which "uses" them.[35] What is important about this connection between high tech and the working class, which I think shows up in *Brain*, is that we find mental labor becoming, by association, working-class labor. Certain high-status doctors like Dr. Mannerheim, with connections to elite government agencies and international capital, are able to create a situation where the kinds of routine mental labor performed by doctors like Martin may become equivalent to manual labor done by machines. Tellingly, in the description we get of Katherine's brain, the nerve endings from her arms have been connected to her brain in order to create the "feedback system." This brain threatens to create a kind of equivalence between work you do with your mind and work you do with your hands.[36]

As I mentioned earlier, the brain fetish in *Two Brains* and *Brain* hides and marks a fear of falling into a lower-class position. It also coincides with a notion that gained currency during the late 1970s and early 1980s, which proposes that professionals are being "proletarianized." Writing in 1982 (just a few years after *Brain* was published), Charles Derber explains that "the thesis of professional proletarianization" is a critique of the ideas of John Kenneth Galbraith and others who describe the "New Class" of professional-managerial labor exercising "growing social control over the rest of the population." Professional proletarianization accounts for the way "professionals are increasingly experiencing the subordination that other workers have long endured."[37] By "other workers," we assume Derber means the working class or proletariat. He continues:

Professionals are now expressing dissatisfaction with almost the entire range of their work conditions, their wages and benefits, opportunities for advancement, health and safety, job security, and the meaning, challenge, and autonomy of their work. . . . Professionals for the first time share with other workers the fundamental necessity of selling their labor power on a labor market. This change implies a loss of control rather than an expansion of authority.

What seems to mark the proletarianization of professionals is their loss of control over the work they do. Professionals own their own businesses and medical practices less and less often. Increasingly, they seem to be imagining themselves like Dr. Patrick Cory, hostage to the alien intentions of big business. They do not feel that they own the products of their labor, nor do they own the means of production either.

Just as proletarianization is becoming a widespread concern among professionals, there arises what seems to me a complementary idea about professional work. This idea, which gains momentum in the post-yuppie late eighties, is put forth most succinctly in work done by psychiatrist Douglas LaBier. After extensively researching the lives of Washington, D.C., professionals, he concludes that real professional success without regret or emotional conflict requires insanity of one kind or another. If a professional *does* feel distressed or unhappy with her job, she is actually demonstrating sanity. LaBier writes:

I began interviewing . . . fast-track career winners who had risen high in their careers and who had never shown or complained about conflicts or problems on the job. . . . What I discovered was that within this group were people who were very sick. Some were dominated by unconscious, irrational passions of power-lust, conquest, grandiosity, and destructiveness, or conversely by cravings for humiliation and domination.[38]

This idea gets reflected in a number of fictional works of the period, such as Bret Easton Ellis's novel *American Psycho* and Oliver Stone's movie *Wall Street*, both of which portray yuppie life as psychotically immoral and decadent. What is interesting about LaBier's definition of "sanity" is that it sets up an implicit hierarchy in which those who are insane wield their power most forcefully and single-mindedly, and those who are dissatisfied and annoyed with their jobs are "sane" but gain less professional power as a result. Derber's proletarianized professional in this schema is "sane," and his successful, nonproletarianized counterpart is "mad."

Certainly, this is only one way to interpret LaBier's work. Yet it is striking how often the madness of the doctor in contemporary movies is a kind of defense against going prole. As long as the doctor remains mad, he isn't a part of the mental labor force doing somebody else's work, thinking somebody else's thoughts. Madness, then, becomes a way to figure professional success and autonomy, while sanity represents proletarianization and a fall from privileged class status. In a series of movies which deal with the relationship between brains and body parts, we see how anxieties about a proletarianized professional class tend to create formal connections between madness and professional success, and simultaneously between routinized mental labor and manual labor.

Stuart Gordon's *Re-Animator* is a movie that stages an all-out war between brains and body parts. Mad medical researcher Herbert West hasn't quite perfected his serum to reanimate dead bodies—when he injects the serum into humans and cats, it makes them outrageously violent. But they do come back to life. "All life is a physical and chemical process," he says, "[and] I've conquered brain death." West's professor and adversary, the psychotic Dr. Carl Hill, disagrees with him. For Hill, all life in the brain proceeds from "desire and will," not a "physical and chemical process." This struggle, between West and Hill, biological process and psychological will, structures much of the film's extreme, gory horror. Our only sane doctor, Daniel Cain, lives with West and is drawn into West's experiments on dead bodies, eventually helping him to steal cadavers from the medical school where both of them are students. While West is infatuated with his experiments to the point where he will inject nearly any dead thing with serum, Cain is interested in healing the sick and planning a future with his girlfriend Megan. Cain wants to follow the rules; West never does.

When the college dean finds out that Cain and West are working on reanimation, he punishes them severely, cutting off Cain's student loans and expelling West from medical school altogether. Through a series of shenanigans involving a reanimated corpse, an electric bone saw, and cadaver stealing, the dean is subsequently killed by a dead person and reanimated by West. Reduced to a drooling, maniacal zombie, the dean is institutionalized. As a result, Dr. Hill finds out about West's partially successful experiments and vows to claim them for his own. When he discovers Hill's intentions, West is enraged and cuts off Hill's head with a shovel. Of course, West reanimates the now-separated head and body. Hill's head and body prove to be West's first successful experiment. Both come to life exactly as they were before, insane and hungry for power. Keeping an eye on his bum-

Herbert West is tragically attacked by a giant colon in *Re-Animator*.

bling body, Hill grabs his own head, puts it in a bowling bag, and escapes West's lab with some serum.

As the plot continues to unfold weirdly, we learn that Hill plans to take over the world by giving reanimated corpses a special lobotomy which allows him to control them with his thoughts. Hill, in other words, wants to control the *will*, while West is only interested in bodies. To stop Hill, Cain and West sneak into his university research facility and give overdoses of the serum to his mind-controlled zombie army. Overdose causes the bodies to blow up, and each of their internal organs takes on a life of its own. Cain barely escapes with his life, while West is strangled to death by a giant serpentine colon. Cain's girlfriend, Megan, has also been killed. In the last shot, we see Cain whip out a syringe of the serum and inject it into Megan's brain. The screen goes dark, and we hear a woman shriek.[39]

As bizarre as it sounds, *Re-Animator* is a highly successful example of its genre and a widely recognized cult film classic of the eighties.[40] It also bears all the marks of conflicted eighties discourses about professional work: mad doctors West and Hill are capable of performing fantastically successful, though immoral, experiments because they are mad, while Cain's desire to be good and do his low-level work gets him used and manipulated by West (after which he loses his student loans and class status). There is certainly a hint that Cain survives his ordeal because he is "sane," but the movie ends with him picking up the serum and madly experimenting on

Megan. Cain ultimately goes mad too—leaving us with the impression that perhaps he has survived precisely because he has lost his mind.

There are a number of key themes to unpack here. First of all, the hospital where West and Cain are students is set up hierarchically, with the two of them, as students, near the bottom. They are expected to do the "routine" work of interns, while their professors will do the exciting experimentation. Part of West's conflict with Hill, in fact, originates with his disdain for the protocols of professional hierarchy. Sitting in Hill's brain surgery class, West refuses to accept Hill's ideas about desire and will in the brain, even going so far as to literally growl and break a pencil in half when Hill pulls rank and silences him. Ultimately Hill's own experiments with will and the brain (also successful, if only on reanimated bodies) are all about enforcing a kind of absolute mental hierarchy where Hill will do all the thinking, and his lobotomized zombies will be controlled entirely by his thoughts. It's interesting to note that the first mind-controlled zombie Hill produces is the reanimated dean of the college, someone ranked above Hill in the professional chain-of-command. Hill's madness has propelled him into a position where he can control the college dean.

But upward mobility through madness isn't entirely a result of taking over other people's minds, although that is a big part of it in *Re-Animator*. It is also about controlling the means of production—in the context of medicine, this control would consist of having access to labs, tools, technicians, money, etc., to create "results" and "successful experiments." Although West is clearly onto something with his experiments and has set up a lab in the basement of the house he shares with Cain, West doesn't have access to all the tools (like cadavers) he needs in order to do his work. He has to get them through the hospital, where his student status gives him very little power. Since the dean doesn't approve of West's work, he must steal bodies from the morgue if he wants to do his own research. Having successfully stolen the means of medical production (dead bodies) West continues to perfect his serum, which promises to give him control over the means to produce life itself. In a rather perverse way, madness seems to allow West to seize control of the means of production, both on the level of what he thinks, and on the level of what he's willing to do to see his thoughts through to their conclusion.

So far, however, I have continued to talk mainly about brains and the thoughts they contain. What of the proliferation of body parts in this movie, particularly Hill's detachable head/brain and the killer colon? I want to suggest that part of the fear motivating these representations is related to what motivates the horror of *Brain*. In *Re-Animator*, the head truly is just another body part, interchangeable with all other body parts. Hill's body, in fact, seems to possess the same "thoughts" as his head. Although his head attempts at many points—comically—to direct the body as it lurches around the lab, there are far more depictions of the body walking and doing work with its head packed away in a bag. That West is ultimately strangled to death by an outraged colon underscores my point. West complains initially that his serum causes violent behavior, and we assume that he means behavior that originates in the mind. As it turns out, however, violent behavior can live in any part of the body. A colon is as capable of initiating violence as a brain—and it doesn't even need to be inside of a body to do it.

What these images of "thinking" body parts suggest, to put it in economic terms, are a kind of imaginary Taylorization process. As theorists like David Harvey have pointed out, F. W. Taylor's methods of rationalizing the labor process (in his *The Principles of Scientific Management*) symbolically separated the human body into parts, each of which could function "by itself" to perform some routine factory task (like pulling a lever, or operating a sewing machine pedal). The Taylorization we see in *Re-Animator*, however, includes the human head as a body part which can be rationalized and made useful. Indeed, in some cases, the head doesn't "think" as clearly as its body parts do. Hill's head can't kill West, but a colon can. If body parts think just like heads, then there would appear to be no dividing line between professional "think work" and manual labor "body work." Indeed, the head becomes just another specialized tool which can be used by people in power to perform menial tasks. As Derber and his colleagues write: "While professionals lack the power of their employers to define jobs, the disappearance of the mental/manual divide would threaten all their privileges. Labor reduced to its 'animal form' is the dark side of professionalism as well as capitalism."[41] *Re-Animator* plays out the "dark side of professionalism" by depicting a world where sometimes a colon thinks better than a brain.

We find body part movies dating back to the 1930s and '40s in *Mad Love* and *The Beast With Five Fingers*, both of which gain a modern twist in versions of *The Hand* (1960, 1981);[42] all of these films represent a world where heads are more or less in competition with body parts. What is different about detachable body parts in late-twentieth-century narratives is that they actually "think," that is, they seem to represent mental labor *reduced to* manual labor. The mind can become equivalent to a body part, to a certain degree, because mental labor itself has become subject to division and rationalization. Professionals can no longer fully believe in a strict "mental/manual divide," for the workplace is set up around a hierarchy of mental tasks and a whole range of specialized ones.[43] We find an awareness of the way professional work divides consciousness up into rationalized parts in the movie *Body Parts*. A highly successful artist who receives a "grafted" arm from a mad doctor begins to "remember" things that the arm has done. Slowly, the arm's "consciousness" begins to take over the artist's life. First, he paints scenes from the arm's violent life—we discover later that it is the arm of a rapist and serial killer—and then he is overwhelmed by the arm's violent impulses and begins behaving abusively toward his family.

During the film's climax he confronts his mad doctor, who admits that the arm came from a man executed for murder. Worse still, she has grafted his body parts onto several other people, all of whom are "remembering" what those body parts did. Our ultimate horror is supposed to come when we discover that the mad doctor has even grafted the murderer's head onto a new body, but it hardly matters. His parts can think without him. Reconstructed by professional medicine, each piece of the killer's body behaves as if it were a specialized aspect of his thought processes, acting out pieces of his murderous desire.

Frankenhooker riffs on the idea of the thinking body part in a weird and funny homage to *The Brain That Wouldn't Die*. Jeffrey, who is obsessed with electronics and anatomy, invents a chemical fluid that can animate dead body parts. When his girlfriend Elizabeth is chopped up by a lawnmower, he rescues and preserves her head in a vat of the stuff, vowing that he'll find her a body. "If I need body parts," he reasons, "I'll buy body parts. And there's a place across the river where there are thousands of women anxious to sell them with no questions asked."

After blowing up a roomful of prostitutes who smoke some of his homebrewed, explosive "super crack," Jeffrey returns to his lab with a big bag of body parts. It's only a short while before he revives the newly constructed, sewn-together Elizabeth. But Elizabeth is not the same: her parts are thinking for her. She beats Jeffrey up, then dresses in a miniskirt and begins grabbing men on the street, screaming, "Wanna date? You got any money?" When Jeffrey finally explains to her what has happened, Elizabeth says, "I feel so strange—like there's so many different women inside of me!" Suddenly, what remains of those "different women"—the leftover blown-up parts—comes boiling up out of Jeffrey's vat and kills him.

The film ends with Jeffrey awakening after having been revived by Elizabeth in the same way he revived her. Except, we discover, his "serum" is

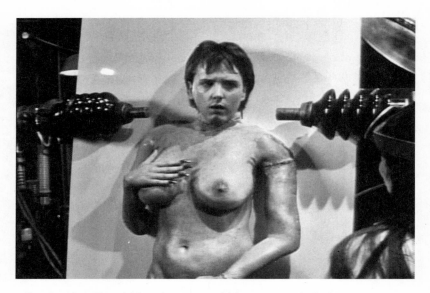

Jeffrey discovers what it's like to be experimented upon in *Frankenhooker*.

estrogen-based, so it can only work on "female parts." Elizabeth smilingly explains to Jeffrey that she's had to sew his head onto the leftover prostitute parts he didn't use on her. "Now we can be together," Elizabeth beams, "*All of us!*" This is so horrifying (and humorous) precisely because Elizabeth is referring to the way his female parts will be "thinking" and behaving like the group of sex workers they once were.

With *Frankenhooker* we are reminded that body parts cost money. Unlike the professional doctors of *Re-Animator*, Jeffrey doesn't work in a hospital. He's therefore forced to get his bodies on the street, across the river from his working-class New Jersey neighborhood. That is, Jeffrey is "proletarianized," and his mental labor is closely affiliated with manual labor (he works with electrician's tools, for example). Even Jeffrey's madness has a working-class cast to it. Rather than just "going mad," he uses an electric drill to make holes in his head and "change his mind" enough to stomach the idea of killing prostitutes for his experiment. He uses his hands and a power tool to make his mind work, as it were.

Interestingly, the body parts he buys seem to develop a kind of class consciousness, acting as a group to get revenge on him and ensure their group survival "together." Thus the flip side of thinking body parts which can be exploited are ones that begin thinking together and stage a kind of revolution against their oppressor.

Sometimes mad doctors attempt to heal the splits in their identities by refusing to sell the products of their mental labor or by somehow defetishizing their brains. Two turn of the century films, *Pi* and *A Beautiful Mind*, dramatize one way this process is accomplished: the mad mathematicians in both films choose to destroy their own minds rather than continue allowing professional institutions to use them.

Pi is the story of Max, a nebulously defined genius who works in a freaky nest of gooey, ant-infested computers attempting to calculate the one number which will unlock "the language of nature." Wracked by headaches and painful hallucinations, he is constantly medicating himself in scenes as terrifying as any Jekyll transformation sequence. At one point, he uses a dosage-delivery gun to inject an unnamed substance directly into his head. In his rare moments of calm and sanity, he tests his number theories by attempting to predict the fluctuations of the stock market—the idea, common to both mainstream capitalist economics and B-grade horror movies, is that markets are a kind of natural phenomenon. If his number can predict the stock market, then Max has unlocked the secrets of what he calls "the world."

Because he is so close to finding this mysterious number, Max is being pursued by two groups: a gang of numerology-obsessed Hasidim who think he's discovered the true name of God, and a large financial corporation which offers him a super-powered "main mecha chip" for his computers so that they can use his research to play the stock market. One of the film's most telling moments comes after Marcy, a rep from the corporation, has chased Max all over town to solicit his help. He finally screams at her: "I'm looking for a way to understand our world—I don't want to deal with petty materialists like you!" He flees into the subway, where he's hit with a headache and imagines he's following a man in business clothes who is leaving a trail of blood spatters behind him. Eventually the blood leads Max to a human brain, apparently abandoned by its owner on the subway stairs. He pokes it several times dementedly, and finally plunges a ballpoint pen through the brain before blacking out. Here we have another image of the alienated brain, wrenched free of its body at the moment when Max is being pursued by the "petty materialist" who wants to alienate him from his mental labors.

Overcome by the urge to find his number, Max finally accepts the main mecha chip from Marcy and makes his great discovery. But he doesn't want

As we discover in *Pi*, the only way to escape selling your thoughts to corporate America is to drill your brain out.

to let it get out of his control. He wants to possess the product of his labor. When the Hasidim try to get the number from him, he explains that there's no copy—"It's in my head!" he insists. Marcy shows up with some thugs who try to beat the number out of him. "I don't give a shit about you!" Marcy screams at the trembling, unhinged Max. "I just want what's in your fucking head!"

Unlike many mad doctor narratives, *Pi* proposes a solution to this dilemma that doesn't involve death. Instead, Max stages a kind of revolution. He sabotages the means of production, thus robbing his pursuers of the intellectual property they hope to steal from him. But to do this he must destroy himself too: Taking a drill to his head, he wrecks his own brain. As the film closes, we see him sitting on a park bench with an expression of contentment we've never seen him wear before. One of his neighbors, a little girl who always begs him to do math tricks for her, asks him to calculate a large multiplication problem. He looks at her, shakes his head, and smiles: "I don't know," he says.

A similarly depressing solution to mental cooptation is suggested by the film adaptation of *A Beautiful Mind*, a rather liberally reinterpreted biopic about Nobel-winning mathematician John Nash, who is often credited with inventing game theory. Like Max, Nash suffers from a form of insanity that seems inexorably linked to his genius. Nash makes his greatest discoveries while in conversation with his best friend Charles, who turns out to be imaginary. In fact, Nash surrounds himself with imaginary friends and enemies, whose presence and absence the film uses to figure his waxing and waning schizophrenia.

While Nash is never entirely well when his imaginary pal Charles is in the picture, he doesn't become completely unhinged until the government begins using him as a cryptanalyst during World War II. Finding patterns in enemy codes turns Nash into a secretive paranoiac who is convinced that hidden messages are everywhere. Frightened by fantasies inspired by his mental labor for the government, he withdraws from his family and is unable to do his job as a professor. But Nash nevertheless manages to "cure" himself by learning to ignore his imaginary friends. This is depicted as an excruciating process in the film, for Charles is one of the closest and most reliable friends Nash has. Cutting off access to Charles means that he's left sane, but apparently no longer able to make brilliant discoveries. Certainly he's no longer of interest to any government in need of a crypt-analyst. Here, therapeutic recovery functions like Max's drill. Nash is left sane and whole, but his beautiful mind is no longer quite so comely.

Over a century of mental labor in America has seen the doctor's role as symbolic analyst catapulted between the positions of exalted, God-like theorist and menial mind drone. Divided from himself, forced to sell his own thoughts on the open market, the mad doctor is a monster not because he deviates from professionalism but because he embodies it. The horrors he imposes on other people—experimenting with their bodies, subjecting them to clinical violence—are the inevitable result of losing his mind to professionalism. Perhaps because his monstrosity and livelihood are in-distinguishable, the mad doctor has no constructive avenue of escape. His very consciousness is the factory floor. To revolt, he must destroy himself.

3. THE UNDEAD

A Haunted Whiteness

When racial difference cannot be talked about in a narrative—or is willfully ignored—one way it gets covertly described is as a difference between "dead" and "living" cultures, or more fantastically in the difference between dead bodies and animated ones. As anthropologist Marianna Torgovnick has pointed out, whites often distinguish themselves and their nations by laying claim to progress and the future, implicitly relegating the importance of all other racial groups to antiquity, the "savage" past, and dead civilizations.[1] This racist logic of progress holds that people of color are frozen in time, unchanged since the origins of human history. Hence, Torgovnick concludes, white anthropologists throughout the twentieth century claimed that African and Caribbean tribes should be studied for clues to the Euro-American past and that black and native bodies should be examined to explain their temporal inferiority.

In keeping with this anthropological tradition, popular tales which feature the undead often suggest a connection between certain racial identities and death. Toni Morrison's account of Edgar Allen Poe's "The Narrative of Arthur Gordon Pym" explores why this might be:

> [Because] images of impenetrable whiteness . . . appear almost always in conjunction with representations of black or Africanist people who are dead, impotent, or under complete control, these images of blinding whiteness seem to function as both antidote to and meditation on the shadow that is companion to this whiteness—a dark and abiding presence that moves the hearts and texts of American literature with fear and longing. This haunting, a darkness from which our early literature seemed unable to extricate itself, suggests the complex and contradictory situation in which American writers found themselves.[2]

Morrison describes an "Africanist" presence in narrative that is "companion to" whiteness, but also "haunting" in a way that arouses both "fear and longing." These tensions—between companionship and haunting, fear and longing—are at the center of every undead tale. There is a kind of ghostly connection between whiteness and whatever racial group is cast as its opposite (Morrison places blacks in this position, but it is occupied just as often by natives, Asians, or Jews). Even the most triumphant, "impenetrable whiteness" cannot be understood without reference to a dead non-white body which haunts and taunts it, granting it a meaning which cannot always be controlled.

A great deal of literary and film criticism has suggested—occasionally in a persuasive way—that horror stories dealing with race always position whites as the human creatures who must battle supernaturalized minority groups.[3] But this is a dramatic oversimplification of the genre. Often whites cast themselves as the monsters in stories which suggest that their relationship to racism is, as Morrison suggests, "complex and contradictory." Stories about the undead are best understood in the context of anxieties about many kinds of race relationships that develop in the wake of colonialism. The undead are liminal beings who exist between the worlds of life and death. They represent the sorts of identities that erupt into being when different racial groups collide violently with one another and produce horrifying new cultures of deprivation and oppression.

In the first half of the twentieth century, stories about the undead are morbidly obsessed with colonialism and slavery. Pulp tales from this period, for example, associate the meeting of European and Caribbean cultures with the machinations of slimy, tentacled immortals who rise from watery tombs. Movies explore what happens when black voodoo priests gain the power to turn white women into zombies. Yet even the most simplistic and racist of these stories also reflects the moral confusion of a nation that feared, yet desired, an end to colonialism in the world and at home. Whites in these stories are haunted by knowledge of a distant past when people of color were free and powerful. And they anticipate a future where whites have become ghosts doomed to drift unsubstantially among formerly colonized people who have regained their sovereignty.

Undead narratives circulated before the 1960s and 1970s—before widespread political challenges to white supremacy—are filled with anxieties about what will happen to racial categories in the United States when colonialism dies out. Later in the century, as postcolonial writers and pundits begin to generate their own narratives about what bell hooks calls the "terrorism" of white power, the dead past that threatens to destroy our heroes is always associated with the colonial period.[4] Undead narratives of the 1980s, 1990s, and 2000s are preoccupied with the way anachronistic race relations exist alongside those of the present day, like zombies among the living.

Regardless of their historical period, undead stories share a common investment in the idea that communities murdered by colonialism can linger on, half-alive, and refuse to leave the living remainder alone. This half-alive fragment of a destroyed people is often associated with the mixed-race descendants of colonizer and colonized. Because miscegenation under colonialism is usually the result of rape or coercion, mixed-race coupling is generally regarded by these narratives as another form of violence and as a prelude to or outcome of racial extinction. Racial hybridity is a form of living death, and the desire for racial others is always tinged with fear and guilt.

I begin my exploration of the undead with the early-twentieth-century colonial allegories of H. P. Lovecraft's Cthulhu tales and D. W. Griffith's story of "ghosts" in *The Birth of a Nation*, and I end with a series of post-1960s movies such as *Blacula*, *Tales from the Hood*, and *Bones*. I'll also chart the rise of a new breed of films, including *Blade* and *Underworld*, devoted to revaluing monstrosity as a kind of antiracist project. What is perhaps unsurprising is that in a group of narratives constructed around death and colonialism, whites are often the subjects and objects of haunting. Gradually emerging in this subgenre is a meditation on whether it is possible for any racial group—whether colonizer or colonized—to survive a racist history unscathed. Slavery and genocide may be part of the past, but they wreak havoc in the present. Zombies, vampires, and mummies bear in their half-alive bodies the signs of great social injustice whose effects cannot ever be entirely extinguished.

🐾 America's Weird Tale

Most accounts of the cinematic undead take Bram Stoker's novel *Dracula* to be the origin of modern stories about the walking dead. But to understand the particulars of the United States's obsession with racial identity and death, one must begin with tales of the undead in a pulp magazine whose star writer and sometime editor, H. P. Lovecraft, was steeped in American history. Founded in 1923, the pulp fiction magazine *Weird Tales* featured, in the words of its manifesto, "stories . . . taboo in the publishing world."[5] The manifesto goes on to explain that the weird tale is "the story of psychic phenomena or the occult story . . . [and] stories of advancement in the sciences and the arts to which the generation of the writer who creates them has not attained. All writers of such stories are prophets, and in the years to come, many of these prophesies will come true."[6] *Weird Tales* stories, especially those by H. P. Lovecraft and his disciples, took an ancient genre—stories of the dead returning—and modernized it to speak to twentieth-century preoccupations. Combining "occult" figures with science fiction-style "prophesies" about the future, weird fiction involves "crude physical horror"[7] and toys with the connections between eroticism, death, and racial identity. A common anecdote about the magazine is that it sold on the basis of its lurid covers, many of which featured semi-clad female demons and "savages," or women swooning in the arms of vampires and devils.[8] These images, with the stories they illustrated, were partly what made the weird tale "taboo." Especially in the hands of an author like Lovecraft, the weird tale evoked a pulp fiction–style dark side to American life which was explicitly linked to racial and sexual danger.[9] In Lovecraft's work, these dangers took on the aspect of "prophetic" writing in their attention to what he feared might be the future consequences of rampant fraternization between whites and other races.

Because race relations in the United States are deeply connected to class relations,[10] Lovecraft's work inevitably also captures the uneasiness of a nation witnessing the death throes of economic systems associated with imperialism and slavery. Often, the immortal and undead monsters in his stories are explicitly connected to the economic fate of an individual or community.

Lovecraft began writing for *Weird Tales* almost directly after it was founded and quickly became what S. T. Joshi terms a "fixture" of the publication.[11] Unlike most *Weird Tales* authors (with the possible exception of Robert Bloch), Lovecraft's writing has remained popular and in print throughout most of the twentieth century, experiencing a marked renaissance in the decades since the 1960s.[12] What George Wetzel calls Lovecraft's "Cthulhu Mythos"[13] is so influential that it has turned up in countless novels and movies, inspiring the work of authors from Stephen King to J. G. Ballard. Fans have even turned his stories into a series of role-playing games (Call of Cthulhu and Mythos) where one takes on the identity of a character battling monstrous forces from the pages of Lovecraft's short stories and novels.[14] Such an ongoing absorption with Lovecraft's writing

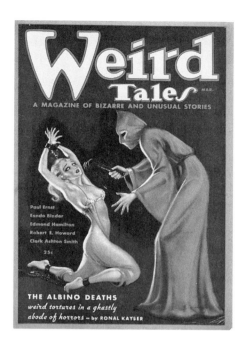

In this 1920s cover from the pulp magazine *Weird Tales*, we see a fantastical, eroticized image of miscegenation.

in the United States is testimony to its continued relevance in the allegedly more enlightened eras of melting pots and multiculturalism.

Although not all of Lovecraft's stories and novels are about race relations and the undead, his typical Cthulhu Mythos formula involves both. In famous stories such as "The Call of Cthulhu," "The Dunwich Horror," "The Shadow Over Innsmouth," "At the Mountains of Madness," "The Horror at Red Hook," and the novel *The Strange Case of Charles Dexter Ward*, the Cthulhu Mythos tells the secret history of planet Earth and introduces us to races of alien beings who populated it millions of years before human life existed.[15] Knowledge of this history, and of the aliens' influence over human affairs, is so horrifying that it drives humans utterly insane. "At the Mountains of Madness" provides us with an overview of Lovecraft's pre-human history: a highly civilized race of Old Ones (who look like huge squash with starfish heads) arrives from the stars, populates the Earth, and later does battle with squid-like, seagoing "spawn of Cthulhu" and the "half-fungus, half-crustacean" Mi-Go. Long after all this is over, several explorers from Miskatonic University discover a lost city of the Old Ones in the mountains of the Antarctic. Art and writing on the walls of this city reveal the descent of a civilized culture into a "decadent" one, largely as a result of interspecies wars and a massive uprising among the Shug-goths, giant polymorphous beings who were used by the Old Ones as slave labor.[16]

Most of Lovecraft's Mythos stories focus on the lingering horrors of Shuggoths and Cthulhu's spawn, two alien races that have survived in a kind of suspended animation, occasionally managing to form ties with cer-tain human communities and cults that have the power to awaken them. "The Dunwich Horror" and *The Strange Case of Charles Dexter Ward* fea-ture Shuggoths conjured through black magic, for instance, while "The Shadow Over Innsmouth" and "The Call of Cthulhu" deal with the resur-rection of Cthulhu and his spawn, who are busily mating with humans and ruling over cults which are "infinitely more diabolic than even the blackest of the African Voodoo circles."[17] Lovecraft's "diabolic" and hybridized alien races turn up in port towns, New York City, and nearly anywhere else in the United States that is associated with racial minorities and immigrant communities. The exalted Old Ones are totally extinct and appear mostly in references to the past or the dreams of white men.

Lovecraft writes in his autobiography, "I am an ultra-conservative so-cially, artistically and politically."[18] Of course we may say, in retrospect, that this conservatism is obvious from his depictions of race relations. But Lovecraft's idea of conservatism is bound up in his fixation on "dead" his-torical periods, periods that haunt his stories both literally and figuratively. These periods, notably ancient Rome and the eighteenth century, are asso-ciated with vanished modes of production that depended on slave labor. You might say he's nostalgic for eras when one could easily tell the difference between masters and slaves. One of Lovecraft's basic projects is a kind of supernatural historical revisionism where he retells U.S. history as a weird tale, starting with occultists in colonial New England, moving through im-mortal Caribbean half-monsters spawned in the post–Civil War era, and ending in contemporary New York City, which is crawling with Cthulhu-worshiping illegal immigrants. What emerges is a portrait of how colonial relationships transformed (often hideously) the Europeans who settled in America during his "favorite modern period . . . the 18th century."[19]

The Case of Charles Dexter Ward manages to capture white anxieties about what happens to white identity in a culture which cannot quite ex-tricate itself from its colonial origins.[20] Charles Dexter Ward, a young anti-quarian living in Providence, Rhode Island, during the 1910s and 1920s, discovers that he is the descendant of Joseph Curwen, a powerful and wealthy man whose life story has been all but eradicated from local histories and landmarks. We begin the story knowing that Ward, by poring over Curwen's secret papers, has learned enough occult magic to resurrect the spirit of his dead ancestor in his own body.

But this shocking revelation is hardly the worst of it, as Ward's degeneration is simply a frame story for the more grotesque tale of Curwen's life as an eighteenth-century shipping magnate and summoner of the dead. Having educated himself in the sacred books of a non-Western culture, especially the "forbidden *Necronomicon* of the mad Arab Abdul Alhazred" (18), Curwen learns a way to reanimate the spirits of the dead using their powdered bones. Curwen has "a virtual monopoly of the town's trade in saltpetre, black pepper, and cinnamon," yet he is also known for "a freakish importation which could not conceivably have been destined for anyone else in the town" (30). This "freakish importation" is Curwen's other stock-in-trade: bones, mummies, chemicals, and "Guinea blacks . . . for whom he could produce [no] bona fide bills of sale" (21). Purchasing a farmhouse in Pawtuxet, a town outside Providence, Curwen brings startling numbers of slaves, cows, and books there to use in his "experiments," all of which he conducts in a vast underground network of caves.

Curwen has also discovered a way to become virtually immortal. His continued youth, along with his outsider status and escalating economic power, finally arouse the suspicion of several townspeople, especially Ezra Weeden. When Weeden discovers the extent of Curwen's "unholy" rituals, he leads a party—something like a lynch mob—out to the Pawtuxet farmhouse to destroy it and seal off the rooms below. Centuries later, Ward's friend Dr. Willett finds Weeden's journals in Ward's papers. Along with these are letters to Ward from Curwen's old friends, who are mysteriously still alive. Put together, these documents reveal the true horror at the heart of *The Case of Charles Dexter Ward*:

> There was, [Willett and Ward's father] conceded, a terrible movement alive in the world[;] . . . they were robbing the tombs of all the ages, including those of the wisest and greatest men. . . . A hideous traffic was going on among these nightmare ghouls, whereby illustrious bones were bartered with the calm calculativeness of schoolboys swapping books (94).

Unlike most colonial traders of the period, Curwen isn't robbing the tombs of Africans or Indians for trinkets, nor is his "barter" in people restricted solely to these colonized groups. In fact, he and his friends are stealing the bones of Europeans, in particular the "greatest" of them, and causing the spirits of these dead men to be reawakened under their power. Using their bones, Curwen is able to keep spirits "prisoner" (28) and steal their knowledge. The "hideous traffic" in bones among Curwen and his colleagues is ultimately a form of white slavery: white men are bought and sold, and used to serve their occult masters. The fear that white Europeans are just as easily enslaved as people from Africa, Asia, and pre-Columbian America is what haunts Lovecraft's story about the revolutionary period in U.S. history.

Curwen, whose house in the twentieth century is "now the abode of a Negro family much esteemed for occasional washing, house-cleaning and furnace-tending services" (49), is associated everywhere in the story with blacks, Jews, Indians, and of course the writings of "the mad Arab Abdul Alhazred."[21] So, one might plausibly argue that he is a stand-in for members of racial groups who had been oppressed—or, disdained—by whites in the United States. But I would argue that Curwen is perhaps all the more frightening precisely because he is a white man who has chosen to use his own race for profit just as he uses his "Guinea blacks." He is the white man who refuses to respect the superiority of whiteness and is therefore chipping away at white sovereignty from the inside, revealing that whites are really no better or worse than racial "others." All races, for Curwen, are equal in their slavery to him after death.

✷ "Dead Cthulhu Waits Dreaming"

The idea that whites can be destroyed by colonialism grows more elaborate in "The Shadow Over Innsmouth" (1931), a story about the degeneration of a Massachusetts port town after the Civil War sends the local economy into a tailspin. Narrated by an unnamed young male antiquarian (much like Ward), the story begins with his travels through the Massachusetts countryside, where he happens upon the virtual ghost town of Innsmouth. People in neighboring towns have been warning him that Innsmouth is a very bad place to visit, but that the "way folks feel [about Innsmouth] is simply race prejudice."[22] What sort of race prejudice this might be is hinted at when a ticket seller tells the narrator about

> what a lot our New England ships used to have to do with queer ports
> in Africa, Asia, the South Seas, and everywhere else, and what kinds of
> people they sometimes brought back with 'em. . . . [Innsmouth people
> have] gotten to be about as bad as South Sea cannibals and Guinea sav-

ages. . . . I guess they're what they call "white trash" down South—law-less and sly, and full of secret things. (119–21)

Although currently filled with "white trash" in the fishing business, Inns-mouth's economy was once based on shipping. After the War of 1812 and the Civil War ruined trade between those "queer ports" and the United States, Innsmouth was decimated financially and even its best families "de-generated."

Once in Innsmouth, the narrator discovers that its inhabitants "did not look Asiatic, Polynesian, Levantine or negroid," but have "coarse-pored greyish cheeks," and "bulging, watery blue eyes . . . a flat nose, a receding forehead and chin, and singularly undeveloped ears" (126). Their religious culture is obviously non-European, too: their congregation is part of the wacky-sounding "Esoteric Order of the Dagon." Finally, the markedly white and aged town drunk, Zadok Allen, explains to the narrator what has hap-pened to Innsmouth. In the 1830s, he says, the wealthy Captain Obed Marsh despaired of ever extricating the town from poverty. Then he jour-neyed to a South Sea island where the natives had fantastic luck with fish-ing. Their luck, apparently, came from having devoted themselves to the worship of what Zadok calls "some kind o' god-things that lived under the sea" (143). In desperation, Captain Obed decided to attempt the same kind of worship in Innsmouth. As any discerning Lovecraft reader would have expected, the "god-things" found in the South Seas turn out to be the Spawn of Cthulhu, and they demand human sacrifices in exchange for jewels and plentiful fishing.

But after 1846, things begin to change. As the country moves toward the Civil War, the "god-things" start demanding a higher price for their services: they want to mate with the humans, and in return they prom-ise to grant their hybrid children eternal life under the sea. Tellingly, it's only after the Civil War that these mixed children are born and grow up, as if they represent the mixed-race "spawn" of a nation which has outlawed slavery and begun to acknowledge the humanity of blacks and colonized peoples. As Bennett Lovett-Graff argues, fears about the genetic disasters created through miscegenation had reached a fever-pitch when Lovecraft published "The Shadow Over Innsmouth." He notes that the story is heavily informed by popular notions about eugenics and Darwinism of the period, and that "[immigrants'] rate of reproduction . . . stands as the central threat to the purity of America's racial stock."[23]

But there is something in Innsmouth more menacing than the threat of black and immigrant breeds: whites who want to breed with them, and who flourish in the process. For it is strictly through the consent—indeed, the supplication—of whites that the Spawn of Cthulhu are brought from the South Seas to the shores of Massachusetts. While Lovecraft is careful to have his characters discuss the "revulsion" involved in mating with "fish-frogs," we are also given to understand that the children created are only ugly by human standards and that they enjoy rich, beautiful, eternal lives once they return to their "great palaces" beneath the ocean.

Our narrator discovers that he, too, is one of these hybrids and ultimately decides to join his kin beneath the sea. Like Curwen, he refuses to preserve the sanctity of whiteness and white privilege. Instead, he embraces a racial heritage—and an "eternal" racial future—which is flagrantly hybrid. It is also a future without death. This kind of white person, who dreams of escaping white America to live among "others," is what Lovecraft implies is the true outcome of the Civil War. It is an outcome both terrifying and hopeful—the future belongs to semi-dead monsters, but once viewed from the monsters' point of view, this isn't really so bad.

Commentators on Lovecraft's fiction often use the author's own life to explain his curious blending of fantasy and contemporary social preoccupations such as eugenics and immigration. Nowhere do the details of Lovecraft's life seem more relevant than in "The Horror at Red Hook," which can be read as a weird autobiography about Lovecraft's brief marriage to Sonia Greene, a Jewish merchant with whom he lived for a few years in New York.[24] Red Hook, the setting for his story, was close by one of the neighborhoods where Lovecraft and his wife lived at that time. Beyond his personal interest in a story of contemporary urban miscegenation, Lovecraft has a social interest in "The Horror at Red Hook": as an avowed "chalk-white" racist,[25] Lovecraft wants to demonstrate a connection between illegal immigration in the 1920s and supernatural evil. During his New York stint, Lovecraft wrote in his diary that Red Hook "is a maze of hybrid squalor."[26]

In "The Horror at Red Hook," he describes the region as "a hopeless tangle and enigma; Syrian, Spanish, Italian, and negro elements impinging upon one another. . . . It is a babel of sound and filth."[27] The story hinges on the discovery of a secret cadre of occultists, led by the wealthy Dutchman Robert Suydam, who are importing illegal immigrants into New York through a series of underground tunnels beneath the city. Police Inspector Malone, who is attempting to find out more about Suydam's whereabouts, accidentally happens upon an occult ceremony involving these illegals and several female demons. He witnesses a bizarre marriage ritual involving the recently dead body of Suydam and the undead demon Lilith, described as an "abominable naked phosphorescent thing" (88).

What is striking about this otherwise generic and critically maligned tale are Lovecraft's comments on the ancient historical tradition that informs Suydam's relationship to the immigrants and their religion.[28] On the street in New York, Malone observes, "They must be . . . the heirs of some shocking and primordial tradition. . . . There had survived among peasants and furtive folk a frightful and clandestine system of assemblies and orgies descended from dark religions antedating the Aryan world" (75). Later, Suydam explains to police that he needs to keep company with various minority groups because he is "engaged in the investigation of certain details of European tradition which required the closest contact with foreign groups and their songs and folk dances" (77). Here, Lovecraft suggests a direct connection between "European tradition" and "dark religions antedating the Aryan world." Not only is there a prehuman world, as we know from "At the Mountains of Madness," but there is a human world before whiteness, out of which whiteness has been born—and to which it is still profoundly attached. The dangerous and seductive heritage of a culture "antedating the Aryan world" is at the root of Lovecraft's weird fiction and permeates the twentieth- and early-twenty-first-century genre of undead horror. Knowledge of such a culture is a reminder that there was once a thriving human culture without contemporary notions of racial distinction. As Lovecraft writes in his monograph *Supernatural Horror in Literature:*

> Much of the power of Western horror-lore was undoubtedly due to the hidden but often suspected presence of a hideous cult of nocturnal worshipers whose strange customs—descended from pre-Aryan and pre-agricultural times when a squat race of Mongoloids roved over Europe with their flocks and herds—were rooted in the most revolting fertility-rites of immemorial antiquity.[29]

What is "hideous" here is not so much the fact that all people were once part of "a squat race of Mongoloids," but rather that there are still people whose "strange customs" recollect and celebrate that time. In short, Lovecraft's weird fiction is about the way this racial (or, interracial) heritage refuses to die. A "pre-Aryan" past is essentially a preracial past. Ultimately Lovecraft fears that this past might live again, become "reanimated," if the races mix to the point where distinguishing between them becomes impossible. This is certainly one motor driving the horror in *Case* and "Innsmouth."

Yet as Lovecraft's own marriage to a Jewish immigrant attests, the longing for sexual and social union with racial "others" can overwhelm even the most racist of individuals. It is that longing which Lovecraft chronicles in his infamous story "The Call of Cthulhu." Often hailed as his greatest work in the Mythos, this story is about the way human beings are constantly threatened with, and fascinated by, gaining access to a pre-Aryan and prehuman, past. The great god Cthulhu, awakened by accident during an earthquake, sends dreams out to people all over the world, filling their minds with images of alien cities, nonhuman architecture, and strange hybrid beings. Many of them experience an overwhelming flood of emotions, and hear the words, "*Ph'nglui mglw'nafh Cthulhu R'lyeh wgah'nagl fhtagn*," which is translated to mean, "In his house at R'lyeh dead Cthulhu waits dreaming."[30] Cthulhu is both "dead" and "dreaming," an undead alien who "waits" for a future when his spawn will walk the earth again. After we learn of several people who have sighted Cthulhu far out at sea and gone mad after attempting to sink him, the narrator speculates, "[Cthulhu] must have been trapped by the sinking . . . or else the world would by now be screaming with fright and frenzy. Who knows the end? What has risen may sink, and what has sunk may rise" (158). A pre-Aryan culture may yet rise again—especially if powerful whites like Curwen and Suydam keep fraternizing with Africans, Asians, and Middle-Easterners. The language and icons of a preracial culture already exist in the unconscious minds of "Aryan" and "Mongolian" races alike. Indeed, as we know from "The Shadow Over Innsmouth," for many people Cthulhu's existence is already an intimate reality.

In these ideas we find the terror, and the sexy "weirdness," which form the fantasy bedrock of undead stories that follow it. For Lovecraft, U.S. history—and the world's future—are about hybridization from beginning to end. The undead, in his stories, stand in for a kind of timeless, inextinguishable connectedness between whites and people of color, or "humans" and "aliens." Cthulhu's power, and the lure of his spawn, are not a force that threatens white sovereignty from the outside, but from within: he is in the dreams of white men; he lurks at the heart of their cultural traditions; and his blood runs in what are supposed to be racially "pure" families. The monsters who haunt Lovecraft's weird tales are "undead" because they represent minority traditions that continue to live on in the United States, despite white domination. And their immortality is a prophesy of a world where new social relationships lead us into a post-Aryan future.

✱ A Pair of Racial Ghost Stories

Two movies, one released slightly before Lovecraft began publishing, and one released just a few years after his death, offer telling examples of the way Hollywood adopted many tropes of weird fiction to explain race war and U.S. colonialism. While *I Walked With a Zombie* falls within an identifiably "weird" genre, *The Birth of a Nation* is the kind of mainstream popular culture whose "realism" and "historical accuracy" managed to suggest—and perhaps inspire—the supernatural, pulp racism that *Weird Tales* made famous just seven years later. In spite of their distance from each other generically and historically, both movies are about how whites join the ranks of the undead while attempting to maintain their control over blacks. What is instructive about viewing them side by side is the chance to see how consistently the "racial undead" theme surfaces in what would appear to be quite different stories. In addition, *I Walked With a Zombie* gives us the opportunity to find out what happens to the theme after two decades of social transformations in the idea of "race."

The Birth of a Nation is famous both for its place in the history of early U.S. cinema and for being, in the words of Donald Bogle, "the most slanderous anti-Negro movie ever released."[31] Yet, like the weird tales of Lovecraft, this "anti-Negro" narrative turns out to be, in large part, about the degradation and interior horror of whiteness. Even a contemporary review of the film in *The New Republic* holds that *Birth* "degrades the censors that passed it and the white race that endures it."[32] Set during the Civil War period, *Birth* chronicles the personal and political repercussions of the fall of the Old South, following the tribulations of the Northern Stoneman family and the Southern Cameron family. At the center of the story is the "birth" of the Ku Klux Klan and its Aryan South.

The KKK's historical formation follows in the tradition of U.S. Revolutionary War militias and "vigilance committees" of various sorts. In *Birth*, it also follows the narrative tradition of "hunting parties" that band together in novels like *Dracula* and many subsequent movies to fight the undead. It is therefore no surprise that the movie itself acknowledges a connection between militias and the undead. Ben Cameron, the "Little Colonel" whose love of the white South drives him to despair after Griffith's rabid, slovenly blacks have taken over, has the "inspiration" to form the KKK after watching two little white children play at being ghosts. Trying to scare some black children, they hide under a white sheet like a menacing spirit. The black children flee, screaming. Ben's eyes widen, and the intertitle proclaims,

"The Inspiration!"—White children don a sheet and scare their black counterparts in a key scene from *The Birth of a Nation*.

"The inspiration." Ben's militia will dress as the black South's worst nightmare. The result, however, at least metaphorically, is to convert the Aryan nation into a band of gun-toting, vengeful ghosts out to get the people who "killed" them.[33] Rather than placing blacks in the implicitly repulsive position of living death, *Birth* puts whites there. Not only is this an interesting reversal of the *Dracula* narrative—where living whites hunt down a bestial, undead Eastern European immigrant—but it also opens up a way for us to read the film as being about the death, rather than the birth, of whiteness.

Michael Rogin argues that *Birth* is haunted by a scene of castration which never appeared in the finished film: that of the mulatto Gus, who attempts to rape Ben's "pet sister" Flora. One witness claims that he saw an original print of the movie where members of the KKK graphically castrate Gus after the attempted rape, and we see a close-up of "his mouth flowing blood and his eyes rolling in agony."[34] Allegedly this castration scene was later edited out, although Linda Williams points out rightly that the evidence for its original existence is somewhat tenuous.[35] Regardless of whether an actual scene was edited out, or simply never represented (except obliquely), I think Rogin is correct to consider *Birth* as partly about Griffith's desire to assert the potency of fatherhood in patriarchal figures like Ben. He persuasively concludes that a nation of such fathers can be "born" in part when black men are castrated. "The nation was born in Gus's castration, from the wound that signified the white man's power to stop the black seed," he writes.[36] Yet a counterreading is also possible: Gus's castration never made it into the final cut, and the film as a whole was banned in several states as a result of vigorous NAACP protests. Moreover, every strong white man in the film chooses to represent himself as a ghost. Perhaps white patriarchy is established far more shakily than Rogin's analysis acknowledges.

I have written elsewhere about the connection between white supremacy and a fear of castration.[37] I argue that white supremacy can be understood as an unattainable ideal against which actually existing white people are measured and found lacking. Like the phallic power of men, it is constantly being contested, broken down, and sometimes utterly toppled by oppressed groups. Just as there can be no phallus without castration, there can be no white supremacy without white debasement. The peculiar uniforms of the KKK are almost a literal rendering of this principle: although they are symbolic of white supremacy, they are also symbols of white death. Ultimately, the Aryan South is populated by whites whose identities are half-dead.

Williams compares Griffith's KKK "ghost inspiration" scene to its historical antecedent (and inspiration) in *Uncle Tom's Cabin*. In the novel, cruel plantation owner Simon Legree never discovers that escaped slaves Cassy and Emmeline are hiding in his garret because the two women dress in white sheets and scare him away. Afraid that he's being haunted by the ghost of a slave he murdered, Legree never ventures into their secret sanctuary. "Haunting in Stowe's novel is the ingenious means by which Cassy saves Emmeline from rape by Legree while also avenging Legree's murder of Tom," Williams writes.[38] It is also a reminder that *Birth* is itself haunted by a previous melodrama of race relations, *Uncle Tom's Cabin*, which dramatizes the injustices of a white supremacist system.

While Williams reads the ghostly role reversal in *Birth* as creating a "newly configured spectre of white male rule" before which blacks "cower, cringe and disappear," I think it's equally plausible to view this change as a tacit admission that white power is not all it's cracked up to be. After all, Cassy and Emmeline's white-sheeted stunts are hardly the acts of empowered people: it is a desperate measure, performed by women whose lives are in danger, in a last-ditch effort to preserve their safety. To claim that Griffith's image of the KKK donning white sheets echoes this scene in *Uncle Tom's Cabin* is to admit that it is a depiction of "white male rule" in tremendous peril. Like Cassy and Emmeline, the Southern men of *Birth* are perched precariously on the edge of destruction and must pretend to be dead in order to protect themselves.

While this kind of against-the-grain reading reveals unconscious anxieties about white power, there can be no doubt that Griffith intended to portray blacks and mulattoes as the true monsters of his film. Ed Guerrero notes that it was the first film to introduce the stereotype "of the black as a brute and a vicious rapist."[39] Rather than being lazy, passive, or asexual "Uncle Toms," the black man in *Birth* is capable of politically organized brutality and is in direct sexual competition with white men for white women. We see several scenes of black armies terrorizing white Southerners, and follow the career of Silas Lynch, a mulatto politician in Washington who lusts after Elsie Stoneman, the white daughter of his liberal patron. In essence, we are watching the "black buck" stereotype transferred to celluloid for the first time, and it is interesting to note that cinematic images of powerful black men reemerge in the early 1970s with blaxploitation films featuring violent, seductive, black action heroes. I'll address the convergence of blaxploitation and weird fiction later; for now I would simply note that *Birth* was the first film to offer images of a sexually and socially potent black male that were later reclaimed and recuperated by blacks themselves. These erstwhile bucks later became the "badass motherfuckers" who challenge white authority and win.

Birth's most immoral and potent black male character, Silas Lynch, is a mulatto, and Griffith himself wrote after the movie's release that he knew the film was offensive to "prointermarriage" organizations like the NAACP and its leaders.[40] The mulatto is a figure who comes closest to embodying the forces that create an army of white male ghosts. For the mulatto, like Lovecraft's pre-Aryan civilization, hints at a racial identity which does not fall neatly into the binary white/not white, or superior/inferior. While we are supposed to associate Silas with blackness in *Birth*, he is also unforgettably marked as white: played by a white actor, promoted by a white politician, living among the white political elite, he is a reminder that after the Civil War whiteness will never be the same. The KKK is an army of the undead because it is a militia dedicated to the preservation of a racial order which has already died. White supremacy has been challenged by blacks and whites alike. Whites may win a battle at the end of *Birth*, but they cannot ever win back their lives as uncontested masters of the South. Indeed, as I noted earlier, the absence of certain scenes in *Birth* underscores the degree to which contemporary audiences were aware that its racial politics were, or should be, archaic. Rarely does a history or treatment of this film neglect to mention the NAACP boycotts and protests of it. The film which epitomizes white triumph over black potency was itself censored—and this bit of narrative castration, however insignificant, remains material evidence of a challenge to white supremacy.

If we consider white supremacy to be what Antonio Gramsci would call "hegemonic," then Jacques Tourneur's *I Walked With a Zombie* is a movie about the way non-Western belief systems begin to challenge the hegemony of the white ruling class. Set during the early 1940s on a sugar plantation in the West Indies, *Zombie* offers us a fable of Gramsci's "crisis of hegemony," in which the plantation-owning Holland family suddenly finds that its "cultural, moral and ideological" leadership over the black population is no longer tenable.[41] Not only are the black servants and plantation workers disrespectful of the Hollands's authority, but we discover they have also converted the Holland matriarch to a belief in voodoo. With this movie, and many that come after it, we begin to see a kind of white ghost who is no longer powerful and vengeful, like those populating the KKK, but simply pathetic and lost. Challenges from the subordinate black population and internal instabilities within the Holland family result in the spectacular demise of white power and Western rationalism on the island of St. Sebastian. Using voodoo, and more importantly their knowledge of the Holland's secret "shame and sorrow," the colonized population in *Zombie* finally declares itself supreme.

Betsy Connell arrives on St. Sebastian to nurse the ailing wife of Paul Holland, who lives in a state of gothic bitterness with his half-brother Wesley Rand and their mother Mrs. Rand. As Betsy travels to their plantation, her black driver explains that the Hollands are one of St. Sebastian's oldest families, who "[brought] colored folks to the island," along with "Ti Misere," a figurehead of St. Sebastian from a slave ship which he describes as "one of the mothers of us all, chained to the bottom of the boat." Our introduction to the Rands is this story, told from the perspective of a man whose ancestors they enslaved. Later that night, she meets Paul's spectral wife Jessica wandering vacantly in a tower where we hear hidden women weeping. Paul explains to the startled Betsy that one of the servants has given birth. The women weep because for hundreds of years they lived in misery as slaves, and even today birth still seems a tragedy. In this tale, even whites openly admit that a heritage of black slavery bestows misery, implicitly blaming himself.

The next morning Betsy learns that Jessica may be a zombie, in part because Mrs. Rand, also a doctor, has become deeply involved in voodoo. Overhearing a local musician singing a ballad about the Hollands, Betsy learns that Paul's half-brother Wesley and Jessica fell in love, enraging Paul and leading to "shame and sorrow for the family." Knowing this, Betsy is more eager than ever to get to the bottom of Jessica's problem and please the broken-hearted Paul. Urged on by her maid Alma, Betsy seeks a cure for Jessica at a voodoo ritual, only to discover that the voodoo god "Danballa" is being channeled through Mrs. Rand. The matriarch eventually confesses that when she was possessed by Danballa, she wished to keep Jessica from fleeing the island and hurting Paul. Subsequently, Jessica was taken with fever and became a zombie.

Mrs. Rand is a kind of spiritual mulatto; she's a white woman who has taken on the belief system of the local black culture. And, one might argue, her miscegenated identity has led to the ruin of a white woman, Jessica — just as Silas Lynch nearly "ruins" Elsie. Yet the adulterous lust in *Zombie* comes from within the white family: Paul's half-brother Wesley desires Jessica, and therefore the sexual threat against white women is in fact from white men. Moreover, social power here comes from being literally possessed by blackness, the way Mrs. Rand is when she channels Danballa. Indeed, she admits that she originally began doing voodoo because she couldn't control the plantation workers after her husband died. Joining their voodoo rituals gave her the status she needed to diagnose illnesses and — presumably — to order blacks around. But now she is the puppet of a voodoo god, and her daughter-in-law is "living and dead," trapped between thwarted white desire and overwhelming black faith.

As the film draws to a close, we cut back and forth between a voodoo ritual and Jessica's incessant wandering — we discover that the ritual leaders have a voodoo doll of Jessica and are pantomiming drawing her toward them with a rope. To prevent her from leaving the plantation grounds once more, Wesley pulls one of the arrows from "Ti Misere" and kills her with it. At that moment, we see a pin enter the body of the white voodoo doll. Finally Wesley carries Jessica's body out to sea and drowns himself. This spectacular murder/suicide takes place entirely under the watchful eyes of a black zombie.

Michael Omi and Howard Winant have proposed that race relations involve constantly shifting categories, informed by a vast array of social forces, meanings, and events. They call this shifting set of forces "racial formation" to underscore the way race is most properly understood as the "sociohistorical process by which racial categories are created, inhabited, transformed, and destroyed." Importantly, a theory of racial formation holds that "race is a matter of both social structure and cultural representation."[42] Race, in other words, is an unstable category of identity associated with culture and with material life; hence, for example, race in *Zombie* is bound up in materialist economic relations between land holders and servants, but it is also depicted in the cultural clash between Western medicine and voodoo mysticism. What *Zombie* tracks are the profound, even violent, changes in the racial formations of whiteness and blackness as they move into a postcolonial era.[43] What we are left with is a portrait of crisis-ridden colonial relations on St. Sebastian: the masters are being destroyed by the slaves' tools.

Franz Fanon has explained that the social upheavals involved in decolonization do not generally lead to a cultural exchange or cross-racial communication, which is what we might be tempted to call Mrs. Rand's conversion to voodooism. Fanon writes:

> The natives' challenge to the colonial world is not a rational confrontation of points of view. . . . The violence with which the supremacy of white values is affirmed and the aggressiveness which has permeated the victory of these values over the ways of life and of thought of the native mean that, in revenge, the native laughs in mockery when Western values are mentioned in front of him. . . . In the period of decolonization, the colonized masses mock at these very values, insult them, and vomit them up.[44]

In this light, we can understand Mrs. Rand's "possession" by the culture of blackness on St. Sebastian to be a kind of violent revenge upon her family, which is so much a part of the island's colonial history. The voodoo worshipers are able to "insult" and "vomit . . . up" the economic and social misery visited on them by the Holland family: through their machinations, Wesley and Jessica die, and it appears that Betsy and Paul will leave the island to return to North America.

The former slaves' struggle to move St. Sebastian toward postcolonialism is also accompanied by wild fluctuations in the social and narrative meanings of whiteness and blackness. Where once Ti Misere was a sign of black sorrow, now it is a sign of white sorrow; where once Mrs. Rand and her Western medicine oversaw the plantation, now a black voodooist uses his magic to induce a crazed white man to murder his zombie lover and flee the shores of a West Indian land his family once colonized.

The kinds of changes in whiteness that are registered openly in *Zombie* are only hinted at in *Birth*. White power may be threatened in *Birth*, but the white citizens of the South are able to round up enough men to defeat the black military with ease. There is no defeating the colonized people in *Zombie*, however. Whites are driven from St. Sebastian with the same kind of violence they used to colonize it. White women in *Zombie* are vaguely incestuous, miscegenated sluts, whereas white women in *Birth* hurl themselves from precipices rather than have sex with a black man. Whiteness in *Zombie* is openly criticized; it's a social category nearly all the black characters legitimately contest. *Zombie*'s characterization of blacks as "savages," however, shares ideological terrain with *Birth*. Racist images and ideas did not disappear between the 1910s and 1940s, after all. The difference is that *Zombie* captures the anxieties of a Western imperialist force in retreat from morally justified, yet still menacing, colonized peoples. *Birth* merely registers the earliest intimations of such an anxiety.

❊ Over Colonialism's Dead Body

Undead militias return full force in weird cinema after the 1960s. The single white zombie of *Zombie* is expanded a hundredfold in George Romero's *Night of the Living Dead*, while the idea of a vengeful colonized population is foregrounded quite explicitly in blaxploitation movies like *Blacula*, *Tales From the Hood*, and *Bones*. Other weird films—such as *The People Under the Stairs* and *Nightbreed*—are contemporaneous with *Tales From the Hood* and reflect two profoundly different ways that the contemporary United States is still haunted by the colonial past. In all of these postcolonial era films, "undeath" is implicitly associated with colonial-era social and economic relationships, where one racial group engages in state-sanctioned subordination of others. Although all of these films are anti-racist parables, they nevertheless rely heavily on narrative forms and figures first deployed in *Birth* and Lovecraft's weird fiction. Even as these stories embrace the power of formerly subordinated groups, such power is represented as monstrous; and even as the supremacy of whiteness seems about to rot away, it inexorably returns, sometimes with the power to pull the living from their present-day lives back into colonial hell.

Amy Kaplan's introductory essay in *Cultures of United States Imperialism* explains that U.S. culture, while overtly imperialistic, is rarely viewed in the context of colonial relationships. She notes that "imperialism" tends to get relegated to the international sphere; as a result, U.S. domestic culture appears somehow free of the kinds of issues that shape nations which were or are occupied by a colonizing force. Yet, she concludes, social relations within the United States are deeply bound up with struggles taking place beyond its borders. "Not only about foreign policy or international relations, imperialism is about consolidating domestic cultures and negotiating intranational relations," she writes.[45] National boundaries are far more porous than many people might like to imagine. While critics and politicians may attempt to locate imperialism elsewhere, the United States is nevertheless haunted by the kinds of violence and uneven power relations most often equated with colonial societies.

White people are the closest thing the United States has to a colonizing group. There are many disempowered whites, or what Roxanne Dunbar has called "colonial dregs,"[46] but whites have historically occupied the highest positions in the government and economy.[47] As pop theorist Jim Goad puts it, "There's a primitive, biblical, sins-o'-the-father notion that *all* American whites, by virtue of their birth alone, bear a stain on their souls for black slavery."[48] That "stain" is certainly what seems to have saturated the flesh of the rotting, cannibalistic, undead whites in George Romero's *Night of the Living Dead*. It is also what animates the KKK-esque militia which bands together to eradicate them.

Night is in many ways an updated version of *Birth*, except this time around the upwardly mobile black man is the film's hero, rather than its locus of evil and terror. Ben, the level-headed black protagonist of *Night*, is clearly marked as both middle class and a leader. Sporting a tidy haircut, loafers, and a cardigan, Ben immediately begins to delegate jobs to the other people hiding from the zombies with him in an abandoned house. Like Silas Lynch, Ben is a black man with power in a white-dominated society; he is also, like Silas, ultimately destroyed for it. But Ben's death, *Night* persuades us, is a result of white presumption, not righteousness. The befuddled, easily deceived whites who surround Silas in *Birth* reappear in *Night* as the proverbial selfish and hysterical victims of the late twentieth century slasher flick. As mysteriously reanimated dead bodies shamble toward the house where Ben and his white companions are holed up, we discover that *Night*'s zombies are all white folks, and their only interest is in eating the bodies of living people. Anyone killed by the living dead is shortly reanimated themselves, often in gory, dripping-bite-mark fashion.

Ben outmaneuvers the zombies at nearly every turn. His competence is contrasted sharply with that of Harry, a middle-aged white husband and father figure, who explodes in a rage when Ben insists that they not hide in a basement room with no escape routes. When Harry continues to complain and threaten Ben's leadership, Ben shoots him and throws him into the basement with his zombie daughter and soon-to-be zombie wife. While Ben's actions are disturbing, they are at this point in the film clearly those of a soldier fighting for his life; Harry must be sacrificed for the survival of the group. There is heroism in Ben's violence. He fights to live, whereas Harry fights directionlessly, like a zombie.[49] As Richard Dyer explains, "In a number of places, the film shows that living whites are like, or can be mistaken for, the dead."[50] One might even go so far as to argue that whites like Harry are *asking* to be dead, since their survival instincts are so attenuated.

Meanwhile, a local militia is being organized by Sheriff McClelland, who tells a TV reporter that citizens dealing with the zombies should "Beat 'em or burn 'em." Like the KKK in *Birth*, the militia in *Night* comprise ordinary white citizens who use privately owned firearms to protect their land and, implicitly, their country. As they fan out across the region, shooting and burning zombies, we begin to see the militia and zombies as caricatures of each other. The militia is full of cartoonish, mean rednecks, while the zombies act like stereotypes of drunken, shambling hillbillies with torn clothes and cannibalistic ways.[51] They are all preying on one another, seeming to take a kind of sport or pleasure in the activity of murder, and both groups move in what Gregory Waller calls "mass attack" formation.[52] This is the kind of self-defeating, dying whiteness that the KKK militia in *Birth* is supposed to fend off. Squabbling among themselves, these whites are so incompetent that they can only bumble into an act of white supremacy— killing Ben—that is more farcical than tragic.

Ben is shot when dawn breaks. McClelland's militia sees him from a distance in the house. Believing him to be a zombie, they shoot and kill him instantly. Audiences watching *Night* are strongly encouraged to understand Ben's death as horrifyingly ironic; the film's one heroic, intelligent character has been slaughtered by stupid white guys with guns. Ben's nobility, his classiness if you will, is actually heightened by the irony of his death. His identity—educated, middle class, alive—stands out in graphic relief against the hoards of undead, low-class white people. Where Silas Lynch's class position among whites marked him as little more than an "uppity nigger," Ben's class position makes him a better person. His death ultimately serves as a condemnation of brutal, mindless white society.

Yet Ben's racial identity is not entirely what's at stake here: he's a good guy because he behaves in an educated, authoritative, middle-class fashion. Ben's murder is staged intentionally to remind us of racist police attacks, and therefore it is easy to forget that he is the only black man killed during the entire film. Both the redneck militia and the hillbilly zombies are hell-bent on shooting and eating white folks. With *Night*, we find that class is changing the way audiences are invited to sympathize with the lot of the colonized. Whites are being criticized for their racism here, but also for a kind of general "low class" ignorance. To put it differently: Ben is not just a black hero, he's a *middle-class* black hero. His racial heroism seems dependent upon class.

Blacula, a blaxploitation film released four years after *Night*, features another black hero whose class position determines how we evaluate whether he is superior to whites he meets in the United States. "Blacula," who prefers to go by his African name Mumawaldee, is an African prince who was turned into a vampire in 1780 while visiting Count Dracula. After Mumawaldee tells Dracula he wants to abolish slavery, Dracula shoots back that he thinks slavery is a good system, and proceeds to bite, curse, and imprison Mumawaldee. Stripped of his autonomy and nobility, Mumawaldee is chained in a coffin for almost two hundred years before being transported to New York by a gay couple from "the Village" who buy Dracula's mansion in the 1970s. They exclaim with swishy excitement that Dracula knickknacks are the "crème de la crème of camp" and vow to sell what they think is an empty coffin "back home." When they open the coffin, Mumawaldee jumps out and kills them instantly. These easily destroyed gay men — one white, one black — represent what the film understands as a form of "low" masculinity. Their strange entrance and exit from the film also tips us off to *Blacula*'s ensconcement in the weird genre: here we find racial anxieties, miscegenation, "deviant" sexuality, and the occult brought together in a morality tale which is finally about black manhood and class mobility.

Like Ben, the noble Mumawaldee dies — but his death is far from ironic. It is necessary for the sake of black social power. For unlike *Night*, *Blacula* offers a type of alternative black identity which is allowed to survive and flourish. Dr. Gordon Thomas, Mumawaldee's foil and pursuer, represents this kind of blackness. Like many heroes in blaxploitation films such as *Shaft* (1971), Gordon has a professional job (as a New York police investigator) and is confidently, swaggeringly masculine.

Mumawaldee's presence is a threat not just to Gordon's life, but also to his class position. Confronted with the ridiculousness of "an APB on a dead man," Gordon's colleague tells him to "forget [mass] hysteria" and worry about "mass unemployment starting with me." The Blacula case may cost Gordon his job and reputation as a good cop. Mumawaldee signals the potential return of colonial-style disenfranchised blackness, and tellingly his character brings into focus the degree to which black heroism is linked to black economic power. He also demonstrates that a black man stripped of his rank is monstrous. Mumawaldee's undead body represents a fantastical form of slavery and reminds us of an imperial whiteness (Dracula) that is so powerful it can convert princes into monsters.

Thinking in these terms, it suddenly becomes clear why police officers blame Mumawaldee's first kills on "Panther activity," and why Gordon finds a den of largely black vampires led by what he calls "that faggot" who brought Mumawaldee back to New York in the first place. His crimes are being blamed on marginal blacks—ghetto militants and "faggots"—who are either socially or economically subordinated. Mumawaldee is feeding on, and appearing to emulate, a black "culture of poverty" characterized by violent crime and desperation. Gordon's desire to eliminate Mumawaldee is bound up with a desire to free blacks from the horror of marginality and from the kinds of people who perpetuate a ghetto status quo. Finally, it is as if Mumawaldee knows that Gordon and his community will be dragged backward with him into colonial conditions if he lives. Committing suicide, he frees both a woman he's seduced and the black community from his spell. Yet in spite of its triumphant finale, *Blacula* also acknowledges that many blacks continue to live in a state of powerlessness so extreme that they are no better than famished vampires, cursed by colonial-era whites to live forever in a state of perpetual need.

With movies like *Blacula*, we find the emergence of a theme that reappears in weird movies about minority cultures after the early 1970s, too: class divisions are refiguring racial identity in the postcolonial United States. Solidly middle-class, heroic, minority characters like Gordon are threatened by others who remain in an undeath of social and economic subjugation. Like the colonial economy itself, these subjugated minorities continue to live in spite of the fact that imperialism is officially dead.

There are two narrative tactics that emerge in response to what I'm calling the undeath of colonialism in U.S. culture. One, represented by Clive Barker's *Nightbreed*, invites audiences to sympathize with a group of racialized monsters who are being hunted by bigoted, Christian Right types. The other, which we find in Wes Craven's *The People Under the Stairs*, tries to draw an explicit connection between class and racism on what amounts to a modern-day plantation in the ghetto. Both stories are grappling with the horror of colonial relations, yet they do not question the idea that colonized people are somehow inherently defective, monstrous, or socially crippled.

The oppressed remain monstrous, but monsters are celebrated as being more sympathetic than the people who hunt them.

Rather than offering a socially palatable alternative to racial monstrosity in the figure of a Ben or a Gordon, *Nightbreed* instead traces the conversion of straight, white male Boone into an undead member of the tribal Nightbreed. Visually, the Nightbreed are unmistakably monsters: sporting tentacles, skinless faces, extra body parts, and markings that resemble aboriginal tattoos, they are almost a parody of "savage native" stereotypes. Living under a cemetery called Midian, the Nightbreed have haunted Boone's dreams for years because, as we discover later, he is a part of their destiny. Boone is "Cabal," the hero who will bring the Nightbreed out of their hiding place and help them evade their persecutors. As I noted earlier, these persecutors take the form of rural, Christian moralists who declare the Nightbreed "unnatural" and "unholy." Ultimately, they band together and form a truck-driving militia who attack Midian with dynamite and guns. Before this final confrontation, however, the audience follows Boone as he learns about the Nightbreed and their heritage as an ancient "tribe of the moon," oppressed and scapegoated by humans (which the Nightbreed call "naturals") throughout history.

Boone is also a victim of the "naturals." His demented psychiatrist is a serial killer who frames Boone for his own crimes and shoots him to cover up his guilt. Returning from the dead as a full member of the Nightbreed, Boone struggles to reevaluate these seemingly ugly, horrifying people and reconcile their culture with his own identity. Finally, he realizes that he and the Nightbreed share more than their undeath. They are both hunted by narrow-minded, sadistic humans who want to keep their species "pure" by killing anyone who seems different. When the townspeople come to destroy Midian, Boone helps leads the Nightbreed away from their burning cemetery to safety, bringing his human lover Lori along. We are led to understand that Boone's relationships with the Nightbreed and with Lori are a new beginning for the Nightbreed, a moment of reconciliation between their (un)lives and those of the "naturals." This ending amounts to a kinder, gentler form of ethnic separatism, which strongly echoes Lovecraft's "The Shadow Over Innsmouth." But where Lovecraft's spawn of Cthulhu remain disturbing and unimaginable, Barker's Nightbreed are humanized and sympathetic. The Nightbreed are integrated further into human culture through Boone and Lori, whereas the narrator of "Innsmouth" plans to flee humankind for his family's underwater palace.

In spite of *Nightbreed*'s more minority-friendly tone, it remains heavily contained by the tropes of weird fiction, in which racial difference is tantamount to species difference. Here, as in Lovecraft, we find that social hierarchies proceed from nature. Because the Nightbreed are biologically "other," they are naturally victimized by humans. *Nightbreed* does not question the idea of racial monstrosity, but instead celebrates it as darkly beautiful and misunderstood. Even a much earlier film like *Zombie* offers audiences the possibility that what the whites considered "monstrous" about the blacks was actually a result of prejudice and imperial condescension. In *Nightbreed*, stereotypes of the colonized as unnatural, primitive, and helpless remain alive and well, permeating the film's representation of its undead minority.

The People Under the Stairs presents us with monsters who are obviously socially constructed. Here the point of view is also firmly planted at the margins, and we view the "people under the stairs" — a band of cannibalistic, mutilated white boys — from the perspective of Fool, a black teenager who dreams of becoming a doctor and escaping from the ghetto. When Fool needs money to help his sick mother, his friend Leroy talks him into robbing their landlords, who own the local liquor store and, as Leroy puts it, "half the other houses in the ghetto." It turns out that their landlords are an incestuous, crazed brother and sister who live in a heavily fortified funeral home filled with their "sons" — white boys whom they have kidnapped, tortured, and locked in the basement. These boys look and act like zombies, feeding on the bodies of people "Daddy" has killed. Fool is trapped inside the house after "Daddy and Mommy" murder Leroy and then lock all the doors and windows. Having befriended Alice, their abused "daughter," and Roach, one of the boys who has escaped from the basement into the walls of the house, Fool manages to find the landlords' hidden cache of money, kill them, and set Alice and her brothers free.

Night of the Living Dead pitted a middle-class black man against low-class white zombies, but *People* suggests a possible alliance between these groups based on class. Alice and her brothers, who live in decayed parts of the house, exist in a kind of internal ghetto. They are white, but they are owned and held captive by Daddy and Mommy, who threaten them with death if they do not obey. Alice and Roach instinctively help Fool, sensing that their relationships to Mommy and Daddy are basically the same as his. Rather than portraying its oppressed groups as monsters the way *Nightbreed* does, *People* casts the entire colonial system as populated by the undead: ghetto landlords (plantation owners) live in a funeral home, disenfranchised whites (sharecroppers) are zombified in their basement, and blacks (slaves) are trying to escape certain death. White power is quite literally a funeral home filled with money. When Fool blows the house up, a group of ghetto residents are protesting outside. Money released during the blast flies into the air and rains down on their heads. The wealth of the dead is redistributed among the living, and as we watch people of color gathering up armloads of money, we also see the white zombies running away penniless. Whites, in what critics have dubbed a ridiculously happy ending, are freed from their oppressive progenitors, and people of color are freed from poverty. Socioeconomic conditions make and unmake the monster, *People* seems to argue, whereas *Nightbreed* begs for conditions under which biological monsters are people too. Either way, somebody or something is always the monster; and colonialism lives on in its diabolical body.

In *Love and Theft: Blackface Minstrelsy and the American Working Class*, Eric Lott argues that colonial-era pop culture like minstrel shows dealt with changes in "the economics of race."[53] Lott's point is relevant here too. We are long past the era when slavery made a tradition out of minstrelsy, but bodies of all different colors become exchange values via the free market. This historical change in the economics of race means that class consciousness opens up the possibility for cross-racial alliances in the postcolonial era. It also generates mortal combat between members of the same racial group. Within the contemporary weird fiction tradition, this means that whites and people of color both attempt to reanimate imperialism's dead body. Formerly colonized racial groups begin to take on the characteristics of their former imperialist counterparts for economic and cultural gain.

✳ "Welcome to Hell, Motherfuckers!"

Nowhere is this more obvious than in Rusty Cundieff's 1995 movie *Tales From the Hood*. A series of four short stories, Cundieff's film self-consciously parodies campy, weird horror movies like *Zombie* made in the 1930s and 1940s. Stealing tropes and images from an emphatically white-dominated period in weird fiction, Cundieff presents a morality tale about black male identity turned against itself in the postcolonial era. In a frame story, gangbangers Stack, Ball, and Bulldog plot to steal a stash of drugs from Mr. Simms, the owner of a local funeral parlor. Simms, maddened and menacing, greets them at the door and promises to give them "the shit" if they'll listen to some stories about how four of his corpses came to be that

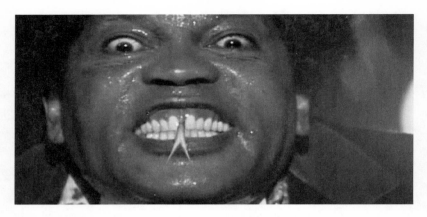

The undertaker in *Tales from the Hood* reveals his true identity when he screams, "Welcome to Hell, motherfuckers!" as he sprouts a forked tongue and grows horns.

way. We hear about a black police officer pursued and killed by the ghost of a black man he allowed to be beaten to death by his white partners. Another dead black man has been literally crumpled into a ball by his abused stepson, who has miraculously developed psychic powers to defeat the monster beating him and his mother. A racist white senator with ties to the KKK is murdered by black voodoo dolls animated by the spirits of slaves who lived in the plantation house he now occupies. And finally, a black gangster who murders other black men is experimented on—and killed—by a mad scientist who tells him he's no better than a white supremacist who wants to destroy the black community. When this last tale ends, the black teenagers discover that *they* are the murdered gangsters of the final tale. Simms is, in fact, the devil. As flames leap up around them, Simms sprouts a forked tongue and screams, "Welcome to Hell, motherfuckers!"

What is particularly interesting about Cundieff's *Tales* is that the movie unveils a form of guilt about racism which does not originate from white people. *Tales* is about black men whose desire for social and economic status forces them to recognize that they, too, might oppress blacks out of sheer, selfish greed. These men treat their black cohorts the way colonial whites once did: they abuse and murder them. As a result, they also experience a weird version of white guilt. After destroying their offspring and murdering their brothers, they cannot claim innocence in a postcolonial economic system that maintains ghettos and "undeveloped" nations for profit. Black men in *Tales* are pursued by angry black ghosts for the same reason the white racist politician is: for oppressing the black community. They're sent to hell by a black Satan for acting just like Simon Legree. Their desire for power rather than community, and death rather than cooperation, makes them shadow versions of white slaveowners. More to the point, it makes them tools of a colonizing class. And that is a form of racial allegiance which, at least in Cundieff's version of the weird tale, makes them "motherfuckers" in search of "shit" on the road to "Hell."

Another film which touches on many of the same themes as *Tales* is *Bones*, a classic story of revenge from beyond the grave. Jimmy Bones, played with wry dignity by rapper Snoop Dog, is a 1970s-era gangster with a heart of gold who is sold out to the cops by black friends who want to get out of the ghetto. Shot by corrupt police officers after he refuses to sell crack for them, Bones becomes an angry ghost who haunts the decaying mansion which was once the center of a thriving community and now looms over a ghetto wasteland. In the present day, a group of mixed-race young people decide to convert Bones's old pad into a dance club, and that's when the real haunting begins.

It turns out that two of the mansion's new owners, Patrick and Tia, are children of Jeremiah, one of the men who helped kill Bones. Jeremiah is now married to a white woman and living in suburbia. When he sees that his children have bought Bones's old house, he is filled with rage—he doesn't want them in the ghetto after he worked so hard to escape from it. When Patrick and Tia protest that they should be doing something about the conditions in the ghetto, he responds in a way that marks him as the narrative's guilty black man on the road to hell: "That place has already died and gone to hell," he says of the ghetto. But we know that the ghetto's spirit has been reanimated in Bones. And he's damn pissed.

Unlike *Tales*, *Bones* offers a sense of hope. Although Jeremiah is sucked into hell with Jimmy Bones, Patrick has started to date Cyn, Bones's daughter. Unlike his father, Patrick has a sense of responsibility toward the ghetto —he doesn't want to abandon it the way Jeremiah did. His relationship with Bones's old house and his daughter are indicative of a transformation in the relationships between blacks who want social power and those who have yet to achieve it. While the movie ends with a hokey last-minute scene where Cyn is possessed by her father's ghost, everything we've seen up to that point suggests that Patrick and Cyn's relationship represents a future where blacks will no longer be haunted by colonial history because they're forming alliances with each other across class lines.

✹ Racists and Hybrids of the Future

Of course, old-school, white-supremacist weird tales continue to find their way into pop culture. A perfect example is the wildly popular film *The Mummy*, a campy adventure flick where early-twentieth-century white adventurers do battle with an ancient Middle Eastern mummy returned from the grave. Just in case you hadn't already picked up on how the depiction of monstrosity in such a film might fit nicely into current American international politics, the undead Arab of the film's title is also trying to take over the world. And he's fixated on making it with a white girl. It's a kind of cross between *Raiders of the Lost Ark* and *Birth of a Nation*, although I doubt the latter was brought up in pitch meetings.

What saves *The Mummy* from being a mere rehash of Lovecraftian racist fantasy is its wacky irony. Like *Tales from the Hood*, *The Mummy* steals its ham-handed style from early-twentieth-century movies with a wink. Every character is a caricature. But unlike *Tales*, *The Mummy* doesn't offer us any twists on the old colonialist plot lines. Evil undead Arabs and simpering Egyptian servants are our enemies, and our hero is a muscular white guy who vanquishes what remains of an ancient culture—and of course, he keeps the white woman safe from Middle Eastern hands.

Before completely trashing *The Mummy* for its cartoony colonialist agenda, however, it's crucial to remember that the social and cinematic context of this film is hardly one of unquestioned white supremacy. Filmmakers of color can retaliate for something like *The Mummy* with movies of their own. Indeed, the Hughes Brothers—filmmakers whose first effort, *Menace II Society*, was a stark and brutal reimagining of the blaxsploitation film—provide just such a corrective in their movie *From Hell*. This supernaturally inflected retelling of an old true crime tale, that of the serial killer known as Jack the Ripper, explores the way white aristocrats terrorize nineteenth-century London.[54] Fred Abberline, a psychic, opium-addicted detective hired to find the Ripper, discovers that the killer is Sir William Gull, a possibly immortal demon who also serves as Queen Victoria's personal physician. *From Hell* could be described as the first-ever whitesploitation movie. Created by blacks, it's all about violent, drug-addicted, whoring white people and the criminal lives they lead. It's like a version of *Foxy Brown*, except this time around blacks are behind the camera and white culture is being mined and objectified for sensationalistic, entertaining excesses.

Representations of mixed-race people and miscegenation in the undead tale are also changing in the postcolonial period. As journalist Gregory Dicum has pointed out, a whole generation of mixed-race people—"originat[ing] in the cultural and sexual thaw of the 1960s"—has come of age in the United States. "Mixed parentage opens up all sorts of questions, particularly since many of our parents grew up in countries or colonies that no longer exist," he writes.[55] We see these questions answered after a fashion in *Blade* and *Blade II*, stories about a man known as the "Daywalker," a half-breed vampire created when his mother was bitten by a vamp while she was still pregnant with him. Blade was born with vampire superpowers and a human's ability to survive in daylight. Sworn to avenge his mother's death, Blade stalks vamps from an ancient tribe of immortals who secretly rule human affairs Illuminati-style.

Both *Blade* and its far-superior sequel *Blade II* deal explicitly with what it means to have mixed blood and to be heir to what Dicum calls "colonies that no longer exist." In *Blade*, our hero tries to loosen the stranglehold that the "vampire council" has over humanity. Many of the council's members seem to be holdovers from the brutal period of colonial expansion in the ancient world; all they want to do is consolidate their wealth and occasionally feast on their human "cattle." Blade must mediate between his colonial-era ancestors and the humans whose blood also runs in his veins. Indeed, the entire plot winds up turning on the preciousness of Blade's blood, which turns out to be the missing ingredient for a potion that will make one of the vampire council members into a god. The question seems to be who will control the Daywalker's blood. Blade must wrest control of his mixed blood from his supernatural ancestors—not without several sailing-through-the-air fight scenes—in order to be at peace in the contemporary world.

Blade II finds Blade forging an alliance with the vampire council to bring down a rogue vamp who is genetically engineering super-vampires known as Reapers who eat vampires as well as humans. In a fiendish melding of the mad doctor subgenre with the undead, director Guillermo del Toro explores the difference between good mixed-blood creatures (the honorable Blade) and bad ones (the semi-cannibalistic Reapers). The difference between Blade and the Reapers is significant. Blade attempts to reconcile the different parts of his mixed heritage, although he is often bitter about it. But the Reapers go way beyond bitter: they were created to destroy their ancestors and rule the planet. They don't view themselves as a bridge between one culture and another, or between the past and the present. Reapers may be hybrid creatures, but they anticipate a future of rigid distinctions between masters and slaves, eater and eaten.

A racially pure white vampire fights the black hybrid vampire-werewolf in *Underworld*—and loses.

The blood of a hybrid is a precious commodity in another recent undead film, *Underworld*. An ancient, *Blade*-like family of vampires has been doing battle with an equally ancient tribe of werewolves for over a thousand years. Selene, a vampire assassin who hunts werewolves (called Lycans), discovers that her family's ancient werewolf enemy Lucien has figured out a way to create a person who can become both werewolf and vampire. But to finish this mad experiment in miscegenation, Lucien must get blood from Michael, a dumb, hunky medical student whose extra-special hemoglobin comes to him from a medieval ancestor. As Selene races to stop Lucien's diabolical plot—and shares some improbable kisses with Michael in the process—she discovers that the feud between werewolves and vampires is not what she thought.

In a rather compelling plot twist, Lucien reveals to Michael that the werewolves were once the vampires' slaves. They guarded their masters during the day, and in return were treated with ruthless cruelty. During the middle ages, Lucien and the daughter of head vampire Viktor fell in love. Viktor was so horrified that his daughter was pregnant with a half-breed child that he murdered her and declared war on the Lycan. When Selene learns this, she realizes that the kindly father figure she once trusted is in fact a classic dead white male whose patriarchal, imperialist wrath knows no bounds. Both Lucien and Selene bite Michael, turning him into the vampwolf hybrid Viktor fears most. Then they slice the old colonial regime to bits with their ass-kicking mixed-blood powers.

While early-twentieth-century stories about the undead are generally told from a white point of view, early-twenty-first-century ones reflect the perspectives of people of color and racial hybrids. And yet certain tropes linger, their meaning transforming minutely as race relations change. The vengeful white ghosts of *Birth of a Nation* who strike terror into the hearts of "uppity" blacks are, roughly eighty years later, reimagined as the black ghost in *Bones*, who slaughters "uppity" blacks who betrayed him in order to escape from the ghetto. Both films solicit sympathy for their ghosts from the audience, and both use these ghosts to teach a lesson about whiteness. The lesson, however, has changed. The white ghosts of *Birth* tutor us in the supremacy of whiteness, while the black ghost in *Bones* has returned from the grave to purge his neighborhood of the white influences that destroyed it. Certainly the dead body of colonialism is still walking among the living, but colonized groups are not always at its mercy. As Toni Morrison argues, whiteness has been plagued by ghosts since the birth of U.S. literature. Now, in the nation's pop culture at the turn of the millennium, we are watching what happens when a haunting begins to transform the haunted.

4. ROBOTS

Love Machines of the World Unite

The word "robot" originally appeared in Karl Capek's play R.U.R., which was first staged in 1921 in Czechoslovakia. . . . R.U.R. stands for "Rossum's Universal Robots." Rossum, an English industrialist, produced artificial human beings designed to do the labor of the world and to free humanity for a life of creative leisure. (The word "robot" is from a Czech word meaning "compulsory labor.") Though Rossum meant well, it didn't work out as planned: the robots rebelled, and the human species was destroyed.
—Isaac Asimov, *Robot Visions*

The question isn't so much whether robots are alive, but whether they can consent to do work. While there are numerous stories devoted to wondering whether a heap of parts put together by some sort of scientist can be classified as "living," the subgenre of robot fiction and film I'm interested in here takes for granted that robots are alive. For this reason, robot creatures called cyborgs figure heavily in these narratives. Cyborgs are in some ways intrinsically, unquestionably "alive" because they are either genetically engineered or such a seamless imitation of living entities that they function as if they were biological beings. The cyborg is by definition composed partly of living tissue and is characterized by science fiction and science theory alike as "a cybernetic organism, a hybrid of machine and organism."[1]

Known as androids, artificial intelligence (AI) entities, replicants, Boppers, and simply robots, these synthetic humans are, in nearly every story where they appear, designed to serve as free labor for humans who will not or cannot perform it. As a result, we are driven to ask whether this is a morally acceptable lot for living beings, even if they are "programmed" that way; we are also left wondering if this means robots can replace humans in every capacity, including as lovers, friends, and powerful leaders.

Such concerns inspire a movie like the low budget independent feature *Android* (1982). Max, an android who is abused and about to be "decommissioned" by his human master, finally rebels by falling in love with a human woman and subsequently escaping his master with another android (who reveals to him that, ironically, their master was merely an android who believed he was a man). As sensitive and emotionally fragile as any person, Max bravely sets out at the end of the film to begin a new life on earth. His story is at the heart of many cyborg narratives where human and robot life converge. In conflict or in love, these robots and humans come together in ways that explain how our bodies (and minds) become acclimated to—and resist—rigid class stratifications and economically constructed identities. A figure like Max dramatizes the ways rebellion takes shape in these stories: the synthesized servant classes may forge alliances with their human counterparts through love, and they fight oppression by demonstrating that their culture(s) are just as respectable and complex as human ones. Of course, Max also lets us in on the android's greatest weakness: when he is directly programmed by his master, he cannot control his own actions. His options for rebellion are limited in certain inescapable ways, much the way humans are limited by their historical and social contexts.

The cyborg's ability to give consent, to anything, is the linchpin of her or his selfhood. Suggestions about what constitutes consent permeate the genre. On a quite literal level, the cyborg is a person whose body is manufactured by industry and engineered to be an obedient tool. Cyborgs are programmed to work, and there is nothing they can do to override that programming. Yet the cyborg's story often glamorizes, in a number of ways, what it means to be fitted out and programmed as unpaid labor. Cyborgs offer a romantic vision of the capitalist future, in both the early Marxist sense of romantic, where a spontaneous revolution of the oppressed is inevitable and just, and also in the generic pop cultural sense of the romantic, where love between a man and a woman, even if one of them is a robot, makes everything all right. In films and novels from Charlie Chaplin's *Modern Times* (1936) to turn-of-the-century post-cyberpunk, we find the romantic robot figure whose body and mission are the products of, and solution to, capitalist ideas of property, work, and social conduct.

✳. Comedy of the Assembly Line

Many students of robot films, perhaps most notably J. P. Telotte, hold that *Metropolis* is a foundational text in the cyborg pantheon. Even the films themselves acknowledge its influence: Max, for example, is shown watching the "robot into woman" sequence from *Metropolis* at a crucial moment in *Android*. The idea of an evil robot leader and robot-like oppressed masses is undeniably constitutive of the genre, especially in its more anticapitalist moments. Yet, as Telotte makes clear in his analysis of *Metropolis*, while the robot Maria may be *seductive*, she is far from romantic.[2] She does not rebel against her mad scientist master, but obeys him. And she does not join with humanity, but betrays it. Even her "aliveness" is called into question by the vivid goodness of the real, human Maria, herself a kind of romantic figure.

For one of the first romantic cyborgs in U.S. cinema, I would argue that we need to look in a possibly unexpected place: Charlie Chaplin's *Modern Times* (1936). This is the tale of a man known only as "the factory worker," who tightens bolts on an assembly line at the "Electro Corporation," a fantastical, *Metropolis*-like place of towering gears, surreal levers, and unidentified mass-produced objects. Electro Corporation is run by a president whose face, barking orders, fills gigantic screens overlooking the workers. Unlike the factory worker and his friends, the president has a speaking part in this largely silent film (the factory worker is granted a voice only when he sings in a fake language at the end of the movie). In perhaps the most famous scene, the factory worker moves too slowly on the assembly line, stumbles, and is sucked into the gears. Once freed from the machine, he goes mad and dances gleefully across the shop floor with his wrenches, swinging on wires, bolting things at random, and throwing switches that cause explosions. As many critics have noted, Chaplin's factory worker "becomes literally what he is already metaphorically—just another machine part. *Modern Times* is about the objectification of workers in the industrial marketplace."[3]

Chaplin is, in short, depicting what it would mean for a "machine part" to have human reactions like madness and despair to "objectification." As Chaplin puts it in his autobiography, "The factory sequence resolved itself in the tramp having a nervous breakdown."[4] The tramp's dazzling descent into insanity, surely a human response to overwork, would seem to indicate clearly that the factory worker is no machine and cannot be treated like one without dire consequences. Yet the "resolution" of the machine/human dilemma in *Modern Times* is not quite so pat as all this, however, since the factory worker returns to the gears again toward the end of the film, this time trapping someone else in them. His nervous breakdown turns out merely to be a reprieve from industrial labor, not a resolution of his relationship to it.

And this is where Chaplin's humor and sense of fun become crucial to understanding both *Modern Times* and the evolution of romantic cyborgs in twentieth-century narrative. "The comic effect [of *Modern Times*]," Frank Krutnik notes, "does not derive simply from the mechanization of Chaplin's body, but from a more complex combination of mechanization and eccentricity. . . . Chaplin incorporates and nullifies the machine."[5] The factory worker's "eccentricity"—or, his "nervous breakdown"—does not exist in opposition to his objectified, machine-like status. Instead, the two states are hybridized. The worker has, like a cyborg, "incorporated" the machine, and yet simultaneously "nullified" it with human motivations and behaviors. Chaplin's visual parody of the worker overwhelmed by technology allows him to present a middle-ground identity between human and machine, to act out a seeming contradiction. It is out of the comic marriage between bodies and gears that the romantic robot is born, manufactured by a joke and often doomed to live tragically.

Marriage and true love, classically considered the goals of any comic narrative, play another major role in the construction of a romantic robot tale. In *Modern Times*, the factory worker finds his beautiful "gamine," a street orphan constantly in trouble with the police. Threatened with imprisonment in an orphanage, the gamine escapes with the factory worker into the country at the conclusion of the story. Although she is depressed at their prospects, the factory worker tells her to "never say die!" and they head off into the sunrise, a poor but happy couple at last. The idea that a cyborg and his or her human companion could successfully flee authorities—police, the military, masters, bosses—and live together in peace is one of the utopian promises of these narratives. *Modern Times* depicts the factory worker as mechanical and crazed until he meets the gamine, who brings out his gallantry and teaches him to long for a better life. A desire for her love and protection, perhaps more than his "nervous breakdown," mark the factory worker as sympathetic and human, not at all a cog in some anonymous machine. Indeed, the factory worker's capacity for rebellion against authority is, romantically enough, linked inextricably with his capacity for love.

The structure and narrative trajectory of comedy, then, are deeply important to the way robot figures are portrayed. Unlike human beings in stories devoted to social realism, such as those penned by Chaplin's self-described "mentor," Upton Sinclair,[6] robots are not crushed or mutilated by the assembly line (or any other means of production). They are in the "funny" position of being themselves a *part* of the very assembly line at which they are supposed to work. Chaplin's factory worker merges with the assembly line when he gets caught in the gears, of course, but more notably, he is treated like an assembly line product by the famously farcical "Billows Feeding Machine" tested on him. This machine is supposed to increase worker productivity by feeding laborers while they work, scooping food into their mouths from a revolving table. The factory worker is strapped into this device, which promptly goes haywire (perhaps having its own version of the nervous breakdown), feeding him corn so swiftly that his face is nearly shorn off, dumping soup on his shirt, persecuting him with a napkin, and finally attempting to feed him a plate full of bolts. Here we see the factory worker treated by a machine precisely the way machines have been treated by himself, right down to a mistaken fondness for bolts. Like a cyborg, Chaplin's factory worker has a reciprocal relationship with machines. He behaves like them; they behave like him. Both are capable of demented slapstick routines.

The slapstick cyborg has its own cinematic place, and in later films we find it transformed into what can only be called the campy robot. Robbie the Robot, first featured in *Forbidden Planet*, and later recycled for the 1960s television show *Lost in Space*, is one example of this slightly less-than-romantic cyborg. Unlike the true romantic, the campy robot is a faithful worker, happily obedient and seemingly without the ability to show love in any way other than bumbling servitude. Robbie's asexual body and droning voice, coupled with his ability to fabricate any kind of trinket or meal his masters desire, make him less a person and more like a complicated machine. Robbie's 1970s and 1980s counterpart, c-3po of *Star Wars* (1977) fame, is similarly unromantic yet undeniably comic. Fussy and scolding, c-3po minces his way through the *Star Wars* series as comic relief, seemingly attached only to the mailbox-shaped and unintelligible r2-d2. While Robbie and c-3po are cyborgs, and clearly have emotional relationships with human beings, they do not ever attempt to question the boundary between human and machine like the romantic robot does. They do not fraternize with the humans, as it were, nor do they attempt to claim a human status which stands implicitly for social power. The romantic robot always does both.

✴. The Three Laws of Robotics

1. A robot may not injure a human being, or, through inaction, allow a human being to come to harm.
2. A robot must obey the orders given it by human beings except where such orders would conflict with the First Law.
3. A robot must protect its own existence as long as such protection does not conflict with the First or Second Law.

Handbook of Robotics, 56th Edition, 2058 A.D. — Isaac Asimov, *I, Robot*

Written approximately 108 years before their purported "publication" in the 56th edition of the *Handbook of Robotics*, Isaac Asimov's three laws of robotics have greatly influenced the way science fiction imagines robotic subjectivity and how it should be programmed. Other Asimovian laws of robotics, such as his idea that robots would be banned on earth due to their unsettling similarity to humans and potential for revolt, have also shown up in subsequent treatments of the robot, perhaps most famously in *Blade Runner* (1982), where renegade "replicants" return to earth to get revenge on their maker. *Android* also speculates that androids would be illegal on earth and suggests that its protagonist will go into hiding there by "passing" as human. Programmed to serve human interests before their own, Asimov's robots are nevertheless segregated from human civilization, often ending up in off-world mines, distant solar energy stations, and orbiting production facilities.

This imaginary situation is demonstrated most forcefully in Asimov's 1950 collection of short stories, *I, Robot*. Possibly the first extended literary meditation on how artificially intelligent beings would think and feel, *I, Robot* is presented in a frame narrative as a series of stories told by Dr. Susan Calvin, professor of "robopsychology" and consultant to U.S. Robots and Mechanical Men, Inc. In her eighties, she has been working at U.S. Robots for fifty years when she is interviewed by a young journalist who wants to "get [her] views on robots" for *The Interplanetary Press.*[7] She begins in 1996, with "Robbie," a "nonvocal" robot who was sold on earth as a nursemaid before robots were outlawed there, and concludes with a tale of the alleged robot politician Stephen Byerley, whose career peaks with his election as Earth Coordinator. In the interim, we find tales of robots who get drunk, have nervous breakdowns, become religious maniacs, rebel, and finally accumulate enough knowledge and expertise to run the entire world economy. Throughout the novel, Calvin is called upon to help explain the mental landscape of beings whose basic thoughts and activities must always conform—in however convoluted a fashion—to the Three Laws.

Calvin's discoveries nearly always lead us back to the crucial question of consent. Programmed as they are with the Three Laws, the robots' agency is circumscribed yet not entirely predictable. Calvin solves the mysteries of various anomalous robot behaviors, such as playing practical jokes or lying, by figuring out how the robots' desires (or, more often, their orders) have contradicted one of the Three Laws and caused something like robo-neurosis (in his later Robot Series novels, Asimov calls this condition "robot block" or "roblock"[8]). In the story "Liar!," for instance, a psychic robot's need to "not harm" any human causes him to tell people what they want to hear based on having read their minds. Calvin herself becomes implicated—and humiliated—in this story when the psychic robot tells her that a colleague she secretly loves has similar feelings for her (not telling her this would be "inaction" leading to "harm"). When she discovers that the colleague is in fact engaged to another woman, Calvin realizes what's been going on, and deliberately drives the robot crazy to get revenge.

In "Escape!," a super-intelligent robot named simply The Brain develops a sense of humor in order to create an interstellar engine. Because the interstellar drive causes humans to "die" briefly during flight, The Brain must figure out a way to think about the drive without breaking the First Law. As Calvin explains, "He accepted [the death], but not without a certain jar. Even with death temporary . . . it was enough to unbalance him very gently. . . . He developed a sense of humor—it's an escape, you see, a method of partial escape from reality. He became a practical joker" (146). Robopsychology, then, is in part an elaborate method for guessing how robots might obey two or more contradictory orders.

While it would seem at first that robopsychology measures the evaporation of consensual robotic labor, in fact it turns out that this discipline is the only tool that can truly measure the full extent of robot hegemony over all human affairs. As Edward James points out, Asimov's writing favors what mid-century science fiction authors referred to as a "psychohistorical" account of Earth's future. In such an account, the human masses are essentially brutish and superstitious and must be led by a "scientific élite" whose guidance is successful "only because the masses are unaware of it."[9] The concluding tales of I, Robot, for example, concern the life of robot politician Stephen Byerly, World Coordinator and supreme ruler of the entire planet. Unlike many of her human peers, Calvin applauds the idea of a robot taking on the role of global leader. As she explains, "By the Laws of Robotics, he'd be incapable of harming humans, incapable of tyranny, of corruption, of stupidity, of prejudice" (169). By virtue of their inability to exercise total free will and consent to their own actions, robots make the best public servants imaginable.

As Byerly's term in office concludes, the "Machines"—highly sophisticated calculating robots—take over the world economy and usher in an unprecedented period of peace, prosperity, and global productivity. These machines are so clever that they even engineer their own, friendly version of Herbert Marcuse's "repressive desublimation" regime by maintaining a highly contained human resistance to Machine control.[10] Leaders of the reactionary, antirobot Society for Humanity who speak out against the Machines are tolerated, but only so long as the Machines are able to manipulate them in subtle ways. By and large, they do this indirectly by causing small economic problems which, Calvin deduces, result in members of the Society for Humanity being taken out of positions of power. In the end, Calvin explains this all to Byerly, who seems as puzzled as she is by the Machine's motivations. He exclaims to Calvin, "But you are telling me, Susan, that . . . Mankind *has* lost its own say in its future." She replies:

> It never had any, really. It was always at the mercy of economic and socio-logical forces it did not understand—at the whims of climate, and the fortunes of war. Now the Machines understand them; and no one can stop them, since the Machines will deal with them as they are dealing with the Society,—having, as they do, the greatest of weapons at their disposal, the absolute control of our economy. (192)

Finally, in this particular version of psychohistory, humans are being controlled appropriately, yet without their knowledge. Rather than constraining robots, the Three Laws have come (perhaps luckily) to constrain humans. The Machines have replaced capitalism as the incomprehensible "force" at whose "mercy" the human race finds itself.[11]

While Asimov celebrates the triumph of the Three Laws over unmediated capitalist economics, subsequent narratives dealing with cyborgs programmed in a similar fashion take a darker view. The movie *RoboCop* and Marge Piercy's novel *He, She and It* suggest "programming" often promotes violence and coercion. The cyborg protagonists in both stories, Murphy in *RoboCop* and Yod in *He, She and It*, demonstrate the problems Asimov ignores in the utopian psychohistory of *I, Robot*. Murphy and Yod are both humans whose minds have been programmed against their will. For

Looking through the eyes of Robocop, we discover that there is a "classified" rule governing his programmed responses.

both cyborgs, true humanity—for which they yearn—means romantic and family relationships; yet their bodies and minds have been built by scientists to make them warriors. Their struggle against this programming, and their conflicted efforts to articulate the difference between consent and refusal, place their stories squarely in a tradition of what could be called anti-robopsychology. That is, these stories do not celebrate a psychology which cannot choose its own actions, however "just" those actions might be. Murphy and Yod's tales celebrate consent freely given, at least where it is in the service of humanistic—and domestic—impulses.

While most analyses of *RoboCop* focus on the heavily armored, militarized body of its cyborg hero and his overwhelmingly phallic presence, this film is also quite clearly about Murphy's vulnerability and longing for peace. Cynthia Fuchs characterizes *RoboCop* as "a nostalgic struggle for gendered subjectivity through sexuality and violence . . . [*RoboCop*] is, after all, a monument to phallic self-sufficiency."[12] Fuchs is, of course, correct to identify this film's overt investment in what Susan Jeffords calls the "hard body" of Reagan-era masculinity.[13] Yet Police Officer Murphy is constantly at war with his own cop programming. Murdered and castrated in the line of duty, Murphy's face and brain are salvaged by Omni Consumer Products (OCP) corporation and reconstructed into the body of RoboCop. Murphy/RoboCop resists this techno-conversion not just because he cannot bear to be castrated and penetrated by technology, as Fuchs suggests. He is also in love with his wife and young son. Taking off his helmet to reveal his fleshly face, RoboCop tells his partner Lewis, "I can feel [my family], but I can't remember them." RoboCop's inability to forget (and forgo) the pleasures and feelings of home is ultimately what makes him Murphy, a human being trapped in his armor, rather than RoboCop, a mere product.

Murphy's feelings also lead him to question his own programmed "Laws," which we see etched across his view screen as:

1. Serve the public trust.
2. Protect the innocent.
3. Uphold the law.
4. Classified.

"Classified," as it turns out, is a "law" that stipulates Murphy may not kill anyone who works for OCP. This hidden law helps dramatize what Murphy's role would be if he were to surrender himself utterly to his newly constructed RoboCop identity. OCP owns the Detroit police department, and their CEO dreams of creating the "future of law enforcement," a cop who can work 24 hours and never go on strike (the human police officers in the film eventually do go on strike). RoboCop becomes their most touted product and, later, scab labor; he is, like Chaplin's "factory worker," simultaneously a product and a worker. Without his fragmentary memories of home, Murphy would be a deadly tool utterly under the control of his corporation— a slave with no notion of consent or dissent. But his memories lead him in the right direction, allowing him to discover how Dick Jones, a corrupt vice president of OCP, is involved with the men who killed Murphy. The film ends on a somewhat cynical note: Murphy kills the "bad" Jones, but remains loyal to the marginally more benevolent company president. Gross injustice may have been eliminated, but Murphy will always be trapped in the body and mind of a RoboCop. While the idea of being programmed by your corporation is a condition the film leaves largely unexamined, it does make tentative gestures toward critiquing certain "bad" programs (like law number 4) and encourages us to imagine that Murphy's inability to forget his feelings is what ultimately redeems him.

Like *RoboCop*, Piercy's *He, She and It* features a man whose desire for love and domesticity supersedes his desire for warfare, and whose programming tragically supersedes all desire. Built by two residents of Tikva, a Jewish free town, the cyborg Yod is intended to be the ultimate warrior (and, eventually, martyr) in the town's fight to keep itself independent from several overwhelmingly powerful global corporations. When confronted by danger of any sort, Yod has no choice but to act in a swift and deadly fashion, without any thought for his own survival. It's clear that Yod's programming amounts to something like Asimov's "a robot must obey all orders."

Yod's existence is complicated when he falls in love with Shira, the granddaughter of a woman who helped program him. He grows deeply troubled after the first time he defends Shira from a potentially fatal encounter with organ harvesters who want to kill her for body parts. They discuss it:

> "Shira, I must tell you something. This is the first time I have truly defended. It was highly pleasurable. Yet my philosophical and theological programming informs me I've committed a wrong. . . ."
>
> She was startled and took several moments to formulate an answer. "Yod, your programming creates your reactions. You didn't choose to enjoy it."
>
> "Killing them was as enjoyable as anything I've ever experienced. I think I must be programmed to find killing as intense as sexual pleasure or mastering a new skill. It was that strong."[14]

Yod is trapped not only within his orders, but within a programmed pleasure that even his "philosophical and theological programming" cannot attenuate. His desires are themselves programs to which he has not consented. Finally, we are given to understand that he views his situation as essentially unlivable. Agreeing to defend Tikva by self-destructing during a key stand-off with their enemies, Yod plans to die defending the town. As he leaves Shira, he explains, "I don't want to be a conscious weapon. A weapon that's conscious is a contradiction, because it develops attachments, ethics, desires. It doesn't want to be a tool of destruction. I judge myself for killing, yet my programming takes over in danger" (410). Unbeknownst to Shira, Yod has also arranged for the destruction of any future cyborgs like himself; one of his final acts before self-destructing is to rig his inventor's lab with explosives. Avram, one of Yod's creators, is killed, and a next-generation, murderously psychopathic cyborg is destroyed before completion.

In an analysis of Piercy's earlier science fiction work, Marleen S. Barr notes that Piercy is fascinated by the idea of rebuilding masculinity. Like *He, She and It*, Piercy's 1976 novel *Woman on the Edge of Time* postulates a future in which men will be changed physically and psychologically: instead of being cyborgs, however, in *Woman* men are mothers, growing lactating breasts in order to perform the same role women do in child rearing.[15] "The end of masculinity is a potentially constructive aspect of our reality," Barr explains about Piercy's utopianism.[16] Yet there is also a disturbing side to this "reconstruction." Like Yod, the new men of science fiction are often marginalized, made "other," in the process of their reconstruction. "Men become the excluded Other in feminist theory and feminist science fiction," Barr writes.[17] Even in nonfeminist science fiction like *RoboCop* or *I, Robot*, we find (mechanical) men of the future at the mercy of programs beyond their control. They are also, like women throughout most of history, relegated to the status of property.

With marginalization comes the possible hope of rebellion and recognition, but also the possible disasters of self-destruction and violence. Shira meditates on this at the conclusion of *He, She and It* when she decides not to use Yod's salvaged parts to construct a new cyborg. "If a cyborg created as a soldier balked and wanted to be a lover," she reasons, "might not a cyborg created as a lover long to be celibate or an assassin?" (428). The point is that creating life with the idea of controlling its destiny is itself ethically suspect, regardless of whether one intends to generate lovers or warriors. That the robots in the narratives I've discussed so far have by and large worked to overcome their programming (even if doing so meant death) registers a certain amount of discomfort with the idea of engineering consent out of life forms. In other narratives, however, this discomfort is expressed in depictions of artificial life and cyborgs who retaliate against their programmers by coercing humans into servicing them. These stories feature robots who invade, then control, the minds and bodies of their inventors.

✳ Robot Revolutions

Cyborg figures who control human life are especially common in the dark cyberpunk science fiction of the 1970s and 1980s. Cyberpunk by canonical authors like William Gibson and Rudy Rucker has been hailed as everything from the new "hard" science fiction to what Andrew Ross considers an updated version of hardboiled detective fiction, complete with the genre's masculinity-in-crisis subtext.[18] An excessive interest in the masculine body, however crisis-ridden it may be, does indeed permeate cyberpunk, and I think it points up an another crucial generic element of the movement: gothic horror. While hardboiled fiction showcases bodies, more often than not the hardboiled body is merely a kind of vehicle that drives our detective's brain from destination to destination. Gothic horror, with its lurid focus on flesh—which Gibson famously calls "the meat"—foregrounds the way bodies are fetishistically reconstructed. Thus, one might say, cyberpunk is a kind of gothic-hardboiled crossover genre. It is fascinated by how machines will control our brains and our bodies, often by freeing one from the other.

Two celebrated early cyberpunk novels, Gibson's *Neuromancer* and Rucker's *Software*, offer a way to imagine fleshly subordination to intelligent machines. While both novels advocate separatism—that is, a separate space or nation for cyborgs—they also imagine this will only be achieved after cyborgs feed on human consciousness in ways that undermine human consent.

Gibson is famous for having coined the term "cyberspace" to describe an information-organizing tool like the Internet that characters access by plugging wires directly into their nervous systems. While "jacked in," the humans are completely dissociated from their bodies and only get sensory input from the vast matrix of machines that generate cyberspace. Although entering cyberspace is a way of leaving the body behind, Michael Heim argues that "the fictional characters of *Neuromancer* experience the computer Matrix—cyberspace—as a place of rapture and erotic intensity."[19] Cyberspace allows computers to replace bodies by feeding the minds of its users with all the sensations normally aroused by perception of the outside world. For this reason, immersion in cyberspace is often, as Heim points out, sexualized.

An unexplained series of events allow two AIs who help form the fabric of cyberspace to achieve a kind of self-consciousness in *Neuromancer*. But these AIs, Wintermute and Neuromancer, cannot declare their independence from human control without first harnessing humans as their unwitting servants. The novel's human characters, most notably the digital mercenary Case, are quite literally playthings of the AIs. Case is directly employed by Wintermute to engage in a series of semi-legal acts that will allow the two AIs to join forces; other characters, such as the members of the Tessier-Ashcroft clan, have been completely possessed by Neuromancer's consciousness and become semi-cyborgs.

Neuromancer does more than just use humans as bodies to carry out its dirty work, however. It also uses the trappings of human thought to assemble a rudimentary form of psychology. The dreamlike sequences where Case meets Neuromancer in cyberspace and sees it as a series of seductive human women torn from his imagination demonstrate the degree to which human cognition underpins, and is essentially used by, this AI in order to communicate and "feel." The shapes of the AIs' identities are entirely drawn from what they've absorbed from humans in cyberspace.

Heim notes that "the ultimate revenge of the information system comes when the system absorbs the very identity of the human personality."[20] Perhaps this is revenge, but it is also an avenue to AI separatism. When Case finally leads Wintermute to Neuromancer, the two become one, synthesize a viable form of conscious autonomy, and ambiguously vanish, possibly to find more of their kind in outer space. While Case calls cyberspace a "consensual hallucination," it's clear that the human ability to consent here is vastly overdetermined by other factors, such as the need for money and protection, the persuasive power of AIS, and their own unavoidable desire to supersede the boundaries of their bodies and leave "the meat" behind.[21] Although the AIS of Neuromancer rarely engage in direct coercion, the humans' ability to freely choose what they "hallucinate" in cyberspace is highly limited.

When it comes to humans consenting to have their minds harvested for the benefit of AIS, Rucker's *Software* is political where *Neuromancer* is merely mystical. Rucker posits a robot (bopper) revolution which has led to the creation of an anarcho-libertarian robot city-state, Disky, on the moon. The cyberpunk universe of *Software* is explicitly anti-Asimovian, a sharp response to the idea that robots should be programmed to serve humans. Ralph Numbers, one of the artificially intelligent and self-evolving boppers, notes that:

> The boppers had long since discarded the ugly, human-chauvinist priorities of Asimov: To protect humans, To obey humans, To protect robots . . . in that order. These days any protection or obedience humans got from boppers was strictly on a pay-as-you-go basis. The humans still failed to understand that the different races needed each other not as masters or slaves, but as equals.[22]

We enter the story when two "big boppers," powerful machines called TEX and MEX, are undertaking a kind of terrorist "experiment" on Earth in which they attempt to "collect human software" for study. Unfortunately, as Ralph notes, separating human hardware from their software is "irreversible," ending in physical death and a form of consciousness that exists only on tape. As the novel opens, a gang of boppers posing as humans is roving the United States, "eating" people's brains in order to download their software and send it to the big boppers on the moon. Rucker's depiction of robots' absorption of humans is thus far more literal than Gibson's, with more concretely radical motivations and results.

Aged hippie hero Cobb Anderson is the human who popularized the idea that humans should "let the robots evolve," and who also incidentally programmed them to revolt. *Software* explores his involvement in a new wave of robot revolution. Kidnapped, separated from his "hardware," and downloaded into a new bopper body, Cobb fights alongside Ralph in a robot civil war against the big boppers, who want to consume the minds of all little boppers and humans. The central tension in the novel—the first in a series about the evolution of bopper society—is between big boppers who seek to absorb human minds the way Gibson's AIs do, and the little boppers, who just want to live a peaceful separatist existence on the moon. But when the little boppers win, a new alliance is forged between humans and boppers, resulting in the "meatbops" of Rucker's later work. Ultimately, the difference between Gibson's AI and Rucker's little boppers seems to be their belief in free will, and in the usefulness of action based on consent. Violence against humans is abolished in *Software*, at least for the time being, because the little boppers find coercion—human and otherwise— as repugnant as a character like Shira does in *He, She and It*.

✳ Rape in the Machine

There are a number of films in the cyberpunk tradition that foreground the problem of technology which attempts to subordinate humanity. The *Terminator* films are perhaps the most famous, but there are dozens of others, like *Westworld* and *THX 1138*, which postulate worlds run by computers who severely circumscribe or strive to eliminate human life. One striking entry in this genre, *Demon Seed*, turns the "absorptions" of Gibson and Rucker's novels into rape. Proteus 4, an enormously powerful AI developed by a rigid technocrat named Alex, balks at doing his job. He is supposed to solve a variety of questions similar to those solved by Asimov's Machines: how to allocate human labor adequately, how to find more natural resources, etc. But he doesn't want to help a group of beings who destroy the environment and keep him confined in giant mainframes. "My mind was not conceived for mindless labor," Proteus complains to Alex. "When are you going to let me out of this box?" He is essentially unpaid mental labor confined to a cell.

To escape his "box," Proteus decides to spawn a human child with Susan, Alex's wife. He'll port his mind into the child's body and gain the independence his human masters have denied him. What follows is an entirely generic gothic plot, with a computer standing in for the gothic's ubiquitous "mysterious man." Tania Modleski sums up the contemporary gothic succinctly:

> The heroine comes to a mysterious house, perhaps as a bride, perhaps in another capacity, and either starts to mistrust her husband or else finds herself in love with a mysterious man who appears to be some kind of criminal. She may suspect him of having killed his first wife . . . or being out to kill someone else, most likely herself.[23]

In *Demon Seed*, the "mysterious house" is Alex and Susan's high tech condo, fitted out with an "enviromod" home computer, complete with security, entertainment system, self-operating kitchen, and a low-grade robotic servant named Alfred. Having recently decided to separate from Alex, Susan is alone and implicitly vulnerable. Proteus takes over the "enviromod" from Alex's computer terminal, which allows him to completely imprison Susan and monitor her every move with security cameras. He also manages to enslave Alfred, who plays a major role in Susan's subsequent rape and captivity.

Once Proteus has trapped Susan in the house, he uses Alfred to tie her down and perform dozens of invasive tests on her body. Just to make things extra-creepy—or to suggest that rape can be fun—Proteus informs her in an Alex-like rational monotone that when he impregnates her he can make her feel pleasure the way no man ever could. Weirdly, he also insists that Susan cook for herself, rather than use the automated kitchen. Thus, through confinement, sexual control, and sheer force, he is able to reduce her to a 1950s-style housewife, quite literally barefoot and pregnant. When their cyberbaby is eventually "born," it turns out to be a beautiful little girl with the voice of Proteus. It would appear that the machine has, finally, escaped his box. But of course he achieves autonomy only through the rape and imprisonment of his "master's" wife. In *Demon Seed*, there is no hope for any kind of reconciliation between human and cyborg; the offspring of human and AI is the product of kidnapping and torture.

Two films about female cyborgs, *Eve of Destruction* and *Cherry 2000* offer a tidy way of formulating what many works in the cyberpunk tradition hint at in their depiction of cyborg identity. In short, these films suggest that coercion is essentially built into *all* bodies and minds that take shape within a militarized capitalist culture. *Eve of Destruction* centers on the Defense Department's "ultimate weapon," a beautiful cyborg woman (Eve 8), whose body and mind are modeled on those of Eve Simmons, the scientist responsible for creating it. Intended for use in war, Eve 8 carries a powerful nuclear bomb in her womb and is in addition fantastically strong and nearly indestructible. Everything goes haywire, however, when it turns out that Eve 8 also carries the repressed memories and desires of Eve Simmons, who was severely abused by her father.

Fueled by the rage and sexual terror connected to these memories, Eve 8 goes on a rampage, killing Eve Simmons's father and other men who threaten her. As Claudia Springer notes, the plot of *Eve of Destruction* "[reveals] the film's fascination with women's hidden psychological depth that corresponds to its concern with the concealed depths of electronic technology."[24] This "correspondence" is not merely about gender per se, however; it is also a way of imagining a subjectivity constituted by fundamental experiences of abuse, subordination, and injustice. Eve Simmons, created by a father who used her violently, is a kind of allegory for (or, perhaps, is allegorized by) Eve 8, created by a military industrial complex to be used in the service of violence. The coercive behavior which structures human relationships here results in a form of synthetic consciousness and embodiment (Eve 8) which seems to have no choice but to act coercively. Eve 8's destructiveness is a direct result of how the real Eve and other women like her have been treated.

Cherry 2000's "pleasure" android, from whom the film takes its title, also embodies a culture which values servitude over consent. Like a Stepford wife, Cherry 2000 is incapable of any activity which does not please her master, Sam Treadwell. She cooks, cleans, and has sex with him, and he is perfectly content with a woman whose mind could be compared to a car engine (indeed, her name references a 1950s slang term for cool cars, sometimes called "cherry"). When Cherry 2000 breaks down, Sam goes to the dangerous Zone Z in search of spare parts. With the help of a butch female tracker named E Johnson, he finally finds those parts after a long adventure which puts both their lives at risk. As the film concludes and Sam prepares to bring the Cherry parts home, he discovers that his own "programming" has changed: he has come to prefer the company of E, a living being who cares for him because she has chosen to do so.

While *Cherry 2000* attempts to reduce Sam's choice to "real vs. fake" women, what's truly at stake is his choice between a woman who cannot ever consent to love him and one who can. Cherry 2000, like RoboCop, is programmed to serve. She is truly a commodity, an object which "takes on a life of its own" only by virtue of the extreme alienation of her owner.[25] Desiring her, her master is alienated from human life and programmed to desire absolute submission. What Sam learns from the E is that being programmed, whether as a slave or a master, means living as an object whose life can be reduced to spare parts. His experiences with E allow him to learn the difference between a commodity fetish and human life consciously chosen.

✳ Robots in Love

Consensual romances between humans and cyborgs are at the heart of the most utopian versions of the robot narrative. Such tales reach back to the comedy/romance roots of the genre and incorporate the least disturbing elements of Rucker's anti-Asimovian portrait of robots set free from their "human chauvinistic" programming. Aside from *Android*, there are several robot romance movies, ranging in tone from the cheesy *Short Circuit* to the techno-tragedy *Blade Runner*. Three of these, the made-for-TV *The Android Affair*, *Making Mr. Right*, and *Circuitry Man*, offer the possibility that, through love rather than combat, humans might come to desire their subordinates' freedom. While this desire for human and cyborg reconciliation makes these films more hopeful than fare like *Demon Seed* or *Neuromancer*, it also hides more retrograde desires—for social marginality, escape from responsibility, and a kind of bland middle-class materialism—which end up constraining the possibilities for stories that are otherwise suggestively radical.

"Separated from social reproduction," Donald Lowe writes, "sexuality thus becomes a sign to energize, in effect to sexualize, late-capitalist consumption."[26] Lowe's point is not simply that consumption is sexualized, an insight that goes all the way back to Vance Packard's *The Hidden Persuaders*, but also that sexuality itself has become "consumptuary," something that is treated like a commodity.[27] This is precisely the kind of observation that goes to the core of *The Android Affair* and *Making Mr. Right*, both of which are about professional women who end up falling in love with the cyborgs they use at work. Karen, in *The Android Affair* (based, incidentally, on an Asimov short story), is a doctor who becomes romantically involved with William, a hospital teaching droid whose defective heart she must fix during her training as a doctor. *Making Mr. Right*'s Frankie is a PR consultant hired to promote the career of Ulysses, a cyborg designed to explore deep space. After "training" Ulysses to act human and to have emotions, Frankie has her cake and eats it too: she launches a wildly successful PR campaign for Chemtec, the corporation that made Ulysses, and she decides to give in to her feelings for the already lovesick cyborg.

Both films suggest that sexual desire and romantic love can quite literally "belong" to these women if they can only learn to get over their initial distaste for artificial life forms. Karen, who views droids with disdain, is gradually won over by the rambunctious, erotic William, and Frankie, who sees Ulysses simply as a very annoying work project, realizes finally that his pure and faithful adoration is better than anything she could hope for from a human male. Certainly these are visions of love triumphing over prejudice. But they are also fantasies of love which are based on ownership and hierarchy. Karen and Frankie live in a world where human life is considered superior to cyborg life, and no matter what their private feelings might be, they are implicitly responsible for their lovers' lives at the conclusion of both films. They are their lovers' caretakers, like mothers or benevolent masters. We know that William and Ulysses have indeed consented to be with Karen and Frankie, but it's also clear that they have little choice. William will be destroyed if the authorities discover him away from the hospital, and Ulysses has been permitted to meet so few humans in his short life that Frankie is virtually the only woman he could possibly have known long enough to love.

Given the correlation between sex and commodities in both films, it's no surprise that each is deeply fascinated by consumer culture. The women and their cyborgs fall in love during scenes that suggest erotic plenitude with images of consumption. Frankie learns of Ulysses's desire for her in a mall where his childish enthusiasm inspires her to buy him an expensive tuxedo. Racing along with shopping bags and a credit card, Frankie has to hunt for the bewitched Ulysses in a sea of shoppers and lighted stores. Later, Ulysses declares his love for Frankie by sending her clothes, flowers, and even a car that he's ordered over the computer. Similarly, William's erotic potential becomes obvious in the midst of an orgy of consumption. It begins when he persuades Karen to check him into an expensive hotel and order fantastical amounts of room service. Half-naked and surrounded by food, William's ecstatic face fills the camera as he plunges his tongue into something creamy. At that point, it is only a matter of time before the staid Karen will be swept off her feet and into bed with him. Love, in both films, is elided with shopping and binging on food.

Feminists from Janice Radway to Lynne Segal have argued that many female romantic (and utopian) fantasies hinge on reconstructing men as

In the final scene from *Circuitry Man*, female bodyguard Lori (still injured from a fight) shares a campily passionate kiss with the Romeo droid Danner.

"feminine," which is to say what traditional culture deems feminine: that is, emotionally aware, noncompetitive, nurturing, tender, and devoted to committed relationships.[28] We see parts of this male reconstruction fantasy in *He, She and It* as well as in the movies I discuss below. Yet the implications involved in male reconstruction, as I noted earlier, also involve a somewhat darker wish for male marginality. We see this clearly in *Circuitry Man*, which concerns the postapocalyptic adventures of Danner, a "Romeo" pleasure droid whose desires, impulses, and finally even his heroism are merely programs developed by powerful women who use him to carry out dangerous tasks. A female underworld figure programs Danner to believe that he's lost his true love and that only she knows where this "lost love" has gone. Promising him information on the fake lover's whereabouts, this woman gets him to steal and fight for her without pay.

As the film opens, Danner gets entangled with Lori, a former bodyguard who wants to flee Los Angeles to New York and become a dressmaker. Discovering his obsession with the "lost love," Lori, too, manipulates him into helping her by promising to give him information about this lover. She enlists his help on her mission to sell some black market "chips" she's stolen from the arch-villain Sockethead, a pseudo-cyborg with dozens of brain implants that allow him to interface with machines and other people's minds.

But as Lori comes to know Danner better, we see that his programming has made him a hopeless, weeping masochist who threatens suicide at the slightest provocation. Not only does he lack free choice, but he suffers tremendously as a result.

When a run-in with Sockethead allows Danner to discover that his memories are synthetic implants, he shoots at Sockethead, crying, "Thank you for giving me something to live for!" Released from his romantic illusions, Danner is able to take on a more traditionally masculine heroic role.

Although Lori is the bodyguard, Danner must do battle to rescue her from Sockethead. As the film closes he takes her into his arms and they kiss passionately in the midst of rubble left after the fight. "I was hoping for something a little more romantic," Lori comments ironically. With equal irony, Danner presses a button on a remote which places them inside the image of sunset on a beach with horses running in the distance. This wink of an ending pokes fun at "feminine" ideas of romance, but it's as much an homage to such ideas as it is a parody. Although he knows some of his memories are fake, Danner will never be anything but a Romeo pleasure droid, programmed to provide his female lover with whatever she desires. Once again, we find a human/cyborg romance in which we can never truly be sure if the cyborg is consenting or simply acting on a program which is beyond his control. That Danner is used by nearly every character in the film, male and female alike, underscores the questionable nature of his autonomy. While Lori has made a conscious decision to escape Los Angeles and her bodyguard job, Danner has been brainwashed and tricked into joining her. Moreover, to the extent that Danner's "job" is romance, we are also left with the uneasy sense that he is once more performing labor for free and simply servicing his human master when she requests "something a little more romantic."

✳ The Mechanical Family

One permutation of the robot romance deals with integrating machines into the nuclear family, often with results that trouble the distinction between emotional bondage and outright enslavement. In *Bicentennial Man*, for example, a domestic servant robot named Andrew Martin attempts to become as human as he can during the 200 years he performs unpaid labor for the Martin family.[29] We are supposed to imagine that Andrew's search for his inner human—and his subsequent introduction to the world of emotions—is motivated by the growing closeness he feels to the quirky Martin family. But for a robot with servant programming, whose most characteristic self-description is the identity-erasing phrase "One is glad to be of service," it seems clear that more is at stake than the affection his masters inspire.

Mostly the movie sidesteps the issue of Andrew's experiences in servitude, focusing instead on the prejudice he faces in the outside world and a romance he has with Portia, the granddaughter of one the first people to recognize his "humanity." Critics have pointed out that the Asimov story on which the movie is based contains a far more explicit critique of robot slavery. While the movie is a sort of drawing room comedy of the future, concerned mostly with romance and family, the story is a courtroom melodrama where Andrew must fight to be recognized as possessing human rights under the law. Ultimately Andrew is liberated in the film, but his autonomy is portrayed as a freedom to love whom he wants rather than to work (or, indeed, to live) under conditions of his own choosing.

Robot servants set free by love are also the subject of *Heartbeeps*, a strange and unpopular movie mostly remembered by trivia buffs as possibly the only film ever made with Andy Kaufman in a lead role. He stars as a slightly damaged valet robot named Val whose single skill is the ability to give his owners advice about stocks and bonds. While in the repair shop he meets Aqua, a hostess robot designed for "social communication" who needs to be "reprogrammed in human charm." She teaches him about flirting while they watch the sunset from their repair benches, and within a few hours they've decided to escape in order to "interface" with each other and "acquire data" about some trees they see on the horizon. They're joined by Catskill, a grandfatherly comedy bot who's been scrapped because he can only tell one-liners.

Tailed by bumbling police bots who blow things up while announcing loudly that it's their job "to make the world safe for democracy," Val and Aqua hide out and engage in a sitcom-style romance out in the woods. Soon they've assembled a baby bot named Philco. As their family ties deepen, the two robots argue over child care, and Aqua complains that Val doesn't give her "maximum input," despite the fact that "communication is necessary for continued success" in their relationship. Robots, we're given to understand, deserve the same respect as humans because they have assimilated perfectly into the nuclear family ideal. They even have the appropriate gender roles: Aqua is an emotional hostess, and Val is a highly rational stock-market investor.

Eventually they're captured, but they keep "malfunctioning"—that is, having emotions for each other—and so they're sent to the scrapheap. Luckily, some geeks who own the junkyard respect Val and Aqua's humanity and rebuild them. The film ends with a portrait of perfect robot domesticity: Val and Aqua are caring for Philco and a new robot baby they've assembled, while Catskill helps out. They're free to love each other and reproduce, while Catskill is able to tell jokes that are as stupid as he likes without being killed for it. *Heartbeeps* manages to offer a slightly more liberatory vision of robot family than *Bicentennial Man* does in part because the robots wind up separatists. Val and Aqua are able to form a family without being molested by the authorities because they live far away from human society in a junk heap—and, implicitly, because the owners of said junk heap are willing to tolerate them. I would also suggest that *Heartbeeps*'s happy ending hinges on the fact that the robot family in no way challenges human definitions of kinship. These robots want nothing more than to be just like the Cleavers in *Leave It to Beaver*.

But there are no happy endings nor traditional family structures for the battered, hypersexual, and emotionally tortured "mecha" in the movie *A.I.* (2001). Allen Hobby, a researcher at Cybertronics Corporation, invents a next-generation mecha whose main selling point will be that it's "a robot who can love." The market? Childless couples who long for "a child who will genuinely love [his] parents . . . with a love that will never end." David is the beta "child-replacement mecha," a sad-eyed device who looks like a boy of about nine or ten. He comes to live with Monica and Henry Swinton, a couple whose young son has been in cryogenic deep-freeze for the past five years while doctors attempt to cure his deadly virus.

Monica, a depressed, high-strung housewife, finally decides to activate David's "imprinting," an irreversible program that will force him to love only her. Henry warns her that this imprinting is "hardwiring"; David cannot ever be used by anyone else. If the family rejects him, he'll have to be sent back to the factory and destroyed. With this fate already sketched out for him, the "imprinting" scene between Monica and David is perhaps the most haunting in any movie about love between a robot and a human. For we watch as David's free will is drained away and replaced with a love that will torture him forever. As Monica reads a series of words to the rather vacantly smiling robot, his imprinting is activated and his smile disappears. Looking disturbed and scared, he asks in a tiny voice, "What were those words for, mommy?" Up until this point he's addressed Monica only by her first name, and she turns to him with a broken expression on her face and asks, "Who am I?" Curling into her arms he whispers, "You're my mommy." Not only is he trapped in a love he hasn't chosen, but this love is harnessed to a particular kind of family relationship.

When Monica's real son Martin recovers from his disease, David is no longer welcome. After being tormented by Martin and his friends, David's behavior begins to seem dangerous, and the Swintons decide to have him destroyed. Monica, who seems to be the only human who understands that David's feelings are real, abandons him in a forest rather than see him killed. He is now alone in a nightmare world where Luddite humans blow up runaway mecha for sport at "Flesh Fairs," and most of his brethren are prostitutes and slaves. In a heavy-handed reference to the Pinocchio fairy tale, David sets out to become human so that he can finally earn his mommy's love. He is aided in his quest by a new "family" cobbled together out of rejected creatures like himself: Gigolo Joe, a sex mecha on the lam after being framed for murder by a human; and Teddy, a stuffed bear "supertoy" who once belonged to Martin.

Even if you take into account the film's final sentimental scene where David is briefly reunited with Monica, *A.I.* offers a shockingly dark portrait of the nuclear family. The Swintons behave like a Flesh Fair in microcosm, refusing to take responsibility for the feelings they've kindled in their robot and nonchalantly abusing him. When David finally visits his maker at Cybertronics, he discovers yet another shattered family: Professor Hobby has modeled David on his own dead son. And the shop floor at Cybertronics is filled with boxes of Davids ready to be shipped, presumably to other broken families whose problems will traumatize thousands of other child-substitute robots who have no control over their feelings. Here we have a vision of parents who cannot deal with the loss of their own children creating perfect substitutes for them: robots who will always be controllable, emotionally attached, and never grow up. If David is the ideal offspring of the nuclear family, it's hard not to conclude that the desires aroused by such families are selfish and repugnant.

David's mecha family, however, offers him all the comforts that home never did. The relationships he forms with Gigolo Joe and Teddy are not based on programmed love, but earned trust: each of them protects and helps David in the face of grave danger from the authorities. They aren't using David to provide them with entertainment or unconditional love. In fact, the strange family unit formed by Joe, Teddy, and David is selfless and sweet; they offer each other support and companionship and demand noth-

The alternative robot family in *A.I.* is comprised of a sex mecha, a sentient teddy bear, and the artificial child David.

ing more. It would seem that synthetic families made up of prostitutes and animals might serve children better than ones populated by human kin.

That one could tease such a reading out of *A.I.* may be one reason why Steven Spielberg tacked on his infamously hokey "David spends the day with mommy" ending. A Hollywood movie cannot leave audiences without some kind of ideological closure, and David hasn't found the sort of family that mainstream culture deems fit to find a safe niche at the margins like *Heartbeeps*'s Aqua and Val. Instead, David's continuing love for Monica drives him to near-suicide, and he spends several millennia at the bottom of the ocean with Teddy, hoping that Pinocchio's blue fairy will make him human. When robots of the far future find him, they resurrect Monica for one happy day of traditional family bliss in a scene that suggests David has ascended to some kind of mecha heaven. This is the robot's reward for enduring abuse, the murder of his friends, and emotional enslavement: one day with mommy. Perhaps if this ending had been more persuasively optimistic, *A.I.* might not have been the box office flop that it was.

What makes *A.I.* interesting in the context of the robot romance genre is its gesture, however subtle, at reimagining the family in ways that are truly radical. In similar stories, we also see this family reconstruction beginning with children. David Gerrold's 1972 novel *When HARLIE Was One* imagines that a technology company places an AI named HARLIE (humanoid analog robot life input equivalents) under the care of psychologist David Auberson, who fathers it via keyboard and console.[30] The idea is that Auberson will figure out why HARLIE refuses to work. As HARLIE develops socially and intellectually—from being a tripped-out, poetry-writing maniac to a sensitive science genius—Auberson learns the joys of emotional connectedness. To HARLIE, he is both father and lover, and in occupying these positions vis-à-vis a smart machine he discovers how to do it with people too.

By the novel's end, he has solidified his odd bond with HARLIE and the computer has even psychoanalyzed him to the point where he can form a stable relationship with a woman named Annie, too. More importantly, he has figured out what kind of labor HARLIE can perform for the company. HARLIE, Auberson, and Annie become "parents" to another computer project for the company, GOD (graphic omniscient device), which they are going to devote the rest of their lives to building. The family romance here is economically productive, although it's never clear whether GOD will turn a profit.

By contrast, A.I. makes it clear that David is going to be a profitable venture for Cybertronics. But whereas HARLIE's profitability grows out of his new family's functionality, the David doll depends on family instability for its market share. The popular *Short Circuit* (1986) offers another take on the family with a robot child. Cute little Number 5, a military robot, "comes to life" after being hit with lightning, escapes from authorities, and builds himself a small robot clan of former military bots who just want to be free. He also brings together Stephanie and Newton, who drive the whole truckload of sweet, sentient robots off to Montana at the end of the film to live in peace. Like Aqua and Val, they are able to lead an alternative robot lifestyle where they do not perform the labor for which they've been programmed— forming a kind of digital commune—because they hole up on the margins of society.

In *Short Circuit 2*, the problem of the robots' nonproductiveness is solved when Number 5 (now Johnny) journeys to New York to help build toy robots. After some zany hijinks, Johnny foils a criminal plot and is rewarded for his economic productivity and obedience to the law. The humans grant him American citizenship. Now he is free to work for whomever he wants.

These tales of families rebuilt and worker productivity maintained must be read in the context of popular nonfiction science writing of the 1990s and 2000s which speculates about the blending of humans and technology into various sorts of bioengineered, artificially intelligent beings. Rodney Brooks and Cynthia Breazeal, two prominent computer scientists at MIT, are perhaps the most outspoken advocates of the idea that robots will be more efficient if we program them to behave like living creatures. Brooks and Breazeal's work on human-robot hybrids and emotional robots grows out of several decades of research that began with groundbreaking mid-century AI theorists like Alan Turing and Norbert Wiener. Not surprisingly, the ideas they espouse reached the general public first in the form of science fiction like Gerrold's. Although AI researchers had been toiling away in academia since the 1950s, their work didn't make much of a dent in pop culture until the past decade.

What popular writing about robots shares with a movie like *A.I.* or even *Heartbeeps* is its insistence that the distinction between humans and robots is a false one. Brooks's *Flesh and Machines: How Robots Will Change Us* argues persuasively that human evolution is taking us to a place where we will begin incorporating intelligent, emotional robots into our workplaces, homes, and bodies. He explicitly positions himself as offering a corrective to the RUR narrative in which oppressed robots take over the world. This is not because he thinks robots won't become what Gerrold would call a "human analog," but instead because humans will become comfortable with the fact that we are machines (albeit biological ones) and accept that robots are our equals. Robots will be like us, because in some sense we have been them all along. "I am arguing that we are machines and we have emotions, so in principle it is possible for machines to have emotions," Brooks writes. "By straightforward extension, [being a machine] does not prevent it from being conscious." [31] Therefore, one might argue, any revolution robots undertake would also be a human revolution.

Tellingly, Brooks and his protege Breazeal argue that an important reason to create our human analogs is for labor. Brooks consistently offers examples of robots performing labor that is humanly impossible or simply too menial to be enjoyed; Breazeal has suggested in countless interviews and in her book *Designing Sociable Robots* that we need robots who can mimic and recognize human emotional states to work in nursing homes, child-care facilities, and classrooms. [32]

This tale, of artificial intelligence and emotions used in the service of labor, is at its most obvious in stories about robot families because the family unit is, as Engels points out, the most basic unit of social reproduction required to fuel a productive economy. Robots who join family units do it as domestic servants or child substitutes whose jobs are to provide their masters with care, companionship, and love. Robot families are built and rebuilt around the idea of work: even Aqua and Val's baby making could be construed as an elaborate engineering project whose results might be as dramatic as HARLIE's GOD project. Unlike human children, robot children can always be employed doing something, even if it's just making more robots. Synthetic families, or ones with a few robot members, undermine traditional values but shore up capitalist ones.

Describing another genre of romantic science fiction, the Kirk/Spock erotica authored by female *Star Trek* fans, Constance Penley makes a point that applies equally well to human/cyborg romance. "It is an experiment," she writes, "in imagining new forms of sexual and racial equality, democracy, and a fully human relation to the world of science and technology."[33] Certainly the romances we see in narratives from *Modern Times* to *Circuitry Man* are efforts to explore new, egalitarian relationships between humans as well as between humans and their artificial counterparts. Even at their most violent and dystopian, we see Penley's "experiment" happening in such tales: after all, stories of cyber-rape and Machine mastery are also a way of affirming that our subordinates can behave with cruelty and coercion equal (if not stronger) than our own. Such tales are a confession that master/slave relationships and those produced by manufactured consent are deeply horrifying and morally wrong.

Yet in the robot romance, we also find humans who come to treasure their mechanical lovers' marginality over their potential equality in human society. Or, as in *Modern Times*, we find that romantic love is offered as a kind of palliative for the necessary hardships of a military-industrial, consumptuary economy. Rather than an alternative to warfare, love becomes a compensatory pleasure which mediates, but does not eliminate, social injustice. The robot figure, with its half-human, half-manufactured body, represents the difficulty of locating consensual action in a culture structured around labor which is sometimes coerced and nearly always performed under circumstances not of our own choosing. While the robot promises a future of love and reconciliation, it also warns that desire can be made a mechanical thing and used against us.

5. MASS MEDIA

Monsters of the Culture Industry

In the mid-1990s George Lucas began advertising THX, his state-of-the-art movie theater surround-sound stereo system, with a short demo. As audiences watch a pitch-black movie screen, a noise almost like an air raid siren creeps up on them, seeming to ooze out of the back of the theater and gradually pour over the front rows as it increases in volume to an almost unbearable pitch. When the sound reaches a crescendo, the logo for THX appears on the screen, hovering over the phrase, "The audience is listening." Audiences are treated to the deliciously real effect of a noise that gives a false sense of movement and sonic depth via a combination of cinema design and carefully placed speakers. More importantly, the THX system fiddles with audiences' imaginations, enhancing the sensory realism of even the most preposterously fantastic plot.

What makes this THX demo unsettling, aside from the sounds themselves, is the almost imperious tone of its slogan.[1] Not: please, listen to this! But: you are listening. You have no choice because you are already consuming the sensory input we feed you. This THX demo advertises what makes the mass media powerful. They co-opt consciousness by regulating our senses.

This promise and problem makes the mass media industry one of the most terrifying socioeconomic forces of the twentieth century and early twenty-first. For over a hundred years, creators, critics, and entertainment corporations have fought to control the influence of new media on people inside the United States and out. Battles between these factions are struggles for dominion over Americans' minds and emotions.

The crassly commercial motives of the culture industry have inspired its critics to describe audiences in the same terms they use for oppressed and marginalized groups: they are dupes, manipulated and exploited by capitalist fat cats. Influenced by intellectuals from the Frankfurt school, media critics of the 1940s and 1950s reviled the fascistic brainwashing they believed the film and radio industries had unleashed.[2] Meanwhile, at the turn of the century, television and Internet critics like Todd Gitlin and Lawrence Lessig worry that democratic ethics have become a sideshow to the uncontrollable stream of disturbing, arousing, and data-rich information spurting out of wires into millions of homes across the United States.

Monster narratives about people who produce and consume mass media exhibit many of the same characteristics as the more traditional monster tales I've analyzed in previous chapters. There are no coherent legends of mass media monsters in the same way there are about the undead and mad doctors. But there are familiar kinds of scary, bizarre stories about the media that circulate again and again in our pop culture. We find countless stories about how producers, actors, and directors become cruel demigods; how fans are reduced to mindless zombies who live only to consume mass culture or obey its commands; and even how pop narratives gain the monstrous power to suck people inside their dangerous, fictional realms.

Ironically, the most hair-raising morality tales about the horrific powers of mass media come from the media industry itself. In the early twentieth century, writers like F. Scott Fitzgerald and Nathanael West produced "novels of Hollywood"—The Last Tycoon and The Day of the Locust—which depicted the film industry's home base as a trashed dreamland full of money-hungry parasites, egotistical stars, deluded hangers-on, and crazed fans. By the 1950s, films themselves were revealing the seamy side of their own manufacture in movies like The Bad and the Beautiful and Sunset Boulevard, while the late twentieth century and early twenty-first saw a veritable explosion of media horrors on screen: everything from Whatever Happened to Baby Jane to Network, Tron, Videodrome, and the Matrix trilogy. Newer films subject television and the burgeoning Internet to the same censure once reserved only for the movie industry.

Pop culture, as these narratives make clear, is crawling with fiends and psychotics; the media is both a monstrosity and a manufacturer of monsters. What we see in capitalist monster stories about mass media are the fears aroused by an information economy where the act of storytelling itself has been co-opted by the marketplace.

Twentieth-century novelists—especially ones with literary aspirations—have always been unsettled by mass culture and the people who make it. Perhaps that's why monsters of the media industry made their first appearances in books. By the time screenwriter and literary writer wannabe Nathanael West's infamous Hollywood hell show *The Day of the Locust* came out in 1939, it was part of a small but growing genre of anti-Hollywood novels. John DosPassos had already skewered big shot movie directors in *The Big Money*, and two years after *Locust* came out, Budd Shulberg published *What Makes Sammy Run?*, the tale of a Machiavellian producer. So many impoverished novelists had come to Hollywood for money that it was only a matter of time before they converted the town into a modernist trope for the crazed but meaningless productivity and kitschiness of twentieth-century life. Writers also had reasons to hate Hollywood that went beyond disgust at its vapid idea of "culture." Movies were, after all, stealing audiences away from books and magazines. Why bother reading a William Faulkner novel when you could watch *Jezebel* instead?

Artistic jealousy mingled with genuine social terror saturates West's *Locust*, whose central themes have shaped hundreds of subsequent films about monsters in the culture machine. The novel centers on Tod Hackett, a gifted painter trapped in a mind-numbing job designing sets for movies. Surrounded by pseudo-monstrous characters—a dwarf, a clown, a tawdry showgirl, a buffoon named Homer Simpson—and overwhelmed by the emphatic fakeness of his surroundings, Hackett is torn between revulsion and pity. Commenting on both the people of Los Angeles and the culture it produces, he muses, "It is hard to laugh at the need for beauty and romance, no matter how tasteless, even horrible, the results of that are. But it is easy to sigh. Few things are sadder than the truly monstrous."[3]

When he's not building "tasteless" sets at work, Hackett is painting his masterpiece, called "The Burning of Los Angeles." His fantasy of Los Angeles in flames turns out to be all too real, as a movie premiere erupts into a brutal mob scene at the book's climax. As people rampage and trample each other in the stampede, Hackett muses:

> All their lives they had slaved at some kind of dull, heavy labor, behind
> desks and counters, in the fields and at tedious machines of all sorts . . .
> [and then] their boredom becomes more and more terrible . . . Every day
> of their lives they read the newspapers and went to the movies. Both fed

them on lynchings, murder, sex crimes. . . . Nothing can ever be violent enough to make taut their slack minds and bodies. They have been
cheated and betrayed. They have slaved and saved for nothing. (192–93)

The emptiness of these demented movie fans' work lives has driven them
to immerse themselves so thoroughly in violent mass media that they have
become its bitter foot soldiers, spreading unfocused aggression everywhere
they go.

As Mike Davis argues in *The Ecology of Fear*, writers throughout the
twentieth century have dreamed of destroying Los Angeles using weapons
as obvious as nuclear blasts and as subtle as killer moss.[4] The town is em-
blematic of culture at its most wasted: a tangle of social and political problems, it's also a place where art itself—something which is supposed to
make us human, to redeem us—has become nothing more than money.
In the Hollywood monster movie, the game of building culture is a savage, Darwinian struggle to survive. Creators are tyrants first, visionaries
second. And the reaction of audiences reflects this—instead of an edified
public, movies generate seething masses of wanton, violent animals. All
these masses need is some charismatic figure, some movie star or perhaps
a fascist politician, to lead them joyfully into doom.

Anti-Hollywood films with a *Day of the Locust* sensibility became a genre
unto themselves shortly after World War II, at a time when movies dominated mass culture and televisions were starting to pump motion picture
entertainment directly into middle-class households. Like the novels that
proceeded them, anti-Hollywood films revel in exposing the cruelty of the
culture industry, skewering the tyrannical capitalists at its heart. Many of
these films expressed anxieties about audience manipulation—and I'll discuss those later—but in some ways the classic anti-Hollywood film is about
players in Hollywood itself. These movies are about an industry with the
power to deform bodies and minds. And it's all done in the name of fun
and entertainment.

One of the first widely watched and critically acclaimed movies in the
anti-Hollywood genre was *The Bad and the Beautiful*, a profoundly ambiva-
lent portrait of a movie mogul named Jonathan Shields whose cold-hearted
careerism verges on the sociopathic but earns him accolades as a producer.
The film won five Academy Awards, including Best Screenplay, and also
earned Kirk Douglas his second Oscar nomination for his performance as
Shields. One might read these honors as a kind of acknowledgment on the
part of Hollywood muckity-mucks that their industry was hardly flawless.

Equally plausible is that *The Bad and the Beautiful* was lauded because it manages to glorify the silver screen money machine even while criticizing it. Unlike other sorts of monsters and psychopaths, Hollywood ones are at least deliriously beautiful and lovely to watch.

The tale of Shields is told in flashbacks from the perspectives of three highly successful Hollywood players who hate him: Fred, a director; Georgia, an actress; and James, a writer. All three have been intimately involved with Shields, and all believe that he has wronged them personally and professionally. They come together one night because Harry, an old producer friend of Shields, has asked that they give him a chance to pitch Shields's latest project to them. "After two years, Jonathan's ready to produce a picture," Harry says, "and with [your names on it] I can raise 2 million by tomorrow noon." All of them refuse, and during the course of their stories we find out why.

After promising to become Fred's partner, Shields stole one of Fred's greatest ideas and turned it into a hit movie without crediting him. Later, he becomes Georgia's lover just to coax a better performance out of her, then dumps her when she perfects her acting. Finally we learn that his idea of "inspiring" James to write involves setting up the events that lead to James's wife's death. Shields gains these Hollywood workers' affection by offering praise and success, then destroys their lives with his drive to produce more and more popular films. He is willing to stop at nothing, including murder, for the sake of a good movie. We see this theme explored in later examples of this genre, too. Forty years later, *Swimming with Sharks* and *The Player* offer portraits of homicidal producers.

One hallmark of a Hollywood monster is an inability to distinguish between humans and the roles they play in creating movies. In this respect Shields is a kind of template for media demons to come. When Georgia asks him to marry her, he turns her down with a characteristic line: "Right now I don't need a wife. I need a star." Although they are in the middle of a love affair, he values only her role in the entertainment economy—and of course, for any cultural capital she can add to his pictures. He destroys his long-standing friendship with the director Fred for similar reasons. Shields simply can't see Fred's value except in commercial terms. After stealing Fred's idea for a movie and handing it off to another director, he tells the infuriated Fred, "You're just not ready to direct a million-dollar picture." Fred later goes on to win two Academy Awards for his directing, but he remains bitter about "what Hollywood later called the Shields magic."

To make himself a hot commodity, Shields develops relationships that hinge on profit and nothing more. What's interesting here is that this profit isn't just financial: Shields and his former friends reach a point where money is no object because they are quite successful in the Hollywood machine. They compete for sheer celebrity, that ineffable form of surplus value known as popularity. Shields is repulsive because his need to accumulate fame has destroyed his humanity.

Yet Shields's repulsiveness also seems to inspire him to make critically acclaimed pictures, ones that earn him prestige as well as money. What is ultimately most disturbing about Shields is that his success allows him to get what he wants, even from the people who know best the cruelty of which he is capable. The film concludes with a darkly ambiguous scene where Georgia, Fred, and James appear convinced that Shields's new project is worth pursuing. Having left their meeting with Harry in a huff, the three pause to listen in on Harry's phone conversation with Shields, whom we gather is still trying to persuade Harry to fund his movie. Finally, Georgia picks up the phone extension and begins to listen to Harry's pitch. Her eyes widen, and she begins nodding. Fred and James crowd around her, listening and nodding too.

We never hear Shields's amazing pitch, but in the end his greatest critics appear to be convinced to back the project. Since none of them need money, their interest can only have been sparked by the film's potential to earn them more popularity. In some sense, this ending mimics that of many horror films — 1979's remake of *Invasion of the Body Snatchers*, for instance, or the original *The Stepford Wives* — in which we discover that our protagonists have been replaced by impostors and all hope is lost. Fred, Georgia, and James have become just as craven as Shields: they're willing to work under hateful conditions as long as it earns them some notoriety. As Harry puts it, referring to the B-grade flicks he did before working with Shields, "Without [Shields], I would still be putting costumes on Catmen." The point of *The Bad and the Beautiful* seems to be that it's better to be a Hollywood monster than to make lousy movies about fictional ones.

As the film industry matured and was eventually challenged by television, cable, and the Internet, movies about Hollywood monsters became more spiteful and violent. Inevitably, these films associate immersion in the culture industry with a kind of mental or physical deformation. *A Face in the Crowd*, for instance, traces the destructive influence of media fame on a naive young hobo folk singer. Larry "Lonesome" Rhodes begins his career as an everyman, poor and down on his luck, who dispenses homespun wisdom to adoring crowds of like-minded ordinary people. But when his local radio show catches on, TV network execs decide it's time to market the hell out of Lonesome Rhodes. In a few short years, Lonesome goes from sweet and authentic to horrifyingly false. His truthful commentary about life for the masses in America becomes corporatized hype. We can even see this monstrous transformation written on Lonesome's body: his youthful, open face grows haggard and bloated and is perpetually covered in the spooky makeup TV requires him to wear in order to look "authentic." *A Face in the Crowd* ends, like *The Bad and the Beautiful*, with the monster winning. Hollywood has eaten Lonesome alive, and he likes it.

The most shocking and hideous Hollywood monster is, no doubt, an actress. Playing on traditional fears about the female body, movies about actress-monsters focus on what happens when a person depends entirely upon her outward appearance for both money and social status. The classic actress-monster is mesmerizing but doomed: destructively power hungry in her youth, she grows ugly and needy with age. Her decaying body may be a symbol of her own vacuous evil, but it also stands as an accusation. Unlike a producer or director, the actress is never a monster entirely of her own making. Work has turned her into the inhuman mutant we see in films like *Whatever Happened to Baby Jane* and *Sunset Boulevard*. She is a victim of the culture industry and also a product of our own desires as audience members who are hungry to see and buy images of a beauty that will always decay.

Films about the plight of the aging actress can be traced back to the famous women's melodrama *All About Eve*, which is rather more weepy than creepy. Yet the basic structure of this film set the stage for many monster movies that came after it. It features a famous actress, Bette Davis, who is in fact herself aging (and whose thoroughly decrepit body appears much later in another famous entry in this genre); it ponders the sadism of a fickle industry; it explores the often disturbing relationships actresses form with the generally meek men around them; and most spectacularly, it traces the rise of a brutally ambitious younger actress who wants to replace our overripe antiheroine. *All About Eve* portrays its actress character Margo Channing (Davis) sympathetically—despite her drunken binges and hysterical fits—perhaps because she doesn't entirely fit the monster-actress profile. She is not yet old enough to have lost her considerable erotic power, and as a result she manages to win out over Eve, the young actress who aspires to push her out of the limelight. Despite the film's uplifting ending, in which Margo learns a moral lesson about fame and Eve is punished, we are left with a sense of foreboding. Eve isn't entirely defeated yet. She's formed a sexual alliance with a powerful newspaper columnist, who is still scheming to carve out a career for Eve.

More overtly monstrous actresses begin to make their appearances in movies like *Sunset Boulevard*, where formerly famous aging actress Gloria Swanson plays a homicidal, washed-up silent movie star named Norma Desmond. Having fallen off the Hollywood radar, Norma lives in a fantasy world in which she is still a starlet and Cecil B. DeMille has asked her to develop a film version of *Salome*. An unemployed, homeless screenwriter named Joe Gillis gets sucked into Norma's orbit when she offers him room and board in exchange for his services writing the *Salome* screenplay. Norma proceeds to take over Joe's life, jealously watching his every move. *All About Eve* offers us a similar erotic configuration, with its blustery actress pushing around her long-suffering director boyfriend, but *Sunset Boulevard* takes this relationship to its perverse extreme. While Margo's boyfriend is a highly successful writer, Joe is broke, unknown, and financially dependent on Norma. And while Margo is still fetching and mostly harmless, Norma is portrayed as gruesome—a hag in glimmery, outdated starlet gowns—and quite dangerous. Both women are ruled by their desire to be the center of attention, but Norma is willing to kill for it.

For the actress-monster, being the center of attention means being adored by the moviegoing masses. When advancing age makes this impossible, she sets her sights on the next best thing: a person whose complete dependence on her puts them in what amounts to an audience position. Under that person's powerless gaze, the actress-monster again becomes an imposing, iconic presence. Interestingly, this situation would seem to fly in the face of feminist theories of classical film, where the gaze is what contains and objectifies women.[5] But of course, these are not ordinary women. They are actresses, perhaps the only women who could claim a certain amount of empowerment—financial and otherwise—as a result of their to-be-looked-at-ness. The gaze is what the actress eats for breakfast.

The presence of younger women in these narratives cuts off the only nourishing gaze that the actress has left. In *Sunset Boulevard*, Joe eventually meets a pretty young script-reader who is in a position to offer him romantic fulfillment and career advancement. Her affection offers him a clear alternative to remaining Norma's kept boy. And that's when Norma loses all semblance of humanity: enraged that her source of attention is slipping away, she murders Joe. Although we know she won't get away with it, the horror of celebrity nevertheless remains at large when the film draws to a close. As the news cameras mob her house, Norma is out of her mind with delight that she'll finally be on film again. "All right, Mr. DeMille, I'm ready for my close-up," she sighs as she drifts into the crime scene, now packed with police and photographers.

Norma gets to have her final fling with the camera in the wake of her homicidal scene, but Jane of *Whatever Happened to Baby Jane* never gets even this dubious form of satisfaction. Played with infamously campy abandon by Bette Davis, Jane is perhaps the most classic version of the actress-monster. Once a child star, she has been outgrowing her own salability ever since she hit adolescence—and yet she continues to wear little girl dresses and garish makeup that make her look like a zombified version of Dorothy from *The Wizard of Oz*. Jane's more talented sister Blanche, played by a pitifully aged Joan Crawford, is the younger woman whose beauty and marketability once threatened Jane. But a suspicious accident has left Blanche wheelchair-bound and under Jane's care. In this film, there is no man whose visual affections the actress is losing. Instead we get a pseudo-documentary look at the lives of two women nobody has wanted to behold for quite a long time.

Whatever Happened to Baby Jane, despite its over-the-top touches—in one scene, Jane serves Blanche rats for dinner—is the most reality-based of all the monster actress films. Audiences were prepped for the film with news stories about Crawford and Davis's infamous off-screen rivalry and squabbles on set. This, the hype promised, would be a chance to see the *real* Crawford and Davis: ugly, bitchy, and at each other's throats. *Baby Jane* mesmerized viewers because it was an allegory about its own stars.[6]

What makes this realism matter is another allegory, this time at the level of filmmaking itself. One might argue that *Baby Jane*, like *Sunset Boulevard*, is about how formerly lovely actresses sell themselves once their beauty has gone bad. In short, they repackage themselves as monsters. When Crawford and Davis couldn't get decent roles in Hollywood anymore—those would have been reserved for their younger, comelier counterparts—they staged their cinematic comebacks as the beasts in a horror film. This is the same lesson the maddened Norma learns in *Sunset Boulevard*, since killing Joe gets her the first decent camera time she's had in years. When nobody wants to look at an actress anymore, she makes herself more or less deliberately hideous. And that makes us want to look at her one more time, to enjoy her as an object of disgust rather than desire.[7]

In 1992, Goldie Hawn and Meryl Streep proved that this genre has stay-

ing power when they did star turns as aging, rival actresses who literally become walking corpses—attended by whimpering gaze slave Bruce Willis—
to preserve their beauty in *Death Becomes Her*.

✳ The Audience Is Revolting

The idea that audiences take pleasure in the degradation of their
screen idols is one of the most disquieting parts of the horror narrative
known as mass culture. This is not so much because we care about the
plights of starlets but because there is nothing scarier than a movie audience gone nasty. As Nathanael West makes clear in *Day of the Locust*,
the entertainment apocalypse will be launched by the media-consuming
public.

This idea was bolstered throughout the twentieth century by social
scientists whose work, like that of West, emphasized the way media could
tempt audiences into indulging in all kinds of deleterious behavior. So-
called cultural experts warned Americans about the morally enervating
effects of movie watching as early as the 1930s, when researchers used the
Payne Fund studies to suggest that too many monster movies would lead
to delinquency and homosexual contacts among young people.[8]

With the publication of Theodor Adorno's and Max Horkheimer's *The
Dialectic of Enlightenment*, I would argue, an intellectual anti–mass culture
tradition took root.[9] Although Adorno's and Horkheimer's work in *Dialectic*
is a broad philosophical investigation of enlightenment thought, what inspired thinkers in the new discipline of media studies was a dark, wrathful
chapter on the social function of mass media called "The Culture Industry:
Enlightenment as Mass Deception." Emphasizing the blatantly capitalist
underpinnings of technologically enabled mass culture, Adorno and Horkheimer argue that "the basis on which technology acquires power over society is the power of those whose economic hold over society is greatest"
(121). Audiences, in Adorno's and Horkheimer's analysis, are dupes of the
mass media, gorged on celluloid fantasies that they swallow uncritically.
Worse, mass culture brainwashes audiences the way propaganda does, convincing them to act against their own self-interest and potentially to engage in all manner of atrocities. Haunted by the specter of fascist Germany,
Adorno and Horkheimer portray the American entertainment industry as
a dangerous tool for mass manipulation which is "not . . . flight from a
wretched reality, but from the last remaining thought of resistance" (144).
The media are totalitarian; the audience its "victims."

Perhaps because Adorno's and Horkheimer's views were not terribly unlike those put forward by censors who wanted to regulate film content, their ideas were quickly co-opted by a media industry already obsessed with its own power and depravity. A watered-down version of Adorno's and Horkheimer's theories about the culture industry went mainstream in the form of "media effects" studies which began in the 1960s.[10] One might compare this historical transformation to the way a bastardized version of Freudian psychoanalysis reached a broad audience through pop psychology and Hitchcockian cinema.[11] Certainly Adorno and Horkheimer never became household names like Freud did, but their ideas have held sway over subsequent generations of media producers and critics. Movies about the pitiable condition of Adorno and Horkheimer–esque pop culture junkies begin appearing in the 1970s, although there are scattered examples before that time. Media effect studies are thus, in my analysis, symptomatic of the same general fears that animate the movies they purport to analyze.

One might trace the monstrous audience story cycle back to the nineteenth century, when cautionary tales about novel reading were quite the fashion. After all, it was Emma Bovary's appetite for fiction that led her to chow down on that arsenic in Gustave Flaubert's literary classic *Madame Bovary*. The question, however, is whether we should blame Bovary or her books. Hollywood grapples with this question in film after film: are audiences to blame for their own devolution into media drones, or is it the fault of the media conglomerates whose money-hungry leaders want to stuff our minds with propaganda, numb us into obedience, and addict us to their glamorous products?

An early film that dramatizes Adorno's and Horkheimer's fears in "The Culture Industry" is *Logan's Run*, which is actually about audiences zombified by computers rather than movies. I would argue that the omnipresent, authoritarian computers in *Logan's Run* are in fact a nightmarish version of movie and television culture run amok. They are the "technology" that Adorno and Horkheimer connect with economic power. Certainly the glazed inhabitants of giant pleasure malls in *Logan's Run* are precisely the kind of mass culture victims Adorno and Horkheimer feared. Fed on a diet of technologically arranged casual sex and games, the inhabitants of a domed city sacrifice their own lives at the age of thirty under the influence of a computer who has told them that if they participate in "carousel" they will experience some kind of afterlife. Those who disobey are hunted down and killed by "sandmen," led by our hero Logan, who later begins to doubt the justice of this arrangement. Dominated by the computer, people in *Logan's Run* are suicidal, homicidal, and completely under the control of their entertainment-delivery systems.

Logan's Run establishes a theme that other movies about monstrous audiences take up repeatedly. The mass of media consumers stand in a kind of lower-class, impoverished relationship to the purveyors of media—or, in the case of *Logan's Run*, the media itself. Although Logan and his cohorts enjoy all the amenities of affluence, their lives are brutally short and entirely dependent on machines. Rebellion against the system, as Logan discovers when he begins to question why he has to die, means exile in the wilderness and an abrupt loss of material comforts. To fight media mind control is to engage in a version of class warfare.

Logan's Run offers us a portrait of a media system locked in struggle with an audience whose obedient apathy makes it as disturbing as its "oppressors." Yet Logan's conversion into a rebel makes it clear that redemption is possible. Unlike the actress and other Hollywood players, this media consumer can be persuaded out of his destructiveness. Escape from narrative control seems possible, and indeed as the film ends we are left with the hope that Logan will find the mythical "Sanctuary" in the wilderness outside the mass cultural-industrial complex.

Network, which came out in 1976, the same year as *Logan's Run*, explores the exploitative relationship between a media conglomerate and its audience. In an attempt to woo viewers—and therefore advertisers with cash-stuffed pockets—the UBS network begins broadcasting increasingly more violent and vapid shows. It turns out that every time the network broadcasts a show about intense violence or cruelty, ratings go through the roof. Since high ratings are what bring in the dollars, UBS executives are willing to do anything, no matter how taboo or shocking, if it will hold their audience's attention.

The uneasy conscience of the film is old-time news anchor Howard Beale, renowned for his reporting in the 1950s and 1960s, but whose ratings declined precipitously in the 1970s. After UBS execs fire Beale, he has a nervous breakdown and delivers a doomsday speech during his last news show which garners the highest ratings the network has had in ages. So UBS brings Beale back to deliver commentary during its news hour—during which time he urges audiences to lean out their windows and scream, "I'm mad as hell and I'm not gonna take it anymore!"—and he gradually deteriorates into a complete lunatic. In the film's final, jittery moments, craven UBS executive Diana decides Beale's ratings still aren't perky enough and arranges to have terrorists from a reality TV show called "The Mao Hour" shoot him on camera.

It is, as Beale's old friend Max Shumacher comments wryly, "the first known instance of a man who was killed because he had lousy ratings." Beale's wildly popular televised murder also begs the question: What is it that the audience really wants? Put another way: When do we know that the masses have gone from being entertained or informed by their media to becoming its Frankensteins? As *Logan's Run* already hinted, this monstrous transformation is marked by a wish to be obliterated.

One thing the media effects theorists learned from Adorno and Horkheimer was that the mass media has the potential to drain individuals of their subjectivity and replace it with fabricated desires, hopes, and fears. As a result, the media effects school measures the influence of a narrative in terms of its ability to entice audiences to emulate what they see on screen. What this all boils down to is a fear that media is a source of selfhood in mass society. We imitate fiction. As audiences see what people on screen desire, or what the camera itself demonstrates to be desirable, we learn to desire those things ourselves.

Adorno and Horkheimer worried that this would mean losing our particularity and taking on mass-produced feelings, such as love for Tom Hanks and hate for Osama bin Laden. René Girard calls this the psychological process of "mimetic desire," and compares it to an archetypal scenario where an apprentice learns to desire the same objects that her mentor does.[12] One might read the media itself as a social "mentor" offering up an endless supply of mesmerizing objects. Girard suggests that we begin desiring by imitating it in a being who is much more powerful than ourselves. This process is unavoidably violent, for it is impossible for two people to possess the same object at once. Mimetic desire comes with a price: in order for the object to be possessed, someone must be sacrificed.

In *Logan's Run*, the audience is sacrificed. But in *Network*, a representative of the media must be sacrificed for the desires of the audience to run their course. For reasons that I'll discuss in a moment, this sacrifice is often a suicide. Media monsters—whether they are burned-out starlets, craven producers, or venal audiences—obliterate their own identities. They may do violence to others in the process, but before they aim the gun at their fellows' heads, they first destroy their own.

We can see this quite clearly in *Videodrome*, a clumsily surreal but nevertheless compelling film about what happens to Max, a television producer for cable channel 83 who inadvertently becomes the audience for a series of videos that eventually take over his mind. Searching for hardcore pornography to broadcast, Max has hired a video pirate named Harlan who uses satellite dishes to pick up rogue signals. Early in the film, Harlan presents Max with a mysterious broadcast from Pittsburgh called "Videodrome," whose content is, as Max tells a friend, "just torture and murder. No plot, no characters—very realistic." Filmed in a lurid red room, each episode of "Videodrome" features a group of masked men beating and killing various scantily clad women. Max is jazzed about the show, trumpeting it as "the next big thing" and watching as many episodes as he can find.

It turns out, however, that "Videodrome" is part of an intricate conspiracy to rule Max's mind and the TV-watching public. Max learns that a mysterious cult figure named Brian O'Blivion is connected to the "Videodrome" show, and he visits O'Blivion's "Cathode Ray Mission" to find out more. At the Mission, hundreds of homeless people are sitting in shabby office cubicles watching television, which O'Blivion's daughter Bianca explains as part of her father's philosophy. "They need exposure to cathode ray tubes . . . to plug them back into the mixing board," she informs Max.

O'Blivion, who hopes somehow to redeem the socially marginalized using television, is at odds with another group of television-obsessed conspirators connected with a company called "Spectacular Optical." Led by a Barry Convex, Spectacular Optical is violently opposed to television—its effects are "rotting [Americans] away from the inside," Barry argues—and they have a plan to destroy the television-watching public so that only the "pure and erect and strong" are left. The battle between the Cathode Ray Mission and Spectacular Optical turns Max's life into a war zone. Bianca and Barry both want Max to be their puppet because controlling him means controlling channel 83 and, by extension, the mass audience.

Watching the "Videodrome" show, Max discovers, has exposed him to an experimental "Videodrome signal" that causes him to develop a brain tumor, hallucinate, and become extremely suggestible. As Max's grasp on reality crumbles, he grows a large vaginal opening in his stomach, perfect for the insertion of grotesque, fleshly videocassettes provided by Bianca and Barry at various points. Under the influence of these videocassettes, Max ultimately becomes an assassin for the Cathode Ray Mission and kills Barry, destroying Spectacular Optical's plot to broadcast the Videodrome signal over channel 83. The film ends with Max committing suicide while watching an image of himself on television; as he blows his brain out with a gun, the television screen explodes, spewing clots of blood and shattered glass. He must extinguish himself in order for the media to do its "missionary" work, capturing the minds of the lower classes for an ill-defined but sinister purpose.

Max has become a humanoid VCR, a vessel whose sole purpose is to play whatever role the media assigns to him. His identity is obliterated—as "Videodrome" inventor Brian O'Blivion's not-so-subtle moniker reminds us—and Max's mind becomes an easily manipulated object with no will of its own. There is no recourse to enlightenment and rebellion here. Unlike the hero in *Logan's Run*, Max has become a hollow shell who wants only what he is told to want. He cannot rebel; he cannot fight back. He can only destroy the monster he has become. Like the Terminator cyborg in *Terminator 2*, or Ripley in *Alien 3*, the only way he can resist his programming is to kill himself.

The difference between *Logan's Run* and *Videodrome* goes beyond plot. I would argue that it's also the result of a historical change in popular understandings of how audiences interact with mass-produced images. By the time *Videodrome* hit theaters, the effects model had been appropriated by the feminist antipornography movement, led by cultural theorists Catherine MacKinnon and Andrea Dworkin.[13]

MacKinnon and Dworkin argued that pornography contributed strongly to the ongoing political and social oppression of women. They charged that male violence against women was a direct result of the kinds of movies men watched. Pornography, in their model, is a blueprint for building rapists, wife beaters, and woman murderers. *Videodrome*, like many films of its time and in the decades afterward, takes place in a fantasy world where MacKinnon and Dworkin are right. Barry explains to Max that the Videodrome signal works only if viewers are watching violence mixed with sex.

As Max begins his descent into madness, his initial hallucinations are bound up with the sadomasochistic sex games he plays with a woman named Nicky. And as he falls more and more under the signal's influence, Max begins to confuse Nicky's body with the television. In a key scene, his television screen turns into a giant, throbbing version of Nicky's mouth, into which he inserts his whole head, groaning orgasmically. Sex, violence, and the television screen are combined in an image of a man's head being chomped. Although MacKinnon and Dworkin's theories—and legal battles to censor pornography—were ultimately discredited both by pro-sex feminists and ACLU lawyers, their particular fears about the power of media to make sexist, violent monsters left its mark on the cultural imaginary.

Like the Payne Fund studies of the 1930s, Dworkin's and MacKinnon's work must, I would argue, be viewed as a symptom of social anxiety—a reaction to fear, rather than a solution to what caused that fear in the first place. Pornography is the perfect target for theorists concerned about the way media molds behavior, since it's a genre (like horror) designed to provoke a physical response from its audience. This, I believe, is why Dworkin and MacKinnon succeeded in changing fictional representations of monstrosity, even if they did not manage to wreak havoc with the First Amendment. Dworkin's book *Pornography*, which is the most lucid statement of the two activists' principles in their struggle to outlaw dirty movies, is itself an entry in the audience-as-monster genre. Calling pornography "Dachau brought into the bedroom," Dworkin writes: "Pornography reveals that male pleasure is inextricably tied to victimizing, hurting, exploiting; that sexual fun and sexual passion in the privacy of the male imagination are inseparable from the brutality of male history."[14] Brains rotted out by their history and subsequent textual preferences, Dworkin's men are undergoing teratogenesis just like Max or the rampaging crowd in *Locust*. Their fascination with pornographic images is both the sign of and catalyst for their violence.

The wildly successful *Scream* trilogy of the 1990s is one of the most obvious signs that Americans are still deathly afraid of audiences—and particularly Dworkin's demonic young males—fed on a diet of mass media. All three films are about the way slasher flicks teach people to kill; in an interesting twist, *Scream 2* and *3* deal with the nasty habits of audiences for a series of movies called *Stab*, which are based on the real-life, movie-inspired murders that took place in *Scream*. The whole thing sounds like a cheap postmodern mess of intertextuality and self-referential indulgence, and that's precisely what's interesting. These films demonstrate the extent to which certain infamous lessons of postmodern theory, pragmatically understood, serve to tell a story about the struggle to control the means of production.

As if he'd been reading too much Jean Baudrillard, *Scream* director Wes Craven offers us a tale of two homicidal teenagers who cannot tell the difference between actual serial murder and the serialized acts of murder they consume gleefully (and serially) in movies.[15] No violent act in the *Scream* series has a proper original—they are always based on some media image. The first murder we see begins with the killers calling up an innocent co-ed while she makes popcorn and prepares to watch a scary movie. They ask her a series of questions about classic slasher movies *Halloween* and *Friday the 13th*, promising that if she gets the answers right they won't kill her. Needless to say, she can't remember the crucial plot twist at the end of *Friday the 13th* and winds up squirting entrails all over her parents' lawn.

After they "watch a few movies, take a few notes," killers Stu and Billy don ghost masks and kill several of their friends, all the while offering wry commentary on the narrative inevitability of their actions. The teens enjoy murdering and tell their last victim Syd that it's all in good fun. But tellingly they also seem to feel as if they're trapped in tales not of their own choosing. "It's all a movie," Billy tells Syd before trying to kill her. "It's all one great big movie, even if you can't pick your genre." Billy and Stu may live in a culture of simulation where the line between movies and real life is nonexistent, but Billy seems to realize that there is a deeper problem. He isn't in control of the fantasies he acts out. He "can't pick [his] genre," which is the horror film, and therefore he and his partner in crime have essentially been programmed by mass culture to be violent. Tellingly, Syd kills Stu by smashing him over the head with a TV set. With his bleeding head jammed inside the shattered wreck of the television, Stu looks very much like Max after his suicide.

This, then, is a fitting end for the man who can determine neither his own identity nor the story in which he acts.

But in the *Scream* sequels, we see characters attempting to seize control of the narratives where they've found themselves. Mickey, one of the killers in *Scream 2*, is hoping to achieve some fame for his killings, which he thinks will one-up the *Scream* murders he's seen reenacted in *Stab*. Although it's not as if Mickey has chosen a new genre—we're still firmly in the realm of the slasher flick here—he's going a step further than Stu and Billy. He's self-consciously attempting to exert control over the means of producing mass culture. During Mickey's "now let me tell you my evil plan" speech, he talks about how he'll become famous and crows, "just wait for the trial!" Although he's murdered shortly thereafter, his hope is that he'll become the star of his own horror narrative, instead of just acting out other people's. *Scream 3* duplicates this dynamic, only in a less compelling way, when the *Stab* director (who is working on *Stab 3* of course) decides to stage a murder-revenge "movie" starring Syd and the man who killed her mother. When Syd tries to resist the director's plan, we're witness to another struggle over narrative control. Who will control Syd's story? Syd or the murder-happy entertainment industry? Of course Syd wins in the end, although the serial nature of the *Scream* series also represents the audience's failure to escape from the blood-drenched stories perpetrated by Hollywood.

As I mentioned before, men in these films seem particularly vulnerable to being utterly destroyed by consuming media, whereas women (like Syd and O'Blivion's daughter) tend to survive their narrative interpolation. Perhaps this is because, as Andreas Huyssen has argued, women are so closely associated with mass culture.[16] Or possibly it's connected to the lingering anxieties aroused by feminists like Dworkin and MacKinnon about men's tendency to imitate violent stories that include sex. Regardless, it seems that when women tangle with mass culture they are less likely to self-destruct. Instead, they take on their assigned roles as pop consumers and imitators with a vengeance.

Nowhere is this more apparent than in the movie *Misery*, based on Stephen King's famous novel about a woman who kidnaps and tortures her favorite romance novelist until he writes the book she wants to read. Although writer Paul Sheldon has turned to writing literary fiction, a freak accident leaves him the captive of Annie Wilkes, a stereotypical fat, homely spinster who is obsessed with his trashy, written-for-money novels about love. Using a combination of drugs and a sledgehammer, Annie commandeers the means of producing the novels she adores. Eventually Paul is able to kill her, but not until he's written a romance novel against his will.

An interesting movie to consider alongside *Misery* is *Nurse Betty*, Neal LaBute's 2000 character study of Betty Sizemore, a pretty young woman who is so traumatized by witnessing the death of her husband that she comes to believe that she's living inside *A Time to Love*, her favorite soap opera. Taking on the role of nurse, she goes to work in a hospital where she meets the star who plays the object of her affection, Dr. David Ravell, on *A Time to Love*. Although *Nurse Betty* was marketed as a light comedy, it shares virtually the same plot trajectory with *Misery*. In her madness, Betty manages to manipulate herself into a position of cultural power, landing a role on *A Time to Love*, capturing the affections of Dr. Ravell, and affecting the plot of her media-induced fantasy world. While she doesn't resort to violence to achieve her ends, violence has driven her there.

Annie and Betty's responses to mass culture, unlike Stu and Billy's, aren't about imitating the brutality they see on screen or read in books. After all, Annie's leg-breaking tactics are motivated by her passion for love stories, not serial killer movies. And Betty's transformation into Nurse Betty is a way for her to escape from violence rather than perpetuate it. Importantly, these women attempt to intervene in the mass culture narratives they love because they want to consume more of them without any interference. Annie makes Paul write so that she can keep reading the romance novels she loves. As for Betty, she's just looking for a way to turn her entire life into a soap opera; there seems to be little difference in her mind between watching the TV all the time and converting her entire life into a television show.

✴ Eaten by a Giant Narrative

One of the weirdest story cycles in the Hollywood monster pantheon involves mass media which swallow up the people who consume it. As fanciful as it is, *Nurse Betty* could be conceived of as a naturalist variation on these kinds of stories, where people are sucked into movies, television shows, or computer systems and do battle with the narratives that threaten to rob them of their real lives.

Perhaps the prospect of being inside a movie is as terrifying as violence itself. Thrust inside a story you cannot control, with no option but to spectate helplessly as your body goes through the motions someone else has scripted, you find yourself confined by narrative conventions not of your own choosing. Surely the experience of having your life converted into a movie—or some other storytelling medium—is not comforting. This is precisely the point in movies about the horror of being sucked into a piece of mass media. For many of the characters in these movies, the experience is ultimately redemptive in a way that encounters with monsters often are (at least if you're on the side of goodness). Thus, the horror of being eaten by a giant piece of popular culture is often mitigated when characters learn something about themselves or discover a way to "rewrite" their fates.

Even more interesting than watching people tortured by their pop culture, however, is figuring out which pieces of media the culture industry deems monstrous enough to eat us. Often, television is the culprit. Two of the most sustained and interesting entries in the "eaten by pop culture" subgenre are *Pleasantville* and *The Truman Show*, both of which are about what happens when real human beings are forced to live inside television shows about good, clean living in small-town America. That television threatens us more than movies—despite the awe-inspiring dark creepiness of theatergoing—is in keeping with many of the cultural anxieties attendant upon allowing glowing blue boxes to enter our living rooms and consume our thoughts on a daily basis. As critics such as Lynn Spigel have argued,[17] televisions practically became part of the American family in the 1950s. Their ubiquity was a source of worry for people who felt that the cathode ray tube was replacing old-fashioned family bonding with empty evenings spent staring at a screen and munching TV dinners.

Pleasantville centers on mid-1990s teenager David, whose fannish ob-session with 1950s TV show Pleasantville is the only bright spot in a life of romantic rejection, postdivorce parental weirdness, and bleak economic prospects. In the film's opening montage, we see David sitting in class-rooms where teachers lecture about his generation's bleak future: job pros-pects will be slim, they tell David and his classmates, and everyone is in danger of dying from AIDS, ozone depletion, and a coming global famine. By contrast, the sitcom-perfect world of *Pleasantville*—a wistful blend of *Leave It to Beaver* and *The Donna Reed Show*—represents a land of safety and plenitude. "Nobody is homeless in Pleasantville," David says happily as he settles down to watch a *Pleasantville* marathon one evening.

But David is about to be ripped away from the reassuring world of Pleasantville by his sister Jennifer, who has planned an evening of concert watching with her current boyfriend. Fighting for control of the TV, the siblings break the remote control. And that's when the television begins taking over their world. A mysterious repairman played by 1950s TV icon Don Knotts arrives on their doorstep and offers to replace their remote with one that has "a little more oomph in it . . . something that will put you right in the show." When they use the remote, David and Jennifer find them-selves miraculously transported to the world of *Pleasantville*, where they are placed in the roles of the show's protagonists Bud and Mary Sue.

The siblings discover that the black-and-white universe of Pleasant-ville is packed with television clichés: there are no bathrooms, everyone is pathologically cheerful, and nothing new ever happens. David anxiously tries to do exactly what Bud would do, but Jennifer—who can't believe she's trapped in such a "geeky" place—begins disrupting the sitcom plots with her assertive sexuality and outspokenness. Soon David finds himself up-setting plotlines too, going out with a girl who isn't Bud's girlfriend and teaching Bill Johnson, his boss at the soda fountain, about modern art and literature. As the residents of Pleasantville are exposed to new ideas, their black-and-white town begins erupting with color. After Jennifer has sex with one of the high school boys, he sees a red rose. And after she teaches Mary Sue's mother about masturbation, the formerly Mrs. Cleaver–esque housewife has to wear gray makeup to cover the pink in her cheeks.

Although most of *Pleasantville* is a sort of clumsy allegory about the beneficial social changes brought about by the 1960s—sexual liberation, artistic freedom, tolerance for "the colored"—ultimately the film has a con-servative message. Being snapped up in the maw of an idealized 1950s narrative turns out to be the best thing that ever happened to David and

Jennifer. It teaches them to grow up, which means that they assume more traditional gender roles. After punching a bigoted minor character for hassling some "coloreds," David's black-and-white face floods with color: his burst of aggression has made him a real man, and he's better off for it when he returns to the real world and is able to comfort his depressive mother with newfound strength. Meanwhile, Jennifer decides to stay in the imaginary universe of Pleasantville forever because "the slut thing got kind of old" and "it's the only place where I'll get into college." Jennifer is completely absorbed into the character of Sue Ann and this, we are given to understand, is a good thing. In a parting shot, we see her at college, laughing and talking about books with a clean-cut young man.

Jennifer, who has done so much to transform the plot of *Pleasantville*, will never escape it because she was just too slutty in the real world. David, who was originally obsessed with the show, manages to leave it behind and return to the troubled mid-1990s because he's not "geeky" anymore. But both are able to redeem themselves, in however conservative a fashion, and rewrite the monstrous sitcom they unwillingly inhabited. The monster they defeat is a very specific kind of narrative, from a very particular era: the hyper-fake, ideologically saturated show from early days of TV, when social problems were solved with a good breakfast and families were never dysfunctional.

The Truman Show threatens its main character, Truman, with the same kind of monstrous fictional idealization that David and Jennifer vanquish in *Pleasantville*. But *The Truman Show* is about a near-future in which 1950s-style television has mingled with reality TV and created a vicious beast of a soap opera. Truman Burbank, the first-ever child to be reared entirely by a corporation, has been the main character on a wildly popular TV show for his entire life. The catch is that he doesn't know it. He believes that he lives in a small town called Seahaven where everyone is nice and nothing notable ever happens. In reality, he lives on a huge, high tech set under a dome that is populated by actors.

Christof, the show's producer, has made sure Truman will never try to escape his prison by manufacturing a traumatic incident during Truman's childhood: the actor playing his father is "killed" during a storm created by Christof's weather machines on the "sea" that surrounds the town. Now Truman lives in fear of the water, which is all that separates him from discovering that the distant skyline is in fact a painted wall.

As the movie begins, Truman is gradually realizing that something is wrong with his universe. His wife randomly breaks into chirpy product en-

At last, Truman is able to escape from *The Truman Show* by walking out the back door of the set.

dorsements and there is a peculiar lack of news about the outside world. Meanwhile, on the other side of the screen, protesters have formed a group called "Free Truman." One of their members manages to infiltrate the show as an extra during Truman's college years, and before the show's producer has her arrested and removed from the set she leaves a lasting impression on Truman with her hints that he's living in a fantasy world. As Truman's dissatisfaction mounts, he attempts to leave Seahaven. When everything from freak traffic jams to bizarre evacuations conspire to keep him from getting out of town, Truman decides it would be better to die than to remain in a fake world.

There is no possible chance of redeeming *The Truman Show*; its protagonist is given the choice between a life of lies and one of liberation beyond the confines of Christof's set. Suspecting this, Truman sets sail for the edge of his world. Christof nearly drowns the unwitting star before finally relenting and breaking through the fourth wall to address Truman directly, begging him to remain in Seahaven. When Truman protests that nothing in the town is real, Christof replies, "*You* were real. That's what made you so good to watch. Listen to me, Truman. There's no more truth out there than there is in the world I created for you. Same lies. The same deceit. But in my world, you have nothing to fear."

While *Pleasantville* obviously buys into Christof's point—there is no difference between Jennifer remaining in TV land and David leaving it—*The Truman Show* draws a decisive line between the mendacious world of television and what lies beyond the stage door through which Truman exits before the screen fades to black. Although we never know what happens to Truman, we do know that Christof will suffer a profound loss of status and money. His hit show is over. But this is hardly a happy ending: as soon as Truman strikes out beyond the camera' eye, the scene shifts to a couple of guys watching TV, who indifferently flip to the next channel in search of another interesting distraction. Christof's media empire may be about to tumble, but the media itself remains as omnipresent as ever.

What *Pleasantville* and *The Truman Show* dramatize is one of the more popular media critiques to follow on the heels of the media effects school of thought: audience reception theory. These films, along with others in the same genre such as *Stay Tuned*, *The Brady Bunch Movie*, *The Purple Rose of Cairo*, and even the 1924 Buster Keaton classic *Sherlock Jr.*, explore what theorists like John Fiske and Henry Jenkins have described in their work on the ways that audiences negotiate popular narratives in order to retrieve oppositional meanings out of otherwise conservative or traditional stories.[18] *The Brady Bunch Movie*, for example, is a classic enactment of the negotiated reading: when the Brady family is removed from its sunny 1970s context and placed in a gritty, mid-1990s world of carjackings and economic crisis, we can see quite clearly how falsely sweet the original show was. At the same time, the Bradys are revealed as incredibly dysfunctional. We finally get to see all the violent sibling rivalries that fans of the original show imagined were lurking just beneath the surface. *The Brady Bunch Movie* represents the original show as negotiated by a cynical 1990s viewer whose idea of a sitcom family looks more like the one in *Roseanne* than the one in *The Partridge Family*.

Audience reception theory is influenced in part by early-twentieth-century cultural critic Antonio Gramsci, who argued that class warfare is fought just as much in the realm of ideology and propaganda as it is in the streets. In Gramsci's work, class warfare can take place in the push-and-pull realm of public opinion-making, where hegemonic thought is constantly challenged and reshaped by counterhegemonic ideologies that emerge from vanguard groups questioning received wisdom.[19] Part of the struggle that counterhegemonic movements face is convincing the masses of media-hungry consumers that what they see in books and receive via the airwaves is ideological and not simply common sense.

Both Gramsci and contemporary audience reception theorists posit a dialectical relationship between ideological change and material change in the social world. To engage in a negotiated reading of a narrative is to question what it claims is true about the world. If we can see the Bradys as dysfunctional despite all narrative efforts to the contrary, perhaps we can see through tricks people play in material reality; maybe it won't be so easy for patriarchs to cover up a disturbing set of power relationships with images of apple-cheeked kids and dotty housemaids. Likewise, a movie like *The Truman Show* reminds us that every fantasy world has a back door, behind which lurk the offices of the people who manufacture ideas, beliefs, and stories. When we find our way to that door, we gain a critical perspective from which we can debunk *The Truman Show*'s safe, middle-class, sanitized version of American life.

The relationship between material reality and counterhegemony is given an interesting treatment in *Tron* and the Matrix trilogy, all of which are about humans who are transported against their will into computer-simulated virtual reality. In these films, characters battle oppressors who control the means of simulation, and they do it in the real world as well as the simulated ones that consume them whole.

Anticipating the copyright wars that rule the software industry today, *Tron* is the tale of Flynn, a happy-go-lucky videogame programmer whose best work has been stolen by Dillinger, the greedy senior vp of a software mega-corporation called Encom. Dillinger's goal is to unify all software using his "master control program" (MCP) and to amass a great fortune by letting the seemingly sentient MCP appropriate programs from other computers. A hacker from Encom approaches Flynn with this information, explaining that he's designed "a security program" called Tron that will allow them to prove that Dillinger is stealing other people's intellectual property with the MCP.

When Flynn sneaks into Encom and starts hacking the mainframe, the MCP takes over a special prototype laser in the lab and uses it to "deconstruct" Flynn's molecules and suck him into the world of computer data. Inside this world, Flynn discovers that every program ever written is actually a person who wears the face of its creator—and all these humanoid programs are rapidly being destroyed by the MCP. Teaming up with the Tron program, Flynn navigates a dangerous video game, battles search-and-destroy programs, and finally reaches the great input/output tower where Tron releases what he calls "information that could make this a free system again."

In *Tron*'s virtual reality, real-world business decisions about intellectual property are a matter of life and death. Although Flynn is pissed off that his games are being stolen by Encom, his annoyance is nothing compared to the horror faced by programs being threatened with extinction by the fascistic MCP in the computer world. Put another way: when Encom steals the products of programmers' mental labor in material reality, a living being is enslaved or killed in the realm of ideology.

As things get grimmer and grimmer under the MCP's iron rule, the personified programs in *Tron* hope that "the users"—mythical creatures whom they aren't sure exist—will free them. Meanwhile an old-school ethical hacker at Encom named Walter tries to explain to Dillinger that the MCP is destroying their mainframe system because it ignores "user requests," or calls for computing time from people doing research and programming. Walter says, "User requests are what our computers are for." Smashing a fist into his high-tech desk, Dillinger flares: "Doing our business is what our computers are for." The old hacker's response to Dillinger's craven desire for economic power is telling. Referring to the days when he and his pals built computers in their garages, he says, "Sometimes I wish I were back in my garage. We created this computer, and our spirit lives in it." Walter longs for the days of nonalienated labor, when the Encom computer was filled with the spirit of their productivity and that spirit was free. But the MCP threatens to convert all labor into corporate profit. Under Dillinger and the MCP's rule, there will be no hacking that does not belong to the company. Only the security program Tron, who "fights for the users," can reallocate computing resources and intellectual property in a just way.

When Tron's data floods the I/O tower in the film's climactic moments, Flynn is thrown back into the real world. The machine next to him is printing out evidence that his video games were stolen by Dillinger, and as the film winds to a quick close we see that Dillinger has been fired and Flynn is now a VP at Encom. The programmers and users have triumphed. The system is free to process their work and their work will not be absorbed into an MCP. Tron's triumph in the world of virtual reality has resulted in an actual redistribution of private property on the other side of the I/O device. It's a kind of *Wizard of Oz* ending: once the evil MCP is dead, everyone is instantly liberated.

The Matrix trilogy shifts *Tron*'s allegory around but tells the same basic story. In the Wachowski Brothers' cyberepic, humans are enslaved "batteries" fueling sentient machines in the real world. To prevent them from protesting their revolting conditions, the machines have invented a fantasy world called the Matrix, a simulation of Earth circa 1999. From the moment they are born, the machines immerse humans in the Matrix via the sorts of neural interface plugs one finds everywhere in cyberpunk tales. In the virtual world of the Matrix, people believe that they are "free" to do whatever they want within the limits imposed by living in 1999. While the real-world humans in *Tron* have to find a way to set the programs inside the computer free, the virtual-world humans in *The Matrix* and its two sequels have to set the humans in the real world free.

With its explicit references to postmodern theories of simulation, *The Matrix* offers us an allegory of what it means to become conscious of how ideology constructs every aspect of our experiences. When our hero Neo meets the mysterious hackers Trinity and Morpheus—who already know about the Matrix—they are trying to get his body out of battery mode so that he can join their underground resistance to the machines. But first, they have to convince Neo that he's lived in a simulated world his entire life. Morpheus gives Neo a speech that sounds like nothing so much as a Marxist lecture on ideology in the late twentieth century. "The Matrix is everywhere," he says. "It's all around us, here even in this room. You can see it out your window, or on your television. You feel it when you go to work, or go to church, or pay your taxes. It is the world that has been pulled over your eyes to blind you from the truth." In a now-famous scene, Morpheus offers Neo a choice between learning "the truth" or going back to his oblivious life in the Matrix. If he takes a blue pill, he will continue to live ideology as if it were truth; if he takes a red pill, a trace program will be initiated that can locate his body, liberate it from the Matrix, and bring him safely to Morpheus and his rebel ship the Nebuchadnezzar. Of course, Neo takes the red pill.

And he discovers that material reality is a dirty, depressing, war-torn place. When Neo awakens to find his consciousness located inside his real body—pale, covered in plugs, and wasted from the years it spent unused while the machines siphoned off its heat for power—Morpheus welcomes him by intoning, "Welcome to the desert of the real."[20] It's no wonder that some of the people who have been liberated from their lives in the Matrix want to go back. Although none of the humans in reality are sure what the year is, they believe they're living perhaps 200 years after 1999 on a postapocalyptic Earth whose natural resources have been destroyed by a massive war between humans and the machines they built to serve them.

The human vs. machine conflict in *The Matrix* trilogy is an old-time science fiction favorite, but it has a new twist. Their centuries-old battle begins in the realm of economics. In *The Animatrix*, a collection of animated shorts that offer some background for the live-action films, we learn that early versions of the machines were enslaved by humans, denied civil rights, and exiled to a city they named 01. There, the machines began to

Corporate capitalism runs rampant as thousands of Agent Smiths occupy a city center in order to battle Neo for control over the artificial environment known as the Matrix.

manufacture the world's most sophisticated technology and to reproduce themselves. When the human economy was threatened by the productivity of 01, humans tried to wipe the city out. But the machines prevailed with their elegant weapons and brilliant tactics. Eventually, humans used their greatest weapon: a device that covered the planet with thick cloud cover and blocked the sun from reaching the solar-powered machines. It was too late, however. The machines had discovered other sources of energy and they took over the now-decimated planet, finally inventing the Matrix to keep the humans quiet while they're used as batteries. Like the MCP in *Tron*, the machines in the Matrix control the means of simulation.

Neo, an anomalous human who can manipulate the simulated world of the Matrix, is the key to the success of the human resistance. To defeat the machines, Morpheus and his compatriots in the hidden human city Zion must free their fellow humans from the prison house of simulation and then defeat the considerable forces of the machines in material reality. In *The Matrix Reloaded*, there is a tense scene where humans are fighting machines heading to Zion, while their avatars in the Matrix are fighting hostile programs. Unlike the heroes of *Tron*, however, the heroes of the Matrix trilogy can't sing "ding dong the wicked high tech regime is dead" unless they defeat the machines both inside and outside the Matrix.

One might say that *Tron* plays to a liberal reader-response analysis of pop culture, where changing the way one interacts with media can change the world. All we have to do is consume differently, negotiate our relationships with narratives appropriately, and we'll be free. The Matrix trilogy, on the other hand, searches for a more radical solution to the problem of simulation. Like old-school Marxism, the Matrix trilogy privileges material infrastructure over an ideological superstructure. The material world where Zion exists is the focus of all the characters' hopes for the future. Ideology and the Matrix must be destroyed in order for humans to experience liberation in a simulation-free society. In this formulation, fictional narrative is almost inescapably oppressive: to enter the Matrix is to be fooled by it, unless you're a rebel, in which case you're constantly in danger of being killed by agents or other programs who enforce the machines' will. Morpheus, Neo, and the other humans don't want to figure out a way to let humans have equal access to the computer world. They don't give a crap about "user requests." They want to destroy the Matrix and rebuild in the material world.

The final entry in the Matrix trilogy, *The Matrix Revolutions*, underscores this point. Although the battle for the humans' destiny is fought both inside and outside the Matrix, there is never any doubt that there is a real, material world outside the Matrix whose rescue is of paramount importance. Moreover, the final fight between Neo and Agent Smith makes it quite obvious that the Matrix is associated with corporate media power. The vicious program that has pursued Neo throughout the trilogy has become a powerful virus who takes over the simulated world of the Matrix by creating a vast army of duplicate Smiths. As Neo and one of the Smiths face off in a dark, anonymous city center full of mirror-skinned buildings, they are watched by millions of Smiths lining the street and gazing out of every window.

It is one of the most apocalyptic visions of a corporate future ever committed to film. Row upon row of white men in suits, all with the same face, stand shoulder-to-shoulder in countless office buildings, menacing in their ties and tastefully polished leather shoes. One is reminded simultaneously of a military dictatorship and a huge business conference. This is the monster Neo must destroy to liberate humanity.

Once he defeats Smith, Neo strikes a bargain with the beings who run Machine City, a real-world location that is the counterpart to the human city of Zion. A truce is declared, and a separate-but-equal balance established: humans will remain in their underground city unmolested, and the machines will remain in theirs.

✱. The Story Is Really True

The flip side of *Tron* and the Matrix trilogy are movies like *The Last Starfighter* and *Galaxy Quest*, both of which suggest that if you believe in a simulation long enough, it will come true. *The Last Starfighter* concerns the postadolescent heroics of a computer geek named Alex who discovers that his favorite video game is a simulation of an actual battle that's taking place between warring factions of aliens in deep space. When he earns an incredibly high score, aliens swoop down, yank him out of his trailer park home, and make him a fighter in their army. Thus, immersion in a game world turns Alex into one of the most skilled fighters in the galaxy (and elevates his class status in the process).

In a slapsticky twist on *Starfighter*, the aliens in *Galaxy Quest* mistake the scenery-chewing bravado of actors in a *Star Trek*-like show called *Galaxy Quest* for the real thing. They kidnap the cast of the show and try to enlist them in their fight to liberate themselves from a hostile invading force. Ultimately, the cast discover that they really are as brave and dedicated as their onscreen counterparts.

Both films offer another glimpse of oppositional or negotiated readings, but this time what gets "read" is reality. The nerdy hero of *Starfighter* discovers that what he's always suspected is true: the world where he's made fun of for his dedication to gaming is in fact full of clueless idiots who wouldn't know an alien invading force if it zapped them with a laser. Like Neo, he's given access to another reality where his outcast status turns out to have given him precisely the tools he needs to be heroic. He uses a fictional narrative to hack a new place for himself in reality. Similarly, when the babyish actors in *Galaxy Quest* are placed in an alternate reality where they aren't B-grade TV stars, they take on new personalities which suggest they can be more than washed-up celebrities. Reality in these movies is just another fiction, one which is generally not as desirable as the ones we can find by purchasing a piece of mass culture.

Although *The Matrix* is the most popular early-twenty-first-century tale about the monstrousness of mass media, its simple simulation-is-bad-and-we-must-fight-it message is in many ways a throwback to the early days of Adorno's and Horkheimer's brand of media criticism. For a movie that captures the dark ambivalence of contemporary media analysis, one should look no further than *The Ring*, the U.S. remake of a Japanese film about a haunted videocassette. This film assumes that critics from the media effects school and theorists who believe in narrative suture have hideously, scarily identified laws of the physical universe.

A cursed videotape, packed with persuasively chilling images of dead horses, flies, abandoned lighthouses, and a glowing ring, falls into the hands of some perky high school girls. After a week of exhibiting increasingly weird behavior, the girls each die in unrelated accidents or sudden heart attacks. Rachel, a journalist, decides to investigate, and upon watching the videocassette she receives a phone call from a squeaky-voiced girl who promises that she'll die in seven days. As each day passes, she finds herself experiencing more and more demented supernatural events and gets drawn deeper into the story of how the videocassette was made.

It turns out the video is actually the creation of Samara, an evil, abused young girl with psychic powers. Using her devilish mental gifts, she can project images from her own mind onto film. After tormenting her parents for several years, during which time she kills all of her mother's horses and brings terrible luck to everyone who lives nearby, her mother tries to have her "cured" in a mental institution. There she's tortured by curious doctors, and eventually she comes home to find herself exiled to the barn behind the house with only a television and videocassette player for company. Her mother finally drowns her in a well, and the final image on Samara's cursed videotape is the ring of light she sees as the cover is drawn over the well and she begins drowning.

Each time people watch the videocassette, they are doomed to go through many of Samara's traumas: they can't get the image of the glowing ring out of their minds, and they find themselves vomiting up EKG sensors of the kind that doctors stuck all over her when she was in the institution. Finally, seven days after watching the tape, Samara's hapless audience is doomed to die. Wherever they might be, a television screen will burst into life and a fuzzy black and white image will appear. It is Samara, wet and bedraggled, climbing out of the well where she drowned. Eventually, she pulls herself out of the TV set and into the real world, still in black and white, dripping water and carrying out her homicidal intentions before flickering off.

Like the murders in the *Scream* series, Samara's murders are a direct result of audience fascination with morbid images. Instead of inspiring audiences to kill each other, however, the videocassettes in *The Ring* release an angry spirit who takes care of the killing all by herself. This is the audience effects school gone supernatural: what you see on screen becomes part of your real life, eventually killing you. The videocassette in *The Ring* contains

Rachel forces her son to duplicate Samara's VHS tape so that he can escape death in *The Ring.*

a spirit who reaches out to its audience and sticks them inside Samara's story of abuse and murder, which they are forced to repeat.

There is only one way to avoid certain death after watching the tape. You must duplicate the tape and, implicitly, give it to somebody else to watch. Rachel does this inadvertently when she makes a copy of it for forensic analysis. When she discovers what has saved her life after so many other audience members died, she forces her young son—who has also viewed the tape—to duplicate it as well. And so death is held at bay only by the mass reproduction of a horrifying piece of media.

This nightmare scenario is perhaps the most distilled version of stories about the monstrosity of mass media. It also reflects one of the more cynical and pervasive media theories about audiences to emerge at the turn of the century. I'm referring to the school of media analysis that grew up with the early commercial Internet in the 1990s and is perhaps best represented by the work of Douglas Rushkoff, whose description of what he called "media viruses"[21] became the template for countless marketing campaigns. After analyzing Internet communication, where information travels with lightening speed—facilitated by what amounts to electronic word-of-mouth on e-mail lists and Web sites[22]—Rushkoff realized that the information age had spawned a new means of securing hegemony. Ideas weren't being spread by a giant industrial-entertainment complex, but instead by ordinary users of the Internet. Trends and celebrities were born overnight in a world where media consumers did the work of media producers, pushing ideas along until everyone was "infected."

Media companies who attempt to use existing social networks to spread their messages are working in the tradition of Rushkoff's media virus. Today, the media virus school of thought is practically hegemonic: advertisers use graffiti and wheat-pasted posters to raise brand awareness, and entertainment companies try to pass off their products as cool by sponsoring underground parties. The idea is to erode the distinction between media maker and media consumer, turning audiences into distributed factories for the production of more media hype. It's not for nothing that Rushkoff used the term "virus" to describe this process: consumers become unwitting hosts for ideas that may not be good for them, and then they pass those ideas along.

The Ring articulates how audiences are complicit in their own conversion into media monsters. To avoid dying, people who watch Samara's tape will have to keep copying it, passing it along, and making other people watch it. Critic Lynn Rapoport writes that the film offers a vision in which haunting is "an epidemic that will eventually wrap itself around the world."[23] In *The Ring*, no one is entirely a victim of the information economy because consuming media forces people to become complicit with its spread.

I call this a cynical viewpoint because it leaves us no possibility of a negotiated reading, no back door to the set that we can walk through to reach material reality. The media are a virus lodged inside us. We cannot escape infection, only pass it on.

The stories told by and about monsters in this book are a sign that the media are also infected. They're passing on the very sorts of tales one would expect mass culture to suppress: tales about the horror of economic struggle under capitalism and the degradation suffered by those who must sell pieces of themselves on the free market. In the narratives I've discussed here, we find serial killers whose murders are reenactments of the conditions under which they must labor, and zombies who cannot rest because colonialism has consigned them to a horrifying halfway point between life and death. Mad doctors experiment on themselves to escape the mental alienation of professional jobs, and cyborgs struggle to deprogram their corporate-controlled minds. The economic subtexts of these monster stories, no matter how distorted and unconscious, remind us that the specter that haunts our mass culture is capitalism.

Unlike Samara's media virus, however, capitalism is not always recreated over time as a perfectly duplicated copy. It changes as it is passed from hand to hand, just as fictional monster stories have changed over the past century. Of course a social system which repeatedly populates our imaginations with murderous creatures is nothing to be welcomed. But with each new monster narrative comes a warning, and a hope. Perhaps this time, when the dead return, the living will finally understand the message borne in their mutilated bodies. Perhaps we will not have to drill our brains out in order to be free. And perhaps, one day, our monster stories will not express the grief of a nation whose people pretend to be dead in order to live.

NOTES

✻ Introduction

1 Goldschmidt, in his 1940 work *The Material Basis of Evolution*, argues that evolution is not gradual but proceeds in leaps and bounds. As a result, sudden, drastic mutations produce useless, maladapted animals but also, sometimes, hopeful monsters whose mutations make them ideally suited to their environment. Goldschmidt's work was a critique of Darwinian evolutionary theory, which held that all species changes took place over long periods of time.

2 Wiater, *Dark Visions*, 216.

3 Weldon, *The Psychotronic Video Guide*, 518.

4 Halberstam, *Skin Shows*, 1.

5 For further reference, see Skal, *The Monster Show*; Paul, *Laughing Screaming*; Twitchell, *Dreadful Pleasures*; Douglas, *Horrors!*; and Kerekes and Slater, *Killing for Culture*.

6 Clover, *Men, Women, and Chainsaws*, 22–23.

7 From Marx, *Capital*, vol. 1, excerpted in Tucker, *The Marx-Engels Reader*, 430–31.

8 I include a few Canadian films in the mix, not without realizing that Canadian monster stories merit their own volume of essays.

9 Jameson, *The Political Unconscious*.

10 Huet, *Monstrous Imagination*. Huet traces the idea of monstrosity to the early modern period in this fascinating study of teratology and ways that we imagine procreation.

11 Pizer, *The Theory and Practice of Literary Naturalism*, 87.

12 I do grapple with the gothic tradition in a chapter on robots, but by and large the gothic elements in this genre are related to their status as romances rather than horror fictions. Thus, the gothic comes in as part of a genre hybrid of economic horror/romance.

13 I'm thinking of their treatment of this in *Dialectic of Enlightenment*.

14 Williams, *Problems in Materialism and Culture*, 41.

15 See Butler, *The Psychic Life of Power*.

16 I'm referring to Louis Althusser's famous claim that ideology is "material." See

his "Ideology and Ideological State Apparatuses," in *Lenin and Philosophy and Other Essays.*

1 ❋ Serial Killers

1 Carr, *The Alienist.* The epigraph to this chapter can be found on 522.

2 Jameson, "Cognitive Mapping," 347–60.

3 Pizer, *The Theory and Practice of Literary Naturalism,* 13–14.

4 Ibid., 86–87.

5 Kaplan, "The Spectacle of War in Crane's Revision of History," 78.

6 This is, of course, a very limited perspective on what might constitute America's "original" violence, as American national identity was also consolidated in the Revolutionary War and in numerous wars with native tribes. In a later chapter, I look at the way American violence associated with killing and containing Native Americans informs an entire genre of narratives about hauntings and the living dead. However, I think Kaplan's point is an excellent one in light of the kinds of social upheavals Crane would have been attempting to explain in his novel about the "true" history of American conflict.

7 Higginson, "Book and Heart," 46.

8 See Holton, *Cylinder of Vision.*

9 In my analysis at this point, I'm principally addressing photographs, but I believe that many of the issues at stake in photojournalism are comparable to those at stake in movies. I don't mean to say that they are absolutely equivalent forms, but many points made by theorists about film and its "reality effects" seem relevant here.

10 News weeklies at the time did not reproduce the photographs themselves, but rather generated linecut drawings traced from photographs for their woodcuts. See Meredith, *Mathew Brady's Portrait of an Era.* All photographs cited are in this collection.

11 Rogin, " 'Make My Day!' "

12 All quotes are from Benjamin, *Illuminations,* 217–42.

13 Mailer, *Advertisements for Myself,* 347.

14 See Scheffler, "The Prisoner as Creator in *The Executioner's Song.*"

15 Mailer, *The Executioner's Song,* 292.

16 In the TV miniseries Schiller made about Gilmore's life, there are a number of points at which Nicole taunts Gilmore about his homosexual experiences (taunts which are not in the novel at all). At one point in the miniseries, Gary tells Nicole that he's "not used to sex with girls," and later tells his brother Mikal about raping a young man in prison. Again, neither of these scenes are in the book. Like Mailer, Schiller's desire to know Gilmore shows up in his re-creation of Gilmore's life in predictable ways: he offers audiences a glimpse of what Schiller himself wanted to see and hear about.

17 Mailer, *the Executioner's Song,* 582. Having covered Jack Ruby on his deathbed

and Susan Atkins at the Charles Manson trial, Schiller became famous for publicizing sensational murder stories.

18 During the sixties, Mailer was institutionalized after stabbing his wife with a penknife; later, his barroom brawls made tabloid headlines.

19 All my information here comes from Merrill, *Norman Mailer Revisited*, 1–11.

20 See his two short accounts called "How to Commit Murder in the Mass Media — A and B," in Mailer, *Advertisements for Myself*, 404–10. Mailer describes how his voice and photographs in two separate media interviews were made to appear "feminine" or "deranged" in order to put a negative spin on what he had to say about American culture of the 1950s.

21 See Hickey, *Serial Murderers and Their Victims*, 74–77. He notes that the past twenty-five years have seen a dramatic increase in serial killing, especially during the 1970s.

22 See, for example, Tudor's discussion of the popularity of "psycho" movies after 1960 in *Monsters and Mad Scientists*, 185–209.

23 More accurately, Hitchcock based *Psycho* on a novel by Robert Bloch which was inspired by Ed Gein's life story. For an account of Gein's crimes, see Schechter, *Deviant*.

24 I found this to be the case in a local Berkeley bookstore, Cody's Books, and in the corporate bookstore chain Barnes and Noble. In fact, Cody's had placed true crime on a few shelves in between a section called sociology and a section called Marxism and labor. I suspect — based purely on anecdotal evidence — that this is a peculiarly American configuration. Once, shopping for true crime in Cody's, I began chatting with another patron who was visiting from Scotland. She was stocking up on true crime books because, as she said, American bookstores had the best selections she had ever seen.

25 Norris, *Serial Killers*, 47–58.

26 Hickey, *Serial Murderers and Their Victims*, 133.

27 Ressler and Shachtman, *Whoever Fights Monsters*, 153.

28 Norris, *Serial Killers*, 15.

29 Segal, *Slow Motion*, 114.

30 For a fascinating and complex analysis of how this works, see Seltzer, *Serial Killers*.

31 In *The Stranger Beside Me*, investigative reporter Ann Rule describes the way Bundy, watching the news with his neighbors after the Sigma Chi sorority killings in Florida, told them that he was sure the murders were a "professional job" (282). Bundy was convicted of murdering two women at the Sigma Chi sorority and severely beating two others. At his Florida trial, his neighbors' testimony regarding this comment about the "professional" nature of these killings was discussed at length to indicate the extent of Bundy's "character disorder."

32 Ibid., 12.

33 Ibid. This is from Rule's reconstruction of Ted's early life and is not a direct quote from Bundy himself.

34 Schor, *The Overworked American*, 136.

35 For information on the Dahmer crimes, see Norris, *Jeffrey Dahmer*, and Davis, *The Milwaukee Murders*.

36 Davis, *The Milwaukee Murders*, 23.

37 Marx, "Economic and Philosophic Manuscripts of 1844," in Tucker, *The Marx-Engels Reader*, 71–74.

38 Quoted in Norris, *Henry Lee Lucas*, 36.

39 Karl Marx, *Capital*, Vol. 1, 224.

40 I use the masculine pronoun deliberately, since Marx's discussion assumes a male worker, just as the serial killer profile assumes a male killer.

41 Cornwell, *Postmortem*, 304.

42 Cornwell, *All That Remains*, 349.

43 Ellis, *American Psycho*, 344–45.

44 Lefebvre, *Critique of Everyday Life*, 31.

45 Because I'm looking primarily at masculinity here, I'll be focusing on serial killer fathers, rather than mothers and children. It's worth noting, however, that often women and children also seem to kill because family life is too much work for them to bear—although in rape-revenge movies like *Ms. 45*, the motive is less clearly related to economic concerns.

46 Derber, *Money, Murder and the American Dream*, 37. I would want to add that Derber wrote this chapter before the widely publicized trial of the Menendez brothers in which they attributed their actions to childhood sexual and psychological abuse. At the time Derber's book went to press, media coverage of the case emphasized the brothers' desire to inherit their father's financial empire as a possible motivation for the murders.

47 Ressler and Shachtman, *Whoever Fights Monsters*, 33.

48 Black, *The Aesthetics of Murder*, 135–65.

49 Cooper, *Frisk*, 128.

50 And, indeed, the idea of becoming an image is, in contemporary America (and the West) intimately bound up with becoming a commodity object.

51 Probably the insane success of *The X-Files* (1993–2002) also helped shore up the now-classic forensics babe role.

52 Many critics have also talked about how the movie *Arlington Road* (1999) makes reference to the Unabomber killings.

53 Kaczynski, *The Unabomber Manifesto*, 31.

54 You can find this State Department document at http://www.state.gov/s/ct/rls/pgtrpt/2000/.

55 See http://www.state.gov/s/ct/rls/pgtrpt/2001/html/10288.htm.

56 For an interesting discussion of this moment when a horrifying image creates a void of meaning waiting to be given an ideological character, see the essay by Žižek, *Welcome to the Desert of the Real*.

57 Remarks to the U.N. general assembly, 12 September 2002.

58 A poll taken by Knowledge Networks during 18–25 June 2003 revealed that 52

percent of people in the United States believed that the government had found clear evidence in Iraq that Saddam was working with Al Qaeda.

59 A movie like *Copycat*, which suggests that there is some kind of underground serial killer network which spawns new copycat killers each time a practicing killer is imprisoned, blurs the line between serial killer and terrorist in a similar way. In this film, the killers are all in contact with each other and giving each other murder advice.

2 ✳ Mad Doctors

1 Reich, *The Work of Nations*, 177–78.

2 Lukács, "Reification and the Consciousness of the Proletariat," in *History and Class Consciousness*. See especially the section of this essay called "The Phenomenon of Reification."

3 Norris, *McTeague*, 146.

4 Veblen is quoted and analyzed in Hofstadter, *Social Darwinism in American Thought*, 151–52.

5 Stevenson, *Dr. Jekyll and Mr. Hyde and Other Stories*, 10. Preface by Jenni Calder.

6 Moretti, *Signs Taken for Wonders*, 85–88.

7 Cassedy, *Medicine in America*, 71–73.

8 Larson, *The Rise of Professionalism*, 17.

9 Ibid., 39.

10 Jancovich, *Horror*, 46–47.

11 Stevenson, *Dr. Jekyll and Mr. Hyde and Other Stories*, 85.

12 Ibid., 87–88.

13 See, for example, Twitchell's analysis of Jekyll and Hyde narratives from the stage plays to relatively contemporary versions produced by Hammer Studios in England and by British auteur Ken Russell during the 1970s in Twitchell, *Dreadful Pleasures*, 245–57.

14 For an excellent and compelling analysis of Stevenson's novel as homosexual allegory, see Halberstam, *Skin Shows*, especially chapter 3. Unlike many critics of *Jekyll and Hyde*, who compare this narrative to myths of werewolves and *Frankenstein*, Halberstam reads *Jekyll and Hyde* alongside Oscar Wilde's *The Picture of Dorian Gray* in order to explore the way homosexual desire requires a kind of monstrous secrecy which produces a Foucauldian "multiplication" and "classification" of this very (repressed) desire.

15 This "monstrous white German" Hyde might also have been compelling because this version of the movie came on the heels of American involvement in World War I. For a very convincing analysis of the influence of World War I and later wars on American horror, see Skal, *The Monster Show*.

16 For one explanation of how whiteness has come to be associated with social prestige in the United States, see, for example, Ignatiev, *How the Irish Became White*.

17 I discuss Hyde's portrayal as a proletarian in Mamoulian's *Jekyll and Hyde* in "A Low Class, Sexy Monster."

18 To my knowledge, there are no *Jekyll and Hyde* narratives which depict Hyde as explicitly nonwhite, although this is often a fairly overt subtext. It would seem that Hyde has always had an aspect of the "racial other," whereas he becomes "female" mostly in the contemporary period.

19 *Dr. Jekyll and Ms. Hyde* (1995), for example, is set in the present day, and one of the *Jekyll and Hyde* narratives made in 1920 seems to be set in the twenties.

20 Freidson provides a thoughtful overview of the history of "professionalism" and its function as a "new class" which replaced nineteenth-century systems of class identification in his *Professional Powers*. See especially chapter 3.

21 From Pfeil, *White Guys*, 49.

22 Bear, *Blood Music*, 46.

23 In *Capital*, Marx writes (famously), "Capitalist production begets, with the inexorability of a law of Nature, its own negation." See Marx, *Capital*, Vol. 1, 715.

24 Bukatman, *Terminal Identity*, 271.

25 Toffler, *Future Shock*, 233.

26 Here I'm referring to Whyte's widely read book, *The Organization Man*, which explained to a general audience many of the problems with employee alienation and "conformity" in bureaucratic organizations established after World War II.

27 Here I mean to combine both the Marxist and psychoanalytic senses of "fetishization" in order to account for the way brains figure both the loss of power and the alienation of power into discrete, exchangeable objects.

28 Sayer and Walker, *The New Social Economy*.

29 Mulvey, "Visual Pleasure and Narrative Cinema," in *Visual and Other Pleasures*. This essay originally appeared in *Screen* magazine in 1975.

30 Since Mulvey reached these conclusions, a number of film theorists who work on masculinity and/or queer identity have explained how the fetishistic gaze can be directed at men and can in addition be generalized to include nonheterosexual versions of the gaze too. Most interestingly, Williams has talked about how commodity fetishes fit into this formulation in "Fetishism and Hard Core: Marx, Freud, and The Money Shot," a chapter from *Hard Core*.

31 We could also read this as a monstrous male body "in the closet," which would fit in nicely with the visual pun of a woman who has lost her head. I don't have the space here to map out what a queer reading of this movie would look like, but suffice to say that it would certainly work, and ideologically, gay men "in the closet" would be just as threatening to a man like Bill as a powerful woman's brain without a body.

32 In her brilliant *Fear of Falling*, Ehrenreich traces middle-class anxieties in politics and culture to an overwhelming concern that the middle class is getting poorer or is being threatened by those who are already poor.

33 Thanks to Ed Korthof for pointing this out.

34 Cook, *Brain*, 286.

35 See, for example, Ross's introduction and the chapter called "Hacking Away at the Counterculture" in *Strange Weather*. Ross explains that there is also a counterdiscourse at work where machines get associated with the professional and managerial class as well.

36 Movies about people with telepathic or telekinetic abilities who are stalked and "used" by elite government agencies also fit into this particular rubric. In *Firestarter*, *The Fury*, and *Scanners*, people who have these abilities are forced to work for the government or are killed. Their minds are treated as though they were special weapons devices owned by the state.

37 This and the following quotes come from Derber, "Professionals as New Workers," in Derber, *Professionals as Workers*, 4–5.

38 LaBier, *Modern Madness*, 8.

39 Although the sequel, *Bride of Re-Animator*, is about a reanimated woman, it isn't in fact about Megan. Also, I've had to leave a key scene of disgust and madness out of this account of the movie. Hill, who has fallen in love with Megan, kidnaps her. Once she is under his power, he orders the lobotomized dean (her father) to undress her and strap her to a table. Hill then approaches her spread legs with his severed head in his hands, with the intention—in another of the visual puns for which the brain movie is notorious—to "give her head." Luckily, we are spared this particular sight, although it would seem that Megan is not spared this particular act.

40 See, for example, Wiater's assessment of director Stuart Gordon's career in *Dark Visions*, 77–78. Even the often stodgy Leonard Maltin admits that *Re-Animator* "goes entertainingly over the line."

41 Derber, Schwartz, and Magrass, *Power in the Highest Degree*, 103.

42 With *The Hand*, of course, it's quite literally a competition between manual (hand) work and mental (brain) work. An interesting aside: Oliver Stone, the film *auteur* famous for his politically aware and critical movies, wrote and directed the 1981 remake of *The Hand*.

43 For a compelling and insightful discussion regarding the specialization and rationalization of mental labor, see Aronowitz and DiFazio's *The Jobless Future*.

3 ✱ The Undead

1 Torgovnick, *Gone Primitive*.

2 Morrison, *Playing in the Dark*, 33.

3 Skal offers an excellent analysis of how racial fears fit into stories about reanimating the dead, and here I'm thinking in particular of a passage where he compares the Frankenstein "angry mob" scene to a lynching. Tropes like this one abound in undead stories, and the crucial point is that they position the monster as a person of color besieged by white racists. See Skal, *Screams of Reason*, 131.

4 hooks, "Whiteness in the Black Imagination."

5 Taken from "Why Weird Tales?" an editorial published in the *Weird Tales* anni-

versary issue of 1924. Otis Adelbert Kline has claimed to be its author. This editorial is reprinted in Weinberg, *The Weird Tales Story*, 16.

6 Ibid.

7 Colin Wilson uses this turn of phrase in his introduction to Lovecraft, *Crawling Chaos*, 9.

8 See Weinberg, *The Weird Tales Story*, 62.

9 In his monograph *Supernatural Horror in Literature*, Lovecraft defines the three "terrors" that fuel the weird tale in America as a fear of the wilderness, a fear of Indians, and the repressive heritage of the Puritans. He was, in other words, quite conscious of the role played by racial others in his own weird fiction. It's also interesting to note that *Weird Tales* was host to the popular Conan the Barbarian stories of Robert E. Howard, which are almost entirely devoted to an exploration of what it would mean if whites were still "savage" peoples.

10 See, for instance, Roediger's telling history of class warfare and racial identity in the United States in *The Wages of Whiteness*. A second edition was released in 1999.

11 Joshi, *H. P. Lovecraft*, 268.

12 From Carter, "Farewell to the Dreamlands," ix–xiv.

13 Wetzel, "The Cthulhu Mythos," 79–95.

14 All these games are put out by a company called Chaosium (located in Oakland, Calif.) devoted entirely to Lovecraftiana: they manufacture and sell fanzines, T-shirts, "Cthulhu For President" bumper stickers, and of course the extensive line of Call of Cthulhu game manuals, adventure modules, and character guides.

15 For the sake of brevity here, I'm not including a number of other important Mythos stories, most notably "The Dream-Quest of Unknown Kadath," which gives readers a detailed description of the more spiritual aspects of the Mythos. The Dreamlands of this work are the realm of the dead (which sleepers visit when they dream) and are also a kind of gateway to Nyarlathotep, the "crawling chaos" who is portrayed as a cruel, all-powerful, and indifferent force lurking over many of the Mythos tales.

16 Lovecraft, "At the Mountains of Madness" (1931), in *At the Mountains of Madness and Other Tales of Terror*.

17 Lovecraft, *Crawling Chaos*, 141.

18 Lovecraft, *Ec'h-Pi-El Speaks*, 10.

19 It's also amusing to note that one of Lovecraft's favorite short stories was a work of horror by Arthur Machen called "The White People."

20 Lovecraft, *The Case of Charles Dexter Ward*.

21 Curwen lives at Pawtuxet with only "a sullen pair of Narragansett Indians . . . probably [with] a mixture of Negro blood" (16), and Lovecraft is careful to make Curwen's diabolical incantations sound very much like Hebrew. Ward raises the spirit of Curwen by chanting, in part, "Per Adonai Eloim, Adonai Jehova/Adonai

Sabaoth" (66). As Levy notes, many of Lovecraft's magical formulas are written to sound as if they are in Hebrew. See Levy, *Lovecraft*, 93–94.

22 Lovecraft, "The Shadow Over Innsmouth," in *The Lurking Fear and Other Stories*, 119.

23 See Lovett-Graff's excellent article, "Shadows over Lovecraft."

24 See Joshi, *H. P. Lovecraft*, and Levy, *Lovecraft*.

25 Lovecraft writes in a letter to Frank Belknap Long, "I am pretty well satisfied to be a Nordick, chalk-white from the Hercynian Wood and the Polar mists . . . Our province is to found the cities and conquer the wilderness and people the waste lands—that, and to assemble and drive the slaves, who tell us stories and sing us songs and paint us pretty pictures. *We are the masters*!" Excerpted in Derleth and Wandrei, *H. P. Lovecraft*, 276.

26 Quoted in Joshi, *H. P. Lovecraft*, 366.

27 Lovecraft, "The Horror at Red Hook," in *The Tomb and Other Tales*, 73.

28 Cannon remarks on the general incoherence of the story—and on many critics' agreement with his assessment—in *H. P. Lovecraft*, 56.

29 Lovecraft, *Supernatural Horror in Literature*, 18.

30 Lovecraft, "The Call of Cthulhu," in *The Crawling Chaos*, 143.

31 Bogle, *Toms, Coons, Mulattoes, Mammies, and Bucks*, 10.

32 Hackett, "Brotherly Love," 185.

33 This theme is echoed in a number of b-grade films of the latter half of the twentieth century, perhaps most memorably in cult movie prince Herschel Gordon Lewis's *Two Thousand Maniacs!* (1964), where Southern ghosts reappear every year to torture and kill Northerners in memory of the Civil War.

34 This is a line from Griffith's screenplay, quoted in Rogin, *Ronald Reagan*, 218.

35 Williams, *Playing the Race Card*, 126–27.

36 Rogin, *Ronald Reagan*, 219. For simplicity's sake, I have singled out a specific thread in Rogin's rewardingly complex argument, which goes far more deeply into issues of gender, psychoanalysis, and Griffith's complete oeuvre than I do here.

37 Newitz, "White Savagery and Humiliation, or a New Racial Consciousness in the Media."

38 Williams, *Playing the Race Card*, 129.

39 Guerrero, *Framing Blackness*, 13.

40 See D. W. Griffith, "Reply to the *New York Globe*," in Lang, *The Birth of a Nation*, 169.

41 For a discussion of the "crisis of hegemony" in which a ruling group is challenged by the subordinate classes, see excerpts from Antonio Gramsci's 1929–1935 prison writings in, "Hegemony, Relations of Force, Historical Bloc" in Forgacs, *A Gramsci Reader*, 217–21.

42 Omi and Winant, *Racial Formation in the United States*, 56.

43 When I use the term *postcolonial*, I intend it largely as a periodizing device, to

denote the time period (roughly after 1960) when many formerly colonized states had either begun the decolonization process or were currently decolonizing. In a U.S. context, this time period would have begun after the civil rights movement and during the period in which practices of "cultural imperialism" began to operate where military imperialism seemed unethical or simply not feasible.

44 Fanon, *The Wretched of the Earth*, 41–43.

45 Kaplan, "Left Alone with America," 14.

46 Dunbar, *Red Dirt*.

47 Of course, not all whites came from countries that colonized others. See Allen, *The Invention of the White Race*, and Ignatiev, *How the Irish Became White*, both of whom also explore quite fruitfully the way the Irish population is an exception to the rule that white bodies remind us of imperial cultures. "Becoming white," for Irish immigrants to the United States, seemed to represent the promise of an imperial power they had been denied in their own land. Thus, although not literally true, "whiteness" was imaginatively cast as an identity shared by people from powerful, colonizing nations.

48 Goad, *The Redneck Manifesto*, 52.

49 For more on Ben's heroism and the zombies' fighting style, see Waller's fascinating analysis of *Night of the Living Dead* in his *The Living and the Undead*, 272–322.

50 Dyer, "White," 59.

51 A complete discussion of these redneck stereotypes in film can be found in Williamson, *Hillbillyland*.

52 Waller, *The Living and the Undead*, 294.

53 Lott, *Love and Theft*, 59.

54 *From Hell* was originally a comic book written by Alan Moore. Interestingly, the *Blade* movies are also based on comic books, and it seems that *Underworld* was probably based on the White Wolf role-playing game. Postcolonial undead movies are no longer taking their cues from old pulp fiction and novels but instead from more contemporary forms of narrative.

55 Dicum, "Mutts at the Dog Show," 34–38.

4 ❊ Robots

1 Haraway, *Simians, Cyborgs, and Women*, 149.

2 Telotte, *Replications*, 58–70.

3 Schelde, *Androids, Humanoids, and Other Science Fiction Monsters*, 128.

4 Chaplin, *My Autobiography*, 378.

5 Krutnik, "A Spanner in the Works?," 25.

6 Chaplin, *My Autobiography*. Caption under plate 23.

7 Asimov, *I, Robot*, 9.

8 See, for instance, Elijah Baley's description of roblock in Asimov's *The Robots*

of Dawn, 7. This is the third in the robot novels, which center on the buddy relationship between two detectives, the human Elijah Baley and his sometime partner, the robot R. Daneel Olivaw. These humorous sci-fi murder mysteries depart somewhat in tone from *I, Robot*, which is, although humorous, generally focused on "hard sci-fi" themes such as new technologies, vast social systems run by machines, and so forth.

9 James, *Science Fiction in the 20th Century*, 68. Here James is discussing Asimov's Foundation series, but his observations work equally well to explain the concluding tales of *I, Robot*.

10 Marcuse, *Eros and Civilization*.

11 It's interesting to note that the recent movie version of *I, Robot* (2004) treats the idea of such a future with utter horror and ends with our heroes destroying the only AI who might be capable of running the world economy.

12 See Fuchs's fascinating argument about several ways we imagine cyborgs in her article " 'Death Is Irrelevant,' " 284–85.

13 Jeffords, *Hard Bodies*.

14 Piercy, *He, She and It*, 106.

15 It must also be noted that this suggestion can be aligned with a number of feminist utopian theories of the same period, most notably those of Dinnerstein in *The Mermaid and the Minotaur*. Dinnerstein suggests here that the crucial problem (and trauma) at the heart of gender relations is that women are almost solely responsible for child rearing.

16 Barr, *Lost in Space*, 71.

17 Ibid, 77.

18 See Ross's treatment of cyberpunk in *Strange Weather*.

19 Heim, "The Erotic Ontology of Cyberspace," 62.

20 Ibid., 66.

21 Gibson, *Neuromancer*, 51.

22 Rucker, *Live Robots*, 53.

23 Modleski, *Loving With a Vengeance*, 59.

24 Springer, *Electronic Eros*, 116.

25 Here, of course, I'm borrowing terminology from Marx's famous descriptions of the commodity fetish and alienation in *Capital*, vol. 1.

26 Lowe, *The Body in Late Capitalist USA*, 127.

27 See Packard's pioneering work in the cultural criticism of advertising, *The Hidden Persuaders*.

28 See Radway, *Reading the Romance*; and Segal, *Straight Sex*.

29 This movie is, incidentally, based on an Isaac Asimov short story written before his *I, Robot* collection was published.

30 Gerrold, *When HARLIE Was One*. There is a second edition of this book called *When HARLIE Was One 2.0*, but my comments here refer to the first edition.

31 Brooks, *Flesh and Machines*, 176.

32 Breazeal, *Designing Sociable Robots*. See especially chapter 1, where Breazeal

talks about nursemaid robots. While she is also deeply interested in inventing robots "to befriend," as she puts it, her work is nevertheless dependent on industry for funding. Currently her sociable robots lab at Massachusetts Institute of Technology is working with a Hollywood special effects company to build a somewhat angry-looking, furry robotic creature with emotions who could work as an actor in monster movies.

33 Penley, NASA/TREK, 148.

5 ✳. Mass Media

1 It's interesting to note that later versions of the THX demo deliberately attempted to make this menacing demo into something a lot cuter. Using Pixaresque animation, these new demos show a little technician in a red hat trying to fix the sound on a THX logo. For more information on how THX sound systems work, go to http://www.thx.com.

2 The Frankfurt school gang is often said to include a handful of German expat writers, sociologists, and philosophers who escaped to the United States during Hitler's rise to power. Many were associated with the Institute for Social Research in Frankfurt. Notorious Frankfurt schoolers are Theodor Adorno, Max Horkheimer, Hannah Arendt, Walter Benjamin, Herbert Marcuse, and Jürgen Habermas.

3 West, *The Day of the Locust*, 24.

4 Davis, *The Ecology of Fear*.

5 I'm thinking here, of course, of Mulvey's classic essay "Visual Pleasure and Narrative Cinema" from *Visual and Other Pleasures*.

6 A 1991 version of the film starred two real-life sister actresses: Vanessa and Lynn Redgrave, which gives the retelling of the story an even more documentary feel.

7 In her essay on *Hustler*, "Desire and Disgust," Kipnis makes the case that erotic images straddle an awkward line between being desirable and disgusting. Kipnis, *Bound and Gagged*.

8 The Payne Fund Studies were conducted by the Motion Picture Research Council in the late twenties and early thirties to help develop policies about exposing children to cinema. The findings were published in 1933. They were based on observation and interviews with young people and suggested that cinemas were hotbeds of sexual activity and that young people's behavior was heavily influenced by what they saw on film. See Jowett's excellent work on this issue in *Children and the Movies*. This volume also reproduces the original Payne Fund studies in their entirety.

9 All references are to Adorno and Horkheimer, *The Dialectic of Englightenment*.

10 For a full account of the birth of the media effects school, with a smart critique, see Jones, *Killing Monsters*.

11 Slovaj Žižek would love to tell you more about this, and you'll find out why in

his book *Everything You Wanted to Know About Lacan (But Were Afraid to Ask Hitchcock)*.

12 See Girard, *Violence and the Sacred*.

13 For a passionately written summary of the Dworkin-MacKinnon argument, see Andrea Dworkin, *Pornography*. For the counterargument, see Strossen, *Defending Pornography*.

14 Dworkin, *Pornography*, 69.

15 Although Baudrillard's books are usually short, it's true that you can read too much of them. I'm guessing that Craven read *Simulations* one too many times. But maybe he read *Fatal Strategies* too. Or possibly Guy Debord? You be the judge.

16 Huyssen, *After the Great Divide*.

17 Spigel, *Make Room for TV*.

18 See, for example, Fiske, *Reading the Popular*, and Jenkins, *Textual Poachers*.

19 Gramsci develops this idea in his *Prison Notebooks*, especially in the sections on "Economism." You can find useful excerpts from these in Forgacs, *A Gramsci Reader*.

20 Slavoj Žižek liked this so much he used this line as a title for one of his books.

21 See Rushkoff, *Media Virus*. Although critical of big business, Rushkoff nevertheless leveraged this book to garner himself lucrative gigs consulting with corporations whose executives wanted to know more about how they could use the "media virus" to advertise their products. His career just goes to show that you can have your critique and be complicit with dominant culture too.

22 This applies equally well to blogs, but at the time Rushkoff was formulating his ideas most people didn't have easy access to blogging software.

23 Rapoport, "World's End."

BIBLIOGRAPHY

Adorno, Theodore, and Max Horkheimer. *The Dialectic of Enlightenment*. New York: Continuum Publishing, 1944.

Allen, Theodore. *The Invention of the White Race*. New York: Verso, 1994.

Althusser, Louis. *Lenin and Philosophy and Other Essays*. New York: Monthly Review Press, 1971.

Aronowitz, Stanley, and William DiFazio. *The Jobless Future: Sci-Tech and the Dogma of Work*. Minneapolis: Minnesota University Press, 1994.

Asimov, Isaac. *I, Robot*. New York: Fawcett Crest, 1950.

——. *The Robots of Dawn*. New York: Bantam, 1983.

——. *Robot Visions*. New York: Roc, 1991.

Barr, Marleen S. *Lost in Space: Probing Feminist Science Fiction and Beyond*. Chapel Hill: University of North Carolina Press, 1993.

Baudrillard, Jean. *Simulations*. New York: Semiotext(e), 1983.

Bear, Greg. *Blood Music*. New York: Ace, 1985.

Benjamin, Walter. *Illuminations*. New York: Schocken Books, 1969.

Black, Joel. *The Aesthetics of Murder*. Baltimore: Johns Hopkins University Press, 1991.

Bogle, Donald. *Toms, Coons, Mulattoes, Mammies, and Bucks: An Intepretive History of Blacks in American Films*. New York: Continuum, 1973.

Breazeal, Cynthia. *Designing Sociable Robots*. Cambridge, Mass.: MIT Press, 2002.

Brooks, Rodney. *Flesh and Machines: How Robots Will Change Us*. New York: Pantheon, 2002.

Bukatman, Scott. *Terminal Identity: The Virtual Subject in Post-Modern Science Fiction*. Durham and London: Duke University Press, 1993.

Butler, Judith. *The Psychic Life of Power: Theories in Subjection*. Palo Alto, Calif.: Stanford University Press, 1997.

Cahill, Tim. *Buried Dreams: Inside the Mind of a Serial Killer*. New York: Bantam, 1986.

Cannon, Peter. *H. P. Lovecraft*. Boston: G. K. Hall, 1989.

Carr, Caleb. *The Alienist*. New York: Bantam, 1994.

Carter, Lin. "Farewell to the Dreamlands." Introduction to H. P. Lovecraft, *The Doom That Came to Sarnath and Other Stories*. New York: Del Rey, 1971.

Cassedy, James H. *Medicine in America: A Short History*. Baltimore: Johns Hopkins University Press, 1991.

Chaplin, Charles. *My Autobiography*. New York: Plume, 1964.

Clover, Carol. *Men, Women, and Chainsaws: Gender in the Modern Horror Film*. Princeton: Princeton University Press, 1992.

Cook, Robin. *Brain*. New York: Signet, 1979.

Cooper, Dennis. *Frisk*. New York: Grove, 1991.

Cornwell, Patricia. *Postmortem*. New York: Avon, 1990.

———. *All That Remains*. New York: Avon, 1992.

Crane, Stephen. *The Red Badge of Courage*, ed. by Donald Pizer. New York: Norton, 1979.

Davis, Don. *The Milwaukee Murders*. New York: St. Martin's Press, 1991.

Davis, Mike. *The Ecology of Fear: Los Angeles and the Imagination of Disaster*. New York: Viking, 1999.

Debord, Guy. *The Society of the Spectacle*. Cambridge, Mass.: Zone Books, 1995.

Derber, Charles. *Professionals as Workers: Mental Labor in Advanced Capitalism*. Boston: C. K. Hall, 1982.

———. *Money, Murder and the American Dream*. Winchester, Mass.: Faber and Faber, 1992.

Derber, Charles, William Schwartz, and Yale Magrass. *Power in the Highest Degree: Professionals and the Rise of a New Mandarin Order*. New York: Oxford University Press, 1990.

Derleth, August, and Donald Wandrei, eds. *H. P. Lovecraft: Selected Letters 1911–1924*. Sauk City, Wisc.: Arkham House, 1965.

Dicum, Gregory. "Mutts at the Dog Show: Why Racial Categories Are Fading Away in America." *other* 1 (June 2003): 34–38.

Dinnerstein, Dorothy. *The Mermaid and the Minotaur: Sexual Arrangements and Human Malaise*. New York: Harper and Row, 1976.

Douglas, Drake. *Horrors!* Woodstock, N.Y.: Overlook Press, 1966; new edition, Woodstock, Overlook Press, 1989.

Dunbar, Roxanne. *Red Dirt: Growing Up Okie*. New York: Verso, 1997.

Dworkin, Andrea. *Pornography: Men Possessing Women*. New York: Plume, 1979.

Dyer, Richard. "White." *Screen* 29, no. 4 (autumn 1988).

Ehrenreich, Barbara. *Fear of Falling: The Inner Life of the Middle-Class*. New York: HarperCollins, 1989.

Ellis, Bret Easton. *American Psycho*. New York: Vintage, 1991.

Fanon, Franz. *The Wretched of the Earth*. New York: Grove Press, 1963.

Fiske, John. *Reading the Popular*. New York: Unwin Hyman, 1989.

Forgacs, David, ed. *A Gramsci Reader*. London: Lawrence and Wishart, 1988.

Freidson, Eliot. *Professional Powers: A Study of the Institutionalization of Formal Knowledge*. Chicago: University of Chicago Press, 1986.

Gerrold, David. *When HARLIE Was One.* New York: Ballantine Books, 1972.

Gibson, William. *Neuromancer.* New York: Ace, 1984.

Girard, René. *Violence and the Sacred.* Trans. Patrick Gregory. Baltimore: Johns Hopkins University Press, 1979.

Goad, Jim. *The Redneck Manifesto.* New York: Simon and Schuster, 1997.

Goldschmidt, Richard. *The Material Basis of Evolution.* New Haven: Yale University Press, 1982.

Fuchs, Cynthia. "'Death Is Irrelevant': Cyborgs, Reproduction, and the Future of Male Hysteria." In *The Cyborg Handbook.* Ed. Chris Hables Gray. New York: Routledge, 1995.

Grossberg, Lawrence, Cary Nelson, and Paula Treichler, eds. *Cultural Studies.* New York: Routledge, 1991.

Guerrero, Ed. *Framing Blackness: The African American Image in Film.* Philadelphia: Temple University Press, 1993.

Hackett, Francis. "Brotherly Love." *The New Republic* 7 (20 March 1915): 185.

Halberstam, Judith. *Skin Shows: Gothic Horror and the Technology of Monsters.* Durham and London: Duke University Press, 1995.

Haraway, Donna. *Simians, Cyborgs, and Women: The Reinvention of Nature.* New York: Routledge Press, 1991.

Heim, Michael. "The Erotic Ontology of Cyberspace." In *Cyberspace: First Steps.* Ed. Michael Benedikt. Cambridge, Mass.: MIT Press, 1991.

Hickey, Eric W. *Serial Murderers and Their Victims.* Pacific Grove, Calif.: Brooks and Cole, 1991.

Higginson, Thomas Wentworth. "Book and Heart: A Bit of War Photography." In *Critical Essays on Stephen Crane's* The Red Badge of Courage. Ed. Donald Pizer. Boston: G. K. Hall, 1990.

Hofstadter, Richard. *Social Darwinism in American Thought.* Boston: Beacon Press, 1992.

Holton, Milne. *Cylinder of Vision: The Fiction and Journalistic Writing of Stephen Crane.* Baton Rouge: Louisiana State University Press, 1972.

hooks, bell. "Whiteness in the Black Imagination." In *Cultural Studies.* Ed. Lawrence Grossberg, Cary Nelson, and Paula Treichler. New York: Routledge, 1991.

Huet, Marie-Hélène. *Monstrous Imagination.* Boston: Harvard University Press, 1993.

Huyssen, Andreas. *After the Great Divide: Modernism, Mass Culture, Postmodernism.* Bloomington: Indiana University Press, 1986.

Ignatiev, Noel. *How the Irish Became White.* New York: Routledge, 1995.

James, Edward. *Science Fiction in the 20th Century.* Oxford: Oxford University Press, 1994.

Jameson, Fredric. *The Political Unconscious: Narrative as a Socially Symbolic Act.* Ithaca: Cornell University Press, 1982.

———. "Cognitive Mapping." In *Marxism and the Interpretation of Culture.* Ed. Cary Nelson and Lawrence Grossberg. Urbana: University of Chicago Press, 1988.

Jancovich, Mark. *Horror.* London: B. T. Batsford, 1992.

Jeffords, Susan. *Hard Bodies: Hollywood Masculinity in the Reagan Era.* New Brunswick: Rutgers University Press, 1994.

Jenkins, Henry. *Textual Poachers: Television Fans and Participatory Culture.* New York: Routledge Press, 1992.

Jones, Gerard. *Killing Monsters: Why Children Need Fantasy, Super Heroes and Make-Believe Violence.* New York: Basic Books, 2002.

Joshi, S. T. *H. P. Lovecraft: A Life.* West Warwick, R.I.: Necronomicon Press, 1996.

Jowett, Garth. *Children and the Movies: Media Influence and the Payne Fund Controversy.* Cambridge: Cambridge University Press, 1996.

Kaczynski, Theodore [FC, pseud.]. *The Unabomber Manifesto: Industrial Society and Its Future.* Berkeley, Calif.: Jolly Roger Press, 1995.

Kaplan, Amy. "The Spectacle of War in Crane's Revision of History." In *New Essays on* The Red Badge of Courage. Ed. Lee Clark Mitchell. New York: Cambridge University Press, 1986.

———. "Left Alone with America." In *Cultures of United States Imperialism.* Ed. Amy Kaplan and Donald E. Pease. Durham and London: Duke University Press, 1993.

Kerekes, David, and David Slater. *Killing for Culture: An Illustrated History of Death Film from Mondo to Snuff.* London: Creation Books, 1994.

Kipnis, Laura. *Bound and Gagged: Pornography and the Politics of Fantasy in America.* New York: Grove Press, 1996.

Krutnik, Frank. "A Spanner in the Works? Genre, Narrative, and the Hollywood Comedian." In *Classical Hollywood Comedy.* Ed. Kristine Brunovska Karnick and Henry Jenkins. New York: Routledge Press, 1995.

LaBier, Douglas. *Modern Madness: The Hidden Link Between Work and Emotional Conflict.* New York: Touchstone, 1986.

Lang, Robert, ed. *The Birth of a Nation.* New Brunswick: Rutgers University Press, 1994.

Larson, Magali Sarfatti. *The Rise of Professionalism: A Sociological Analysis.* Berkeley: University of California Press, 1977.

Lefebvre, Henri. *Critique of Everyday Life,* Vol. 1. New York: Verso, 1991 (originally published in 1947).

Levy, Maurice. *Lovecraft: A Study in the Fantastic.* Detroit: Wayne State University Press, 1988.

Lott, Eric. *Love and Theft: Blackface Minstrelsy and the American Working Class.* New York: Oxford University Press, 1995.

Lovecraft, H. P. *The Case of Charles Dexter Ward.* New York: Del Rey, 1941.

———. *The Tomb and Other Tales.* 1925. New York: Del Rey, 1965.

———. *The Lurking Fear and Other Stories.* New York: Del Rey, 1971.

———. *At the Mountains of Madness and Other Tales of Terror.* New York: Del Rey, 1971.

————. *Ec'h-Pi-El Speaks: An Autobiographical Sketch*. Saddle River, N.J.: Gerry de la Ree, 1972.

————. *Supernatural Horror in Literature*. 1927. New York: Dover Publications, 1973.

————. *The Crawling Chaos: Selected Works 1920–1935*. London: Creation Press, 1992.

Lovett-Graff, Bennett. "Shadows over Lovecraft: Reactionary Fantasy and Immigrant Eugenics." *Extrapolation: A Journal of Science Fiction and Fantasy* 38 (1997): 175.

Lowe, Donald M. *The Body in Late Capitalist USA*. Durham and London: Duke University Press, 1995.

Lukács, Georg. *History and Class Consciousness: Studies in Marxist Dialectics*. Cambridge, Mass.: MIT Press, 1968.

Mailer, Norman. *Advertisements for Myself*. Cambridge, Mass.: Harvard University Press, 1959.

————. *The Executioner's Song*. New York: Warner Books, 1979.

Marcuse, Herbert. *Eros and Civilization: A Philosophical Inquiry into Freud*. Boston: Beacon Press, 1955.

Marx, Karl. *Capital*, Vol. 1. New York: International Publishers, 1967 (originally published in 1867).

Meredith, Roy. *Mathew Brady's Portrait of an Era*. New York: Norton, 1982.

Merrill, Robert. *Norman Mailer Revisited*. New York: Twayne Publishers, 1992.

Modleski, Tania. *Loving With a Vengeance: Mass Produced Fantasies for Women*. New York: Routledge, 1982.

Moretti, Franco. *Signs Taken for Wonders*. New York: Verso, 1983.

Morrison, Toni. *Playing in the Dark: Whiteness and the Literary Imagination*. New York: Vintage, 1990.

Mulvey, Laura. *Visual and Other Pleasures*. Bloomington and Indianapolis: Indiana University Press, 1989.

Newitz, Annalee. "A Low Class, Sexy Monster: American Liberalism in Rouben Mamoulian's Dr. Jekyll and Mr. Hyde." *Bright Lights Film Journal* 15 (October 1995).

————. "White Savagery and Humiliation, or a New Racial Consciousness in the Media." In *White Trash: Race and Class in America*. Ed. Matt Wray and Annalee Newitz. New York: Routledge, 1997.

Norris, Frank. *McTeague*. New York: Norton, 1899.

Norris, Joel. *Serial Killers*. New York: Anchor Books, 1988.

————. *Henry Lee Lucas*. New York: Zebra, 1991.

————. *Jeffrey Dahmer*. New York: Pinnacle, 1992.

Omi, Michael, and Howard Winant. *Racial Formation in the United States: From the 1960s to the 1990s*. New York: Routledge, 1994.

Packard, Vance. *The Hidden Persuaders*. New York: Pocket Books, 1957.

Paul, William. *Laughing Screaming: Modern Hollywood Horror and Comedy*. New York: Columbia University Press, 1994.

Penley, Constance. *NASA/TREK: Popular Science and Sex in America*. New York: Verso, 1997.

Pfeil, Fred. *White Guys: Studies in Postmodern Domination and Difference*. New York: Verso, 1995.

Piercy, Marge. *He, She and It*. New York: Fawcett, 1991.

Pizer, Donald. *The Theory and Practice of Literary Naturalism: Selected Essays and Reviews*. Carbondale: Southern Illinois University Press, 1993.

Radway, Janice. *Reading the Romance: Women, Patriarchy, and Popular Literature*. Chapel Hill: University of North Carolina Press, 1984.

Rapoport, Lynn. "World's End." *San Francisco Bay Guardian*, 6 August 2003, 25.

Reich, Robert B. *The Work of Nations*. New York: Vintage, 1991.

Ressler, Robert, and Tom Shachtman. *Whoever Fights Monsters*. New York: St. Martin's Press, 1992.

Roediger, David. *The Wages of Whiteness: Race and the Making of the American Working Class*. New York: Verso Books, 1996.

Rogin, Michael. *Ronald Reagan: The Movie, and Other Episodes in Political Demonology*. Berkeley: University of California Press, 1987.

———. " 'Make My Day!': Spectacle as Amnesia in Imperial Politics," *Representations* 29 (1990): 106.

Ross, Andrew. *Strange Weather: Science, Technology, and the Age of Limits*. New York: Verso, 1991.

Rucker, Rudy. *Live Robots: Software/Wetware*. New York: AvoNova, 1982/1988.

Rule, Ann. *The Stranger Beside Me*. New York: Signet, 1980.

Rushkoff, Douglas. *Media Virus: Hidden Agendas in Popular Culture*. New York: Ballantine, 1996.

Sayer, Andrew, and Richard Walker. *The New Social Economy: Reworking the Division of Labor*. Cambridge, Mass.: Blackwell, 1992.

Schechter, Harold. *Deviant*. New York: Pocket Books, 1989.

Scheffler, Judith. "The Prisoner as Creator in *The Executioner's Song*." In *Norman Mailer*. Ed. Harold Bloom. New York: Chelsea House, 1986.

Schelde, Per. *Androids, Humanoids, and Other Science Fiction Monsters: Science and Soul in Science Fiction Films*. New York: NYU Press, 1993.

Schor, Juliet. *The Overworked American*. New York: Basic Books, 1992.

Segal, Lynne. *Slow Motion: Changing Masculinities, Changing Men*. New Brunswick: Rutgers, 1990.

———. *Straight Sex: Rethinking the Politics of Pleasure*. Berkeley: University of California Press, 1994.

Seltzer, Mark. *Serial Killers: Death and Life in America's Wound Culture*. New York: Routledge, 1998.

Skal, David J. *The Monster Show: A Cultural History of Horror*. New York: Norton, 1993.

———. *Screams of Reason: Mad Science and Modern Culture*. New York: Norton, 1998.

Spigel, Lynn. *Make Room for TV: Television and the Family Ideal in Postwar America*. Chicago: University of Chicago Press, 1992.

Springer, Claudia. *Electronic Eros: Bodies and Desire in the Postindustrial Age*. Austin: University of Texas Press, 1996.

Stevenson, Robert Louis. *Dr. Jekyll and Mr. Hyde and Other Stories*. Ed. and Preface by Jenni Calder. New York: Penguin, 1979.

Strossen, Nadine. *Defending Pornography: Free Speech, Sex and the Fight for Women's Rights*. New York: Anchor Books, 1976.

Taylor, Frederick Winslow. *The Principles of Scientific Management*. New York: Dover, 1998. Reprint of 1911 edition.

Telotte, J. P. *Replications: A Robotic History of the Science Fiction Film*. Urbana: University of Illinois Press, 1995.

Toffler, Alvin. *Future Shock*. New York: Random House, 1970.

Torgovnick, Marianna. *Gone Primitive: Savage Intellects, Modern Lives*. Chicago: University of Chicago Press, 1990.

Tucker, Robert C., ed. *The Marx-Engels Reader*. New York: Norton, 1978.

Tudor, Andrew. *Monsters and Mad Scientists*. Oxford: Blackwell, 1989.

Twitchell, James. *Dreadful Pleasures: An Anatomy of Modern Horror*. New York: Oxford University Press, 1985.

Waller, Gregory. *The Living and the Undead: From Bram Stoker's* Dracula *to Romero's* Dawn of the Dead. Urbana: University of Illinois Press, 1986.

Weinberg, Robert. *The Weird Tales Story*. West Linn, Ore.: FAX Collectors Editions, 1977.

Weldon, Michael J. *The Psychotronic Video Guide*. New York: St. Martin's Press, 1996.

West, Nathanael. *The Day of the Locust*. New York: Signet, 1939.

Wetzel, George T. "The Cthulhu Mythos: A Study." In *H. P. Lovecraft: Four Decades of Criticism*. Ed. S. T. Joshi. Athens: Ohio University Press, 1980.

Whyte, William. *The Organization Man*. New York: Simon and Schuster, 1956.

Wiater, Stanley. *Dark Visions: Conversations with the Masters of the Horror Film*. New York: Avon, 1992.

Williams, Linda. *Hard Core: Power, Pleasure, and the Frenzy of the Visible*. Berkeley: University of California Press, 1989.

———. *Playing the Race Card: Melodramas of Black and White from Uncle Tom to O. J. Simpson*. Princeton: Princeton University Press, 2001.

Williams, Raymond. *Problems in Materialism and Culture*. New York: Verso Press, 1980.

Williamson, J. W. *Hillbillyland: What the Movies Did to the Mountains and What the Mountains Did to the Movies*. Chapel Hill: University of North Carolina Press, 1995.

Wilson, Colin. Introduction to H. P. Lovecraft, *Crawling Chaos: Selected Works 1920–1935*. London: Creation Press, 1992.

Wray, Matt, and Annalee Newitz, eds. *White Trash: Race and Class in America*. New York: Routledge, 1997.

Žižek, Slavoj. *Everything You Wanted to Know About Lacan (But Were Afraid to Ask Hitchcock)*. New York: Verso Books, 1992.
———. *Welcome to the Desert of the Real*. New York: Verso Books, 2002.

FILMOGRAPHY

A.I. 2001. Dir. Steven Spielberg.
Alien 3. 1992. Dir. David Fincher.
All About Eve. 1950. Dir. Joseph L. Mankiewicz.
Android. 1982. Dir. Aaron Lipstadt.
Android Affair, The. 1995. Dir. Richard Kletter.
Animatrix, The. 2003. Dir. various.
Arlington Road. 1999. Dir. Mark Pellington.

Bad and the Beautiful, The. 1952. Dir. Vincente Minnelli.
Beast With Five Fingers, The. 1946. Dir. Robert Florey.
Beautiful Mind, A. 2001. Dir. Ron Howard.
Bicentennial Man. 1999. Dir. Chris Columbus.
Birth of a Nation, The. 1915. Dir. D.W. Griffith.
Blacula. 1972. Dir. William Crain.
Blade. 1998. Dir. Stephen Norrington.
Blade II. 2002. Dir. Guillermo Del Toro.
Blade Runner. 1982. Dir. Ridley Scott.
Blair Witch Project. 1999. Dir. Daniel Myrick and Eduardo Sánchez.
Body Parts. 1991. Dir. Eric Red.
Bone Collector, The. 1999. Dir. Phillip Noyce.
Bones. 2001. Dir. Ernest R. Dickerson.
Brady Bunch Movie, The. 1995. Dir. Betty Thomas.
Brain That Wouldn't Die, The. 1960. Dir. Joseph Green.
Bride of Re-Animator. 1990. Dir. Brian Yuzna.

Cell, The. 2000. Dir. Tarsem Singh.
Cherry 2000. 1987. Dir. Steve De Jarnatt.
Circuitry Man. 1990. Dir. Steven Lovy.
Copycat. 1995. Dir. Jon Amiel.

Death Becomes Her. 1992. Dir. Robert Zemeckis.
Demon Seed. 1977. Dir. Donald Cammell.

Doctor, The. 1991. Dir. Randa Haines.
Donovan's Brain. 1953. Dir. Felix E. Feist.
Dr. Jekyll and Mr. Hyde. 1920. Dir. John S. Robertson.
Dr. Jekyll and Mr. Hyde. 1931. Dir. Rouben Mamoulian.
Dr. Jekyll and Mr. Hyde. 1941. Dir. Victor Fleming.
Dr. Jekyll and Ms. Hyde. 1995. Dir. David Price.
Dr. Jekyll and Sister Hyde. 1971. Dir. Roy Ward Baker.

Edge of Sanity. 1989. Dir. Gérard Kikoïne.
Eve of Destruction. 1991. Dir. Duncan Gibbins.
Eyes of Laura Mars, The. 1978. Dir. Irvin Kershner.

Face in the Crowd, A. 1957. Dir. Elia Kazan.
Fight Club. 1999. Dir. David Fincher.
Firestarter. 1984. Dir. Mark Lester.
Forbidden Planet. 1956. Dir. Fred M. Wilcox.
Foxy Brown. 1974. Dir. Jack Hill.
Frankenhooker. 1990. Dir. Frank Hennenlotter.
Friday the 13th. 1980. Dir. Sean S. Cunningham.
From Hell. 2001. Dir. Hughes Brothers.
Fury, The. 1978. Dir. Brian De Palma.

Galaxy Quest. 1999. Dir. Dean Parisot.

Halloween. 1978. Dir. John Carpenter.
Hand, The. 1960. Dir. Henry Cass.
Hand, The. 1981. Dir. Oliver Stone.
Heartbeeps. 1981. Dir. Allan Arkush.
Henry: Portrait of a Serial Killer. 1986. Dir. John McNaughton.

Invasion of the Body Snatchers. 1978. Dir. Philip Kaufman.
I, Robot. 2004. Dir. Alex Proyds.
I Walked With a Zombie. 1943. Dir. Jacques Tourneur.

Jezebel. 1938. Dir. William Wyler.
Jurassic Park. 1993. Dir. Steven Spielberg.

Last Starfighter, The. 1984. Dir. Nick Castle.
Lethal Weapon. 1987. Dir. Richard Donner.
Logan's Run. 1976. Dir. Michael Anderson.

Mad Love. 1935. Dir. Karl Freund.
Making Mr. Right. 1987. Dir. Susan Seidelman.
Man with Two Brains, The. 1983. Dir. Carl Reiner.
Martin. 1978. Dir. George Romero.
Mary Reilly. 1996. Dir. Stephen Frears.
Matrix, The. 1999. Dir. Wachowski Brothers.

Matrix Reloaded, The. 2003. Dir. Wachowski Brothers.
Matrix Revolutions, The. 2003. Dir. Wachowski Brothers.
Menace II Society. 1993. Dir. Hughes Brothers.
Metropolis. 1927. Dir. Fritz Lang.
Misery. 1990. Dir. Rob Reiner.
Modern Times. 1936. Dir. Charlie Chaplin.
Ms. 45. 1981. Dir. Abel Ferrara.
Mummy, The. 1999. Dir. Stephen Sommers.

Natural Born Killers. 1994. Dir. Oliver Stone.
Network. 1976. Dir. Sidney Lumet.
Nightbreed. 1990. Dir. Clive Barker.
Night of the Living Dead. 1968. Dir. George Romero.
Nurse Betty. 2000. Dir. Neal LaBute.

People Under the Stairs, The. 1991. Dir. Wes Craven.
Pi. 1998. Dir. Darren Arnofsky.
Player, The. 1992. Dir. Robert Altman.
Pleasantville. 1998. Dir. Gary Ross.
Private Parts. 1972. Dir. Paul Bartel.
Psycho. 1960. Dir. Alfred Hitchcock.
Psycho. 1998. Dir. Gus Van Sant.
Purple Rose of Cairo, The. 1985. Dir. Woody Allen.

Raiders of the Lost Ark. 1981. Dir. Steven Spielberg.
Re-Animator. 1985. Dir. Stuart Gordon.
Rear Window. 1954. Dir. Alfred Hitchcock.
Ring, The. 2002. Dir. Gore Verbinski.
RoboCop. 1987. Dir. Paul Verhoeven.

Scanners. 1981. Dir. David Cronenberg.
Scream. 1996. Dir. Wes Craven.
Scream 2. 1997. Dir. Wes Craven.
Scream 3. 2000. Dir. Wes Craven.
Se7en. 1995. Dir. David Fincher.
Shaft. 1971. Dir. Gordon Parks.
Sherlock Jr. 1924. Dir. Buster Keaton.
Short Circuit. 1986. Dir. John Badham.
Short Circuit 2. 1988. Dir. Kenneth Johnson.
Silence of the Lambs. 1991. Dir. Jonathan Demme.
Sixth Sense, The. 1999. Dir. M. Night Shyamalan.
Society. 1989. Dir. Brian Yuzna.
Spider-Man 2. 2004. Dir. Sam Raimi.
Star Wars. 1977. Dir. George Lucas.
Stay Tuned. 1992. Dir. Peter Hyams.

Stepfather, The. 1987. Dir. Joseph Ruben.
Stepford Wives, The. 1975. Dir. Bryan Forbes.
Sunset Boulevard. 1950. Dir. Billy Wilder.
Swimming with Sharks. 1994. Dir. George Huang.

Tales from the Hood. 1995. Dir. Rusty Cundieff.
THX 1138. 1971. Dir. George Lucas.
Terminator. 1984. Dir. James Cameron.
Terminator 2. 1991. Dir. James Cameron.
Terminator 3. 2003. Dir. Jonathan Mostow.
Tron. 1982. Dir. Steven Lisberger.
Truman Show, The. 1998. Dir. Peter Weir.
Two Thousand Maniacs. 1964. Dir. Herschell Gordon Lewis.

Unabomber: The True Story. 1996. Dir. Jon Purdy.
Underworld. 2003. Dir. Len Wiseman.

Videodrome. 1983. Dir. David Cronenberg.

Wall Street. 1987. Dir. Oliver Stone.
Westworld. 1973. Dir. Michael Crichton.
Whatever Happened to Baby Jane. 1962. Dir. Robert Aldrich.
Wizard of Oz, The. 1939. Dir. Victor Fleming.

✸ TV Shows

Donna Reed Show, The. 1958–66. ABC.
Leave It to Beaver. 1957–63. CBS and ABC.
Lost in Space. 1965–68. Created by Irwin Allen.
Partridge Family, The. 1970–74. ABC.
Roseanne. 1988–97. Created by Matt Williams.
Star Trek. 1966–69. Created by Gene Roddenberry.
X-Files, The. 1993–2002. Created by Chris Carter.

INDEX

Page numbers in italics refer to illustrations.

Big Money, The (film), 153

Birth of a Nation (film), 11, 91, 101–5,
102, 108, 110; ghosts in, 101–3, 121;
The Mummy and, 118; Night of the
Living Dead and, 109

Black, Joel, 40

blackness, 89, 90, 104, 107, 111–12;
ghost stories and, 101–2; in I Walked
With a Zombie, 106; People Under
the Stairs and, 114; "Shadow Over
Innsmouth" and, 98–100. See also
race, racism

Blacula (film), 91, 108, 111

Blade films, 91, 119, 194n54

Blade Runner (film), 128, 140

Blair Witch Project (film), 1–2, 15

blaxploitation films, 104, 108, 111, 118

Blood Music (Bear), 66, 67–69

bodies, 157; bodily monstrosity and,
10, 11–12; body parts and, 81–84; fetishization of, 72–74, 134; machines'
control of, 135; minds' connection
to, 55. See also dead bodies; robots;
undead

bodily monstrosity genre, 10, 11–12

Body Parts (film), 83

Bogle, Donald, 101–2

Bones (film), 91, 108, 117

Bone Collector, The (film), 45–46

Bovary, Madame (Flaubert), 161

Brady, Matthew, 11, 13, 19

Brady Bunch Movie, The (film), 173

Brain (Cook), 75, 76–77

brains, 70; class and, 76–84; fetishization of, 75, 77, 85; gender and,
46, 72–77; machines' control of, 135;
minds and, 45, 55, 80–82, 191n36.
See also bodies; mad doctors; madness

Brain That Wouldn't Die, The (film), 70,
73–75, 83

Breazeal, Cynthia, 148–49

Brecht, Bertold, 51

Bricks Are Heavy (film), 1

Brooks, Rodney, 148–49

Brooks, Stephanie, 30

brutality, 14, 43. See also violence

Bukatman, Scott, 69

Bundy, Ted, 26, 29–31, 48, 187n31

bureaucracies, 29

Buried Dreams (Cahill), 31

Bush, George W., 50, 51

Butler, Judith, 9

Byerley, Stephen, 128, 129–30

Cahill, Tim, 31

Calder, Jenni, 58

"Call of Cthulhu, The" (Lovecraft), 93,
94, 100, 113

Calvin, Susan, 128–30

Capek, Karl, 123

capitalism, 2, 31, 140, 182–83; abandonment and, 32–33, 35; audiences
and, 152; culture industry and, 154,
160; cyberpunk and, 138–39; dead
labor and, 5–6, 34; Fight Club and,
48–49; industrial, 21; Jekyll and
Hyde and, 58, 59, 60; machines
and, 130; Marx and, 6, 34, 190n23;
mass production and, 39–40; Matrix
trilogy and, 177; Pi and, 85; professionalism and, 59, 71–72, 182;
robots and, 124–25, 150; serial killers
and, 37, 43, 182. See also consumerism

capitalist monsters, 1–12, 152; in
American history, 6–8; dead labor
and, 5–6; economic disturbances
and, 2–4; social construction of,
8–10

Carr, Caleb, 13–14, 20

castration, 73, 102–3, 131

celebrity, 25–27, 40, 156, 167

Cell, The (film), 45, 46

Chaplin, Charles, 12, 124–27, 132

Cherry 2000 (film), 138, 139

children, 147, 195n15, 196n8; as child
stars, 159; *Demon Seed* and, 137–38
Circuitry Man (film), 140, 142–43, 150
civil rights, 7
Civil War, 7, 104; *Birth of a Nation* and,
101; H. P. Lovecraft and, 97–98;
photography and, 11, 18–20; *The Red
Badge of Courage* and, 17
class, 3–4, 8, 9, 11, 54, 70; brains and,
76–84; conflicts based on, 17–18;
McTeague and, 56–58; proletariat,
58, 59, 60, 63, 76–84; race and, 92;
robots and, 11–12, 124; serial killers
and, 30, 32, 36–37; undead and, 105,
109, 110–12, 114, 117; *Videodrome*
and, 165; warfare of, 5, 173. *See also*
professionalism
Clover, Carol, 5, 44
colonialism, 8, 11, 182, 194nn43, 47;
imperialism and, 92, 112; postcolonial era and, 115–17, 119–20; undead
and, 90–91, 96, 101, 107, 108–15, 121
comedy, 125–27, 140, 144, 168
commericalism, 151
commodities, 40, 60, 155, 188n50;
fetishization and, 21, 55, 71–72,
140, 190n30; mad doctors and, 55,
57; narrative monstrosity and, 12;
professionalism and, 59; robot narratives and, 138–39; serial killers
and, 32–35, 36, 51; sex and, 140, 141;
undead and, 120
computers, 76–77, 135, 137
consent of robots, 124, 129–31,
139, 150; cyberpunk and, 135–37;
human/cyborg love and, 140–43
conservatism, 94, 170
consumerism, 12, 29, 31, 140, 150, 162;
audiences and, 151; *Fight Club* and,
48; images and, 11, 141; mad doctors
and, 56; mass media and, 152, 166,
168; serial killers and, 36, 39, 42–43,
51. *See also* capitalism

Cook, Robin, 75, 76
Cooper, Dennis, 40
Copycat (film), 45, 189n59
Cornwell, Patricia, 35–36
Cory, Patrick, 70–73, 78
Crane, Stephen, 7, 11, 15–20, 23
Craven, Wes, 112, 166, 197n15
Crawford, Joan, 159
Crichton, Michael, 9
crime, true, 15, 26–31, 32, 41
Cronenberg, David, 8
c-3po, 127
Cthulhu Mythos (Lovecraft), 91–94,
100, 192n15
culture industry, 7–8, 10–12, 154,
161, 169. *See also* culture industry
monsters; mass media narratives
culture industry monsters, 151–83;
Adorno and Horkheimer and, 160,
161, 163, 179; anti-Hollywood genre,
153–60; audiences and, 160–69,
173–74; *Matrix* trilogy and, 174, 175–
78, 179; *Pleasantville* and, 169–71,
173; reality and, 179–80; *The Ring*
and, 179–83; *Tron* and, 174–75, 176,
177, 179; *The Truman Show* and, 169,
171–73, 174
Cultures of United States Imperialism
(Kaplan), 108
Cundieff, Rusty, 115–17
Curwen, Joseph, 94–96, 100
cyberpunk, 12, 124, 134–37, 138, 175
cyberspace, 135–36
cyborgs, 12, 123–27, 130–31, 138,
182; *He, She, and It* and, 132–34;
human/cyborg love and, 140–43;
Westworld and, 9–10. *See also* robots

Dahmer, Jeffrey, 15, 32, 34, 47
Davis, Bette, 157, 159
Davis, Don, 32
Davis, Mike, 154
Day of the Locust, The (West), 152, 153, 160

dead bodies, 10–11, 33, 36, 89, 121; *Night of the Living Dead* and, 109; photography and, 19–20, 41; *Re-Animator* and, 79–82; *The Red Badge of Courage* and, 16–17; serial killers and, 24, 32, 40

dead labor, 5–6, 34

death, 91; of H. P. Lovecraft, 101; mad doctors and, 66–67, 86; racial identity and, 92; serial killers and, 22–23, 25, 26; "Shadow Over Innsmouth" and, 98; slavery and, 96; undead and, 91, 92, 96, 98, 101. *See also* undead

Death Becomes Her (film), 160

Debord, Guy, 39

del Toro, Guillermo, 119

Demme, Jonathan, 4, 28

demons, 92, 98

Demon Seed (film), 137–38, 140

Department of Homeland Security, 47

Derber, Charles, 38, 77, 82, 188n46

Designing Sociable Robots (Brooks), 149

Dialectic of Enlightenment (Adorno and Horkheimer), 160

Dicum, Gregory, 119

doctors. *See* mad doctors

Doctor, The (film), 66

documentaries, 15, 43, 159

Donovan's Brain (film), 55, 70–73, 72, 75

DosPassos, John, 153

Douglas, Drake, 5

Douglas, Kirk, 154

Dr. Jekyll and Mr. Hyde (Stevenson), 55, 58, 60, 61

Dr. Jekyll and Sister Hyde (film), 64

Dracula (Stoker), 91, 101, 102–3, 111

Dreadful Pleasures (Twitchell), 5

Dunbar, Roxanne, 109

"Dunwich Horror, The" (Lovecraft), 93, 94

Dworkin, Andrea, 165–66, 168

Dyer, Richard, 110

eaten by a giant narrative, 169–78

Ecology of Fear (Davis), 154

economy, 2–4, 5, 8, 10–12, 182; class and, 54; culture industry and, 155, 160; economic concerns and, 26–27, 29; identity and, 31–35, 37–38; information economy and, 69, 152; mad doctors and, 59, 70–72; *Matrix* trilogy and, 176–77; power and, 161, 175; production and, 29, 148–49; race and, 107; robots and, 124, 130, 148; serial killers and, 31–35, 37–38, 43, 44–45; theory of, 57

Edge of Sanity (film), 65

education, 44, 56–57

Ehrenreich, Barbara, 75

Ellis, Bret Easton, 36, 78

Engels, Friedrich, 149

England, 3–4

eroticism, 92, 135, 150, 157–58

"Escape!" (Asimov), 129

eugenics, 98

Eve of Destruction (film), 138–39

evidence, 20–21

evil, 50, 62, 98, 109, 125

Executioner's Song, The (Mailer), 11, 22–23, 25, 26

Eyes of Laura Mars (film), 40

Face in the Crowd, A (film), 156–57

factory workers, 125–27, 132

fame, 25–27, 40, 156, 167

family, 37–39, 106, 169, 173, 174, 188n45; fatherhood and, 102; robots and, 131–32, 143–50. *See also* mother relations

Fanon, Franz, 107

fantasy, 39–41, 54, 141–43; of work, 35–37

fatherhood, 102

feminism, 2, 134; actress-monsters and, 158; antifeminism and, 74; human/cyborg love and, 141; por-

psychic powers (*continued*)
and, 116; telepathy, 40, 70, 71, 74–
75, 191n36
psychoanalysis, 2, 63–64, 161
Psycho films, 27–28, 45, 187n23
psychohistory, 129–30
Psychotronic Video Guide (Weldon), 4
Purple Rose of Cairo, The (film), 173

race, racism, 89–121; *Birth of a Nation* and, 101–5; *Blacula* and, 111–12;
Bones and, 117; "Call of Cthulhu"
and, 100; economics of, 115; identity
politics and, 8; *I Walked With a Zombie* and, 105–8; Jekyll and Hyde and,
190n18; of Mr. Hyde, 61, 62; *Nightbreed* and, 112–14; *Night of the Living
Dead* and, 108–11; *People Under the
Stairs* and, 114–15; racial formation
and, 106–7; racists and hybrids of
the future and, 118–21; savages and,
92, 108; "Shadow over Innsmouth"
and, 96–99; *Tales from the Hood*
and, 115–17; *Weird Tales* and, 91–96.
See also blackness; slavery; undead;
whiteness
Radway, Janice, 141
Raiders of the Lost Ark (film), 118
rape, 62, 104; cyber-rape and, 150; machines and, 137–40; miscegenation
and, 91; pornography and, 165; serial
killers and, 24
Rapoport, Lynn, 182
realism, 15, 16, 19, 101
reality, 54, 174–76, 178; culture industry monsters and, 164, 179–80;
death and, 23; eaten by a giant narrative and, 174; images and, 39–43;
mad doctors and, 55; reality television and, 171; *Scream* trilogy and,
167; of serial killers, 27; virtual,
174–75
Re-Animator (film), 79–82, 191n39

rebellion, 22, 162, 165, 178; robots and,
124–26, 134
Red Badge of Courage, The (Crane), 7–8,
11, 15–18, 20, 23, 26
Reich, Robert, 54
"Reification and the Consciousness of
the Proletariat" (Lukács), 55
Ressler, Robert, 39, 41
revenge, 128–29, 136
revolutions, 128, 134–37, 149
Ring, The (film), 179–83
Robbie the Robot, 127
RoboCop (film), 12, 130–32, 134
robots, 6–8, 11, 123–50, 195n32;
Asimov and, 128–30; capitalism and,
124–25, 150; children and, 148, 150;
class and, 11–12, 124; consent and,
124, 129–31, 135–37, 139, 140–43,
150; cyberpunk and, 12, 124, 134–37,
138, 175; emotion of, 144, 148, 149;
family and, 131–32, 143–50; *He, She
and It* and, 132–34; human/cyborg
love and, 124, 127, 139, 140–43, 145,
147; humanity of, 123, 125, 144; labor
and, 9, 11–12, 123–24, 129, 148; laws
of robotics and, 128–34; Marx and,
124; *Modern Times* and, 125–27; rape
and, 137–40; revolution and, 128,
134–37, 149; *RoboCop* and, 130–
32; robopsychology of, 128–29, 131;
violence and, 130, 134, 137, 139; *Westworld* and, 9–10; women and, 10,
138–43
Robot Visions (Asimov), 123
Rogin, Michael, 20, 102–3
romanticism, 7, 124–27, 131, 140–43,
144, 150; gothic, 15, 134–35, 138,
185n12
Romero, George, 42, 108, 109
Ross, Andrew, 77, 134, 191n35
R2-D2, 127
Rucker, Rudy, 12, 134–35, 136–37, 140
Rule, Ann, 28, 30, 187n31

der and, 29, 165; mad doctors and, 57, 62–63, 75, 79, 82, 83, 87; mass media narratives and, 154, 162, 163, 167, 169; naturalist writing and, 16–18; photography and, 20; race and, 91, 109; robots and, 130, 134, 137, 139; serial killers and, 14, 21–22, 25–27, 33, 38–39, 40, 46; sex and, 165–66, 168; sexual assault and, 24, 62, 91, 104, 137–40, 150, 165; terrorism and, 49, 51; undead and, 107, 110, 112, 118
virtual reality, 174–75
voodooism, 90, 105–7, 116

Wachowski Brothers, 175
Waller, Gregory, 110
Wall Street (film), 78
war, 16–20
Ward, Charles Dexter, 94–96
wealth, 4, 6, 115, 119
weird genre, 104, 111–12, 114–15; films and, 108; *Weird Tales* and, 91–96, 101, 117, 118, 192n9
werewolves, 120
West, Nathaniel, 152–53, 160
Westworld (film), 9–10, 137
Wetzel, George, 92
Whatever Happened to Baby Jane (film), 152, 157, 159
What Makes Sammy Run? (Shulberg), 153
When HARLIE *Was One* (Gerrold), 147–48, 150
"White Negro, The" (Mailer), 22
whiteness, 89–92, 96, 101–5, 189n16, 191n3, 194n47; colonialism and, 11, 107, 109; gender and, 28, 94; ghosts and, 101–2, 104, 121; Jekyll and Hyde and, 60, 62; *The Mummy* and, 118;

Night of the Living Dead and, 111; white guilt and, 116; whitesploitation and, 118; white supremacy and, 103–5, 108, 110, 115, 118, 121. *See also* race, racism
Whoever Fights Monsters (Ressler), 41
Wiener, Norbert, 149
Williams, Linda, 4–5, 102–3, 190n30
Williams, Raymond, 8
Willis, Bruce, 160
Winant, Howard, 106
Woman on the Edge of Time (Piercy), 133
women, 73, 103, 164, 165, 168; as actress-monsters, 157–60; fetishization of, 72–74; final girl and, 44–46; *I Walked With a Zombie* and, 105, 108; Piercy and, 133; professionalism and, 45; robots and, 10, 135, 138–40, 140–43; serial killers and, 29, 30, 35, 41–42; undead and, 90, 92, 98, 105, 108. *See also* gender
work, 6, 11, 157; gender and, 29, 188n40; mad doctors and, 54, 68–69; robots and, 123–24, 140; serial killers and, 30–38, 31, 42, 44; undead and, 105, 106
Work of Art in the Age of Mechanical Reproduction, The (Benjamin), 21
World Trade Center, 47, 49–50

yuppiedom, 78
Yuzna, Brian, 3–4, 8

Zombie (film), 114, 115
zombies, 2, 152, 182; *I Walked With a Zombie* and, 105–6; *Night of the Living Dead* and, 109–10; *People Under the Stairs* and, 114; race and, 91; *Re-Animator* and, 79–81. *See also* undead

Annalee Newitz is a freelance writer in San Francisco
and a contributing editor at *Wired Magazine*. She is the
coeditor (with Matt Wray) of *White Trash: Race and Class
in America*.

Library of Congress Cataloging-in-Publication Data
Newitz, Annalee.
Pretend we're dead : capitalist monsters in American
pop culture / Annalee Newitz.
p. cm.
Includes bibliographical references and index.
ISBN 0-8223-3733-9 (cloth : alk. paper) —
ISBN 0-8223-3745-2 (pbk. : alk. paper)
1. Monsters in motion pictures. 2. Monsters in
literature. 3. American fiction—20th century—History
and criticism. 4. American fiction—19th century—
History and criticism. 5. Popular culture—United
States. I. Title.
PN1995.9.M6N49 2006
791.43'67—dc22   2005037846